1389918

Co

1/29/08

BELOVED
WOMEN

The Political Lives of

LaDonna Harris and

Wilma Mankiller

Beloved Women

Sarah Eppler Janda

Northern Illinois University Press *DeKalb*

© 2007 by Northern Illinois University Press

Published by the Northern Illinois University Press, DeKalb, Illinois   60115

Manufactured in the United States using acid-free paper

All Rights Reserved

Design by Julia Fauci

Library of Congress Cataloging-in-Publication Data

Janda, Sarah Eppler.

Beloved women : the political lives of Ladonna Harris and Wilma Mankiller / Sarah Eppler Janda.

p.   cm.

Includes bibliographical references and index.

ISBN-13: 978-0-87580-372-2 (clothbound : alk. paper)

ISBN-10: 0-87580-372-5 (clothbound : alk. paper)

1. Harris, LaDonna. 2. Mankiller, Wilma Pearl, 1945– 3. Indian women activists—North America—Biography. 4. Cherokee women—Biography. 5. Comanche women—Biography. 6. Indian leadership—North America. 7. Indian women—North America—Politics and government. I. Title.

E98.W8J36 2007

305.48′8970092276—dc22

[B]

2006030948

For **Robert L. Griswold,**

who first taught me to love history,

and **Paul A. Gilje,**

who guided me through graduate school so that I could write it.

CONTENTS

ACKNOWLEDGMENTS

I have amassed numerous debts of gratitude (both intellectual and personal) over the past several years while working on this project. I benefited tremendously from working with so many talented scholars. Notably, Albert L. Hurtado has been a strong source of inspiration and advice. I am forever impressed by the insight he brings to his own work and his ability to bring the pages of history books to life. Clara Sue Kidwell and Cindy Simon Rosenthal sharpened my understanding of the connection between race, gender, and power. Linda Williams Reese aided me at various stages of this project. Early on, she helped me clarify and organize my ideas, and her support and enthusiasm have sustained me at difficult junctures along the way. Robert L. Griswold and Paul A. Gilje, to whom this book is dedicated, have each played an instrumental role in my training as a historian. I found their own passion for history contagious, but more important, I am deeply indebted to them for their advice and support.

While writing is by nature a solitary endeavor, for me the process was made less so by the friendship and support of my friends and colleagues. William Bauer, Holly Berkley Fletcher, Douglas Catterall, Heather Clemmer, Linda English, Brian Frehner, Robyn McMillin, and Jana Vogt each played a role in improving my work through reading, editing, or acting as sounding boards at different stages in the process.

I have also benefited significantly from the support of archivists and editors. Much appreciation goes to the archivists at the Carl Albert Congressional Research Center and the Western History Collection at the University of Oklahoma. Archivists at Native American Educational Studies College in Chicago, the Museum of the Great Plains in Lawton, Oklahoma, the Chero- kee National Archives in Tahlequah, Oklahoma, and the

National Archives and Record Administration in College Park, Maryland, were also very helpful. I also wish to thank Charles A. Braithwaite and the *Great Plains Quarterly* for helping to improve my work and for allowing me to reprint portions of an essay on LaDonna Harris in this book. I have been most fortunate to work with Melody Herr at Northern Illinois University Press. Her professionalism and hands-on approach have been invaluable in helping me complete this project.

Although the bulk of my research was conducted in archives, I also had the opportunity to interview a number of people associated with my topic. I am grateful to everyone I interviewed, because their perspectives added a personal component not always found in documents. In particular, I would like to thank LaDonna Harris for her willingness to work with me. Having a historian write a critical analysis of your life's work must indeed be a strange—and perhaps unenviable—thing. Yet Harris shared her stories and even her family pictures with me. Although many people have contributed to my work through their advice and editorial suggestions, any mistakes are mine alone.

Finally, I would like to say a word about my family. I wish to thank my siblings, Angela Chandler and Andrew Eppler, for their love and friendship and my parents, Ray and Carmen Eppler, for giving me the strength to find my own path. My daughter Sydney, who was born as this book neared completion, is a constant source of delight and is a wonderful reminder of the things that matter most in life. The love, support, and editing of my husband and colleague, Lance Janda, were instrumental at every stage of working on this project. He has never hesitated to drop what he was doing to listen to an idea or offer advice. The role he has played in my work looms large, but pales in comparison to his place in my life. For that, I am deeply thankful.

BELOVED
WOMEN

Introduction

Several years ago, when this project was still a skeletal draft, a student wandered into my office to inquire about undertaking a study of the impact of gaming on Oklahoma Indians. I turned away from working on my manuscript to ask exactly what she had in mind. In the course of our conversation, I asked her how familiar she was with federal Indian policy. She responded by saying, "I am Indian twenty-four/seven. I sing and dance all the time." Somewhat taken aback, I rephrased my question and we finished our conversation, but her words often came back to me as I tried to conceptualize and articulate the interplay between image and identity in my own work. When confronted with what she interpreted as a question about her *being* Indian, this student tried to convey her own sense of Native American identity by framing it in a stereotypical image of Indianness. In other words, by saying that she sang and danced all the time, she articulated not what it actually means to be Indian, but what she thought someone else would recognize as Indianness. That chance encounter deepened my understanding of the complex relationship between personal identity and manifestations of image, and this book is, in part, about that relationship and how it affects media depictions, federal Indian policy, and identity within the context of the life's work of LaDonna Harris and Wilma Mankiller.

The formation of identity lies at the very core of human experience. It shapes not only the view of self but also the lens through which people view the world around them. Rarely is identity static; it evolves and changes over time, just as people do. There exist any number of components in an individual's identity; race, ethnicity, gender, and life experience all play a role. At times, one aspect of a person's identity may yield greater prominence than others. Paula Gunn Allen, however, described tribal identity as the most central element in defining what it means to be a Native American woman. She explained that from the perspective of an Indian woman, "her destiny is necessarily that of her people, and her sense of herself as a woman is first and foremost prescribed by her tribe." Certainly, this description does not apply to all Native American women, but LaDonna Harris's and Wilma Mankiller's senses of being Indian women underpinned their constructions of self, their identity, and the public image they projected.[1]

Both self-identified feminists, Harris and Mankiller affected national policy as they worked on behalf of Native American and women's issues throughout the latter decades of the twentieth century. As the wife of United States Senator Fred Harris of Oklahoma, LaDonna Harris became the first congressional wife to testify before Congress, founded Oklahomans for Indian Opportunity in 1965 and Americans for Indian Opportunity in 1970, and served on scores of federal committees whose work pertained to both women and Native Americans. Wilma Mankiller became the first female deputy chief of the Cherokee Nation in 1983, the first female principal chief in 1985, and then led her tribe for the next decade. Each altered the place of women in politics—Harris as a congressional wife and Mankiller as an elected tribal leader. Steeped in the understanding of their cultural traditions, each found a way to situate her accomplishments, her desires, and her life's work within the context of being Indian. By promoting the belief that native tradition esteemed women, Harris and Mankiller simultaneously challenged dominant society and uplifted the status of Native Americans through their activism while creating a new place for women in politics.

A comparison of LaDonna Harris and Wilma Mankiller reveals that *being* Indian and growing up during a turbulent period in federal Indian policy profoundly shaped their images of self and their later humanitarian efforts. In fact, Harris and Mankiller have a great deal in common. Although Harris is older than Mankiller and has been active in national and Indian politics longer, they share several commonalities in expressions of identity, their methods of activism, and the issues they address. Both were born into large, poor families in rural Oklahoma. Harris and Mankiller are liberal Democrats and have actively supported a wide array of Democratic initiatives and Democratic presidents and presidential candidates. Harris has discussed Indian affairs with every president since Lyndon B. Johnson, and Mankiller met with both the Reagan and elder Bush administrations in addition to serving on the Clinton-Gore transition team and consulting with the Clinton administration on health care and the environment.

Each woman has an Irish parent but identifies strongly with her Indian heritage. They grew up in homes that stressed their respective Indian cultures and drew strength from their tribal traditions. In fact, in their autobiographies, each woman took a similar approach by telling her personal story within the context of the larger history and traditions of her tribe. Mankiller, whose autobiography was published first, explained the centrality of her heritage: "My own story has meaning only as long as it is a part of the overall story of my people. For above all else I am a Cherokee woman." Similarly, Harris's autobiography began with the story of her ancestors. After setting up the context of her tribal history, Harris explained, "And that's where I come from. Those are my folks. That's my heritage. That's what influences everything I do and how I do it."[2]

The cultural identity expressed by Harris and Mankiller played a defining role in their work. The use of that identity permeated all that they did, with each drawing strength from her understanding of Indian culture. In fact, each time one did something exceptional or seemingly unconventional by the standards of dominant society, she explained it as a natural outgrowth of her heritage and tribal customs. Harris and Mankiller placed everything they undertook, from their participation in politics to their support of women's rights and emphasis on social justice, in the context of tribal customs. In light of the use of Indianness in their images and activism, it is crucial to explore how cultural beliefs shaped each woman and, at times, how each shaped her beliefs to legitimize otherwise unconventional behavior.

Harris and Mankiller are also women who underwent real and meaningful change over the course of their lives, and the work that follows is a story of how their identities were shaped over time and the types of images they projected as national leaders. By no means is this intended as a definitive biography of either Harris or Mankiller. Nor is it a comprehensive history of Indian policy or feminism. Rather, it is an interpretation of the interplay among image, identity, activism, and, indeed, the intersection of feminism and Indianness in the lives of Harris and Mankiller. Although there are many definitions of "feminism," the word is used throughout this book as meaning a belief in the equality of men and women. "Indianness" signifies the various components of Indian identity, including self- and group identification, cultural beliefs, and heritage.

The way in which the intersection of feminism and Indianness shaped the political life of each woman, as well as her image and identity, lies at the core of this study. It is important because an examination of the way in which each experienced Indianness and femaleness ultimately contributes to a wider understanding of the avenues open to women in politics and the possibilities afforded them to affect federal Indian policy in the late twentieth century. The lives of LaDonna Harris and Wilma Mankiller shed light on the two most critical elements in twentieth-century Native American history: the shift from termination and assimilation policy to self-determination and the cultural revitalization and growth of pan-Indianness and activism. An examination of the experiences and work of both women provides substantial insight into each of these issues. Their place in twentieth-century Native American history, however, speaks to only part of their significance. Both Harris and Mankiller also engaged in activism as women, and gender significantly informed their experiences.

In view of the lack of scholarship on the role of Native American women in the American Indian movement, in the feminist movement, and in politics, biographical and autobiographical works currently offer the best insight into the experience of these women. Although these works offer a glimpse into the budding dialogue on American Indian feminism, they nevertheless reveal the need for greater scholarship in the field. A handful of books and articles refer to Harris or Mankiller, but there is no detailed examination of the role of feminism and Indian identity in the activism of either one of them. What has increasingly emerged in the historiography of Indian women is an effort to understand how women perceived their lives in relation to their tribal histories. Just as Paula Gunn Allen asserted the centrality of tribal identity in the lives of Indian women, there are a growing number of both primary and secondary accounts that do the same. For instance, Susan Williams and Joy Harjo explain that many of the women who have contributed to the recent increase in female tribal leadership came from tribes that "have always treated men and women as equally sacred." More important, as Devon Mihesuah argues, the women themselves characterized their leadership roles as "a way of regaining the prestige and power their ancestors once held." These issues lie at the center of the growing body of literature on modern Indian feminism, but much remains to be done.[3]

There are, in fact, very few books on Native American women, feminism, and politics in the latter half of the twentieth century, and this volume helps fill that gap. To this end, part 1 focuses exclusively on LaDonna Harris and her transition from a young wife and mother with only a high school education to a nationally prominent Indian and women's rights advocate. Harris's childhood, her relationship with Fred Harris, and her activism and political involvement are examined in addition to issues of both racial and gender identity—and how they changed over time.

Part 2 focuses on Wilma Mankiller and includes a discussion of her family's relocation to San Francisco during her childhood as well as her shift from activism to politics. Her activism in San Francisco, her return to Oklahoma in 1976, and her subsequent employment with the Cherokee Nation is explored, as is her role in Cherokee politics and the twelve years she spent in elected tribal office.

Part 3 consists of two comparative chapters, the first of which examines the impact of Harris and Mankiller on federal Indian policy in the United States. It also discusses how they were themselves products of the shift in federal Indian policy from termination to self-determination. Attention is given to Indian activism since the 1960s, Indian identity, and public perceptions of Native Americans. As two of the most visible Native American women in the second half of the twentieth century, Harris and Mankiller played an important role in shaping public opinion of Native Americans.

The final chapter is an attempt to place Harris and Mankiller within the larger historical context of women in politics as well as within the feminist movement. Both women helped redefine the role of women in politics and how they play this role. This chapter also compares the different styles of leadership between the two and the different set of circumstances each confronted. In addition to the generational differences, Mankiller also entered into a different kind of political arena—one of tribal politics, as opposed to national or even state politics. Another significant difference between these two women is that Harris first became involved in politics as the wife of a senator, not as an elected official. These differences are explored in greater detail as a means of assessing the impact that each has had on opportunities afforded to women and their participation in politics.

That Harris and Mankiller hold an important place in twentieth-century Native American and women's history is clear. The challenge lies in discerning the way in which their concepts of traditional tribal values, feminism, and mainstream culture converged during a critical juncture in the dialogue on both gender roles and federal Indian policy and shaped their lives and activism. It is that effort to which the following pages are dedicated.

I

"Freddie and the Indian"

"What is it like to live in a tent?" asked Robert F. Kennedy's five-year-old daughter, Kerry, when she met LaDonna Harris for the first time in 1965.[1] When Harris assured her that Indians no longer lived in "tents," Kerry's mother, Ethel, jokingly told Harris not to disillusion the child. Harris insisted that she wanted Kerry to have an accurate understanding of what Indians were like, to which Kerry responded by asking whether she shot a bow and arrow. This exchange between Harris and the Kennedy family resembled many of Harris's experiences with the media, the public, and government leaders as she rose to national prominence as a leading advocate of Native American rights in the latter half of the twentieth century. It also undoubtedly echoed the struggle many Native Americans faced when they confronted the all-too-common stereotypes about Indians held by so many Americans. What made Harris's experience different, however, and what gave her access to the corridors of power in which she could affect change, was her marriage to a white U.S. senator from

Oklahoma. Their relationship provided, for example, the impetus for the story of Harris's conversation with the Kennedys to be related in an article tellingly entitled "LaDonna Harris May Be Answer to TV Myth." To understand the path that took Harris from the poor farm community where she grew up to the national spotlight that provided the backdrop for this exchange, however, it is first necessary to examine the formative years of her childhood.[2]

Comanche Childhood

LaDonna Harris was born in the rural southwestern Oklahoma town of Temple on February 15, 1931, and spent most of her childhood living eight miles east of her birth place in Walters, Oklahoma. Harris's father, a white man of Irish descent named Donald Crawford, and her Comanche mother, Lily Tabbytite, divorced while Harris was very young, and her mother went to work at the Fort Sill Indian Hospital in Lawton, Oklahoma. From her earliest memories, elements of both Comanche tradition and mainstream white culture infused Harris's life. Harris learned to speak the Comanche language and became acquainted with Comanche traditions and culture while growing up in the care of her maternal grandparents, John and Wick-ie Tabbytite. Harris's grandparents had a farm on the land that they selected in the late nineteenth century as a part of the 1887 Dawes Severalty Act. While the Tabbytite family lived close to thirty miles from the Comanche Nation headquarters in Lawton, Oklahoma, their farm was still considered a part of "Comanche Country." In fact, a sizable portion of what became southwestern Oklahoma had included the Kiowa, Comanche, and Apache Reservation until the U.S. government opened the land to white homesteaders in 1901, just six years prior to Oklahoma statehood.[3]

The combined population of Kiowa, Comanche, and Apache Indians living in southwest Oklahoma in 1931, when Harris was born, totaled only 5,500. Nevertheless, the Native American population in the area managed to sustain a continuity of community —even in the face of such obstacles as allotment, continued dispossession of their land, and the Great Depression, which lasted from 1929 until American entry into World War II.[4]

For Harris and other Comanches who grew up in Oklahoma, the sense of belonging to a community underpinned what it meant to be Comanche. According to Morris W. Foster, "What is most conspicuous about the enduring enterprise of 'being Comanche' is the ability of a people to continue to associate with one another, not the preservation of a specific territory, language, or social structure through which to do so." Harris's recollections of her childhood bear out the significance of social interaction and extended kinship families to Comanche culture. Summertime for Harris meant an inundation of family in the home of her grandparents, and at Christmas her great-grandmother's house swelled with family activity. Harris says this interaction made her close to all of her great-aunts, great-uncles, and cousins, who "were like brothers and sisters" to her. As Thomas W. Kavanagh argues in his examination of Comanche sociopolitical structures, historically the "nuclear family was usually not an independent entity but cooperated with others to form a bilaterally extended household." Both the interdependence of the group and the prevalence of extended kinship ties in Comanche culture can be seen in Harris's perception of her relationship to the world around her. For example, Harris credits her Comanche heritage with teaching her the importance of being a strong individual, not for its own sake, but for the good of the group. She also learned to value all life as sacred and intertwined.[5]

Despite Harris's sense of being connected to a larger community that consisted of extended family, fictive kin (those not actually related by blood but who were considered family), and the Comanche tribe, she still lived within the parameters of a poor, rural, predominately white community. Negative stereotypes of Native Americans persisted among many whites living in southwest Oklahoma during the 1930s and 1940s, when Harris was growing up. Foster argues that Comanches were viewed as inferior, lazy, and financially irresponsible. As such, "they were essentially locked out of the Anglo economy" and "found themselves marked as a separate category of people in their interactions" with the white community. Such prejudice was not automatically clear to a child growing up in a loving household. For instance, her grandmother made all of Harris's childhood clothes, and she remembers feeling well-dressed and proud of the respect people in Walters showed toward her grandparents. Eventually, however, she experienced firsthand the problems encountered by Indians. Harris described herself as "more fortunate than other Indians who came from bitter, poverty-stricken homes," explaining that "it took me longer to feel that I was 'different' and therefore inferior to non-Indian children. But gradually I got the message too—through the subtle downgrading that is constantly taking place and the general atmosphere of prejudice that chips away at the self-esteem of Indian children."[6]

Confronting Racism

Harris had blue eyes and lighter skin than many Native Americans and realized at an early age that this made a difference in how people responded to her. She became acutely aware that white people treated her better than they treated many of her family members who had much darker skin than she did. Even with Harris's fair complexion, she still experienced many painful encounters with racism. In grade school, like many Indian children, she suffered from name calling and other forms of abuse. To shield her hurt feelings, Harris retreated into a shy and reserved demeanor. She watched people and tried to figure out their personalities instead of interacting with them. Her first recollection of encountering racism came when a classmate at school called her and her cousin "gut-eaters," for which her female cousin promptly "whipped up" on the boy who had made Harris cry. She had no idea that not everyone ate intestines, a traditional Comanche food, and for the first time she found herself painfully confronted with what it meant to be different. When Harris tearfully told her grandmother about the incident that evening, her grandmother cheered her up by telling her that white people ate mussels and crawdads. This of course shocked Harris.[7]

As much as being called a gut-eater hurt her feelings, it paled in comparison to the discrimination she encountered under the guise of religion. On Sundays Harris's grandfather drove the

family to church. Not being a Christian himself, he stayed outside with the car during the service. Meanwhile, Harris's grandmother, who was one of the first Comanches baptized in the
area, accompanied Harris and the others inside. Often the
preacher would rail against non-Christians in his sermons by
saying that those who practiced other religions (such as the traditional Comanche religion, which included the use of peyote)
would be doomed to hell. Harris's youngest daughter, Laura, explains that the "Comanche way is to respect other people's medicine," which made it very difficult for Harris to understand the
preacher's awful condemnations. In fact, the anger Harris felt
over these insults threatened to consume her, but for the teachings of her grandmother. Wick-ie Tabbytite told her young
granddaughter that allowing someone to make her angry meant
that she had lost control of her spirit. Harris learned to channel
her hurt feelings and cope with anger, but she never forgot
those early encounters with prejudice. They stayed with her and
later fed her determination to fight against discrimination.

Early on then, Harris drew on the lessons taught by her Comanche grandparents to make sense out of the world. In the critical process of identity formation, Harris encountered two important factors: first, being Comanche made her different. Second,
being Comanche gave her a lens through which to view and respond to the world. Although it is impossible to know the exact
point at which this worldview took hold for Harris, she clearly articulated it years later on the title page of her autobiography with
the assertion: "I filter everything through Comanche values."[8]

Situational Ethnicity

Although the encounters with racism and discrimination hurt
Harris's feelings, she benefited from growing up in a home that
blended Comanche tradition with an understanding of mainstream white society. Her grandfather was a traditional peyote
man and her grandmother a Christian during a period in which
a significant polarization "between peyote and church factions"
existed within Comanche politics. From her earliest memories,
Harris says she internalized what seemed a natural merging of

two cultures and adopted skills to function in both. And yet hundreds of years of failed assimilation policies by the federal government and persistent racism toward Native Americans invite deeper analysis. As Joane Nagel asserts, ethnic identity is "a socially negotiated and socially constructed status that varies as the audiences permitting particular ethnic options change." She explains that the end result is "an array or layering of ethnicities, with different identities activated at different times." In other words, Harris's ability to operate in both mainstream white society and within the Comanche community was made possible by situational ethnicity. That is not to say Harris ever stopped *being* Comanche, but rather that at certain times in her childhood (and later as an adult) some aspects of her identity took a backseat to others, depending on her surroundings, to afford her a greater level of acceptance in a given group.[9]

The interplay between Comanche and mainstream culture during Harris's childhood shaped her understanding of politics as well. Although Native Americans did not get the right to vote until the passage of the 1924 Indian Civil Rights Act, her grandparents raised her to be politically aware. They made a habit of following national politics even though her grandfather could not read and her grandmother had only an eighth-grade education. They voted regularly and were strong supporters of Franklin D. Roosevelt and his New Deal programs during the Great Depression. In fact, Harris thought that President Herbert Hoover's first name was "God Damn" because she always heard her grandfather talking about "that God damn Hoover." That an illiterate Comanche peyote man saw New Deal politics as relevant to his life and encouraged his granddaughter to become knowledgeable about political issues typifies the melding of ethnic identity. To be sure, the nuances of ethnic identity formation were far from her mind when Harris played in the creek on her grandparents' farm on hot summer days. And yet it is here where the seeds of Indianness that would later render Harris one of the most important Native American activists of the twentieth century were first planted. Quite simply, Harris saw her early life shaped by loving grandparents, a strong infusion of Comanche culture in her everyday experiences, and a growing awareness of political issues.[10]

A Partnership Is Born

As a teenager in the mid-1940s, her life took a significant turn when she met Fred Harris while attending Walters High School. At the time LaDonna Harris suffered from undiagnosed dyslexia, and, after realizing that she could not perform well in school in the usual sense, she coped by studying her teachers to determine what she could do in order to get through her classes and gain their approval. The difficulty she experienced in school contributed even more to her shyness, but she eventually began coming out of her shell. She exuded a natural grace that attracted people and by this point had grown into a striking young woman with long legs and big blue eyes. Fred was a year ahead of LaDonna in school, and even though their families owned neighboring farms the two had never met. Fred worked at a local print press to earn extra money. Although she "wasn't very impressed with his physical appearance" at first, LaDonna eventually responded to his overtures. He offered to run her campaign for turkey queen of Cotton County, and, though she did not win, this local beauty contest marked the beginning of a partnership that lasted for more than thirty years. LaDonna and Fred married in 1949 at the end of his first year of college at the University of Oklahoma and just before she graduated from high school. Shortly after their wedding, they moved to Norman and she became pregnant with their first child, Kathryn. LaDonna worked as a babysitter and at other odd jobs to help support Fred as he attended school. In 1952 Fred graduated with his bachelor's degree in history and political science and went on to attend law school at the University of Oklahoma.[11]

At the time of their marriage, the fact that Fred was white and she was Comanche did not seem to be an issue—certainly not to the two of them. Harris's daughter Laura explained that this, in part, had to do with a long-standing Comanche tradition of taking captives and bringing them into the tribe. For all practical purposes, Fred simply became one of them. Yet the fact that this interracial marriage did not seem unusual to Harris—especially given that her own mother had also married a white man—is itself significant because it was informed by her understanding of

Comanche culture. In a period in which racial tension in the United States was becoming increasingly explosive, this Comanche woman's marriage to a white man constituted an expression of tradition rather than a deviation from it. From LaDonna's childhood to her marriage to Fred Harris, being Comanche lay at the center of her experience and her articulation of self. And yet it would be her exposure to racism against African Americans that first aroused her sense of outrage at the treatment of minority groups and gave her a context within which to understand the discrimination that she had encountered.[12]

Introduction to Civil Rights

The time Fred and LaDonna spent in Norman coincided with the emergence of the civil rights movement. Beginning with the end of World War II, numerous cracks in the system of segregation appeared. In 1947, Jackie Robinson broke the color line in major league baseball by signing with the Brooklyn Dodgers. In 1948, President Harry S. Truman ordered the desegregation of the armed forces. And on behalf of the National Association for the Advancement of Colored People (NAACP), Thurgood Marshall announced a plan to challenge segregation in higher education in Oklahoma.[13]

Even Norman, Oklahoma, witnessed volatile challenges to segregation during the late 1940s and early 1950s. A notorious "sun down town," African Americans had not dared to stay in Norman after dark for most of the town's short history. In the mid-1940s, however, a handful of African American students, with the help of the NAACP, began challenging Oklahoma segregation laws. The 1896 United States Supreme Court decision in *Plessy v. Ferguson,* which laid the legal foundation for segregation by allowing that separate but equal facilities could be provided for blacks and whites, came under increasing fire both in the nation at large and in Oklahoma in particular. According to Oklahoma law, anyone of African descent was recognized as "negro" or "colored" in the constitution. All other people fell into the category of "white." This language not only set up significant prejudice against African Americans, but underscored the ambiguous status of Native Americans in the state.[14]

As a result of lengthy court battles fought by the NAACP, George W. McLaurin became the first African American admitted to the University of Oklahoma's graduate college in 1948. In the summer of 1949, just a few months after Fred and LaDonna Harris were married, Ada Lois Sipuel Fisher became the first African American admitted to the University of Oklahoma School of Law. When Fred and LaDonna made their first home together in Norman that same summer, racism still infested the town on the heels of forced integration of the graduate college. Living in Norman in the early 1950s, Harris became aware of racism in a way she had never fully appreciated. The daughter of the principal of the black school in Norman babysat Fred and LaDonna's daughter, Kathryn. One afternoon, LaDonna saw her babysitter standing outside a movie theater protesting racial discrimination and realized that people she knew were participating in the battle against segregation.[15]

In Oklahoma and across the nation, there was nothing subtle about racism toward African Americans. In a 1941 attempt to head off desegregation, the Oklahoma legislature made it a misdemeanor for blacks and whites to attend schools together. For Native Americans, however, a different story existed. Oklahoma had, after all, been the site of many Indian reservations prior to statehood in 1907 and boasted a significant population of Native Americans. Many native Oklahomans who identified themselves as "white" had retained quaint stories of Indian ancestry. And yet, while the discrimination against Native Americans did not follow the same conspicuous pattern as that against African Americans, it still served the same function. When Harris watched African Americans challenging racism in Norman, she began to relate it to her own experiences. She remembered an occasion as a young girl in Walters when the Native American children were separated from the white children for purposes of immunization. Recalling that incident, she now had a larger framework in which to place her experience of racial discrimination.[16]

For Harris, the blatant manifestations of racism against African Americans fostered within her a deeper understanding of prejudice. Her own recognition of the similarities in racism toward blacks and Indians, however, did not necessarily mean that others made the same connection. In fact, one problem with the emerging dialogue on racism in the mid-twentieth century was the tendency to view racism narrowly. More often than not, the quest for civil rights signified an effort to end discrimination against African Americans rather than other ethic groups also facing oppression. Connections between the struggle for equality by various ethnic groups increased in the 1960s and 1970s, but there remained a tendency to view racism as largely an issue between blacks and whites. Historically, whiteness and blackness have been defined as opposites, making the status of Native Americans unclear. Blacks were perceived as a threat and, therefore, a source of white loathing while Indians grew ever more invisible until becoming almost mythical tokens of old Wild West imagery. As a young wife and mother in the early 1950s, Harris did not consciously work through the complicated nuances of racial discrimination, but she began to identify with those victimized by racism. Just as growing up steeped in Comanche culture shaped Harris's early years and sense of identity, living in Norman as a young newlywed in the midst of the emerging civil rights movement clearly shaped her perception and understanding of racism against both African Americans and Native Americans.[17]

Politics and Partnership

The public relationship of Fred and LaDonna Harris became one of the defining characteristics of Fred's political persona because of the centrality of LaDonna in her husband's career. Fred's involvement in politics began as a college student, when he participated in the Young Democrats organization at the University of Oklahoma. He even ran for the Oklahoma state legislature while still in law school. He lost in that first attempt but won the 1956 election and became an Oklahoma state senator. Fred remained in the Oklahoma Senate until 1964 when he left to fill a United States Senate seat after the death of Robert S. Kerr. Fred always included LaDonna in his political career, and she became a crucial asset. This young pair from rural Oklahoma ultimately became one of the most prominent political couples of the period. Just as Fred had discussed his course work with LaDonna while studying at Oklahoma, he continued to share his work in the state legislature with her. Both described their marriage as one in which they shared everything with each other and were each the other's best friend. Although making his wife an integral part of his political career seemed natural to the two of them, it raised more than a few eyebrows and did not come without criticism from friends and colleagues alike. Kathryn Harris remembers a neighbor being "very critical" of LaDonna for being so involved in Fred's career and for not being home more often.[18]

After Fred graduated first in his class from law school, he and LaDonna moved to Lawton, Oklahoma, where he began practicing law in 1954. Although they left Norman behind, their introduction to racial tension and the struggle for civil rights had just begun. That same year, United States Supreme Court Justice Earl Warren handed down the unanimous decision in *Brown v. Board of Education of Topeka,* which deemed the doctrine of separate but equal "inherently unequal" and called for the desegregation of public schools. Nevertheless, the process of integration came slowly and not without considerable effort by grassroots activists. Ada Lois Sipuel Fisher and other African Americans had gained entrance to the graduate college at the University of Oklahoma, but the undergraduate college was not integrated until 1955, after the *Brown* ruling.[19]

Indeed, cities all across the United States resembled Norman in the tumultuous process of securing basic rights for African Americans. In 1956, more than ninety Southern members of Congress signed the Southern Manifesto, which condemned the *Brown* decision and pledged to fight desegregation. The following year, President Dwight D. Eisenhower sent soldiers from the 101st Airborne Division to Central High in Little Rock, Arkansas, to protect nine African American students attempting to enroll in the previously all-white school. Racial tensions teetered on the brink as federal troops were sent into the South to enforce federal law for the first time since Reconstruction. Fortunately, the Little Rock situation did not escalate into a second civil war, but much of the country held its breath in the face of such dramatic racial turmoil. The civil rights movement swept the nation and polarized its citizens over the issue of equality.

Integration of Lawton

Fred and LaDonna Harris brought the lessons of the national civil rights movement, as well as the demonstrations they witnessed in Norman, such as the one in which their babysitter participated, with them to Lawton. They took to heart these lessons as they worked with others in their new community to fight racism and integrate the city. In September 1963, a small group of about thirteen people comprising African Americans, whites, and Native Americans in Lawton began meeting to discuss strategies for integrating the city. According to local civil rights activist Maggie Gover, "The idea of a meeting came from a group of women who had been getting together for lunch to mull over what was happening and what might be done about it." These meetings generally took place on Wednesday nights at the home of one of the members. Harris was one of the founding members of what came to be called simply "The Group." She recalled how their meetings "grew like magic," and said, "we would have a covered-dish supper and then talk about the issues and integrating Lawton, particularly restaurants." In a 1965 brief history of The Group, members described it as a "disorganized organization" with no constitution, bylaws, charter, membership roster, or anything else that signified an official organization. Intent on maintaining the informal structure of their organization, the members took turns leading the meetings. Dubbed the "Honcho," as in "Head Honcho," the leader of the meetings changed from one week to the next. Harris explained that "everybody had to chair [the meetings] so there wouldn't be any fighting for leadership." She also pointed out that "being a leader of an integration movement wasn't very popular," which gave The Group an added incentive to spread around the responsibility of leadership.[20]

Because The Group kept so few records, it is difficult to gauge the total number of people who participated in the organization. One account suggests that "more than 1000 is probably a fair estimate," and that "attendance at a single meeting has been as high as 50." According to The Group's own history, the purpose of the organization was to "make Lawton a truly integrated community." The Group's first meeting established that African Americans "felt alone in their efforts to secure equal opportunities" and that they had no "desire to demonstrate or engage in violent actions." The significance of that first meeting can be seen through an examination of how The Group proceeded from that point forward. Significantly, the organization brought together people from a variety of ethnic and socioeconomic backgrounds, and this diversity enabled its members to share their experiences and learn from one another. The Group described its membership as including "business men, civic leaders, NAACP officials, educators, clergymen, labor officials, military men, civil service personnel, and just plain folk." Equally important to the diversity of The Group was the their desire to find a peaceful solution to the problem of discrimination and segregation.[21]

The Group began compiling a list of all of the segregated restaurants and other establishments in Lawton and then "black and white members would visit a segregated facility together." In fact, this list "actually determined The Group's method of operation" because if a given establishment "was determined to be segregated," then "one of the persons in The Group who knew the owner or proprietor would try to convince him that he should integrate." Although The Group found this approach to be "successful in most cases," Harris recounted an all-too-common response from proprietors of such businesses who seemed not to grasp the inherent inequality of segregation. One woman who owned a diner not far from the nearby military base, Fort Sill, said, "'Well, if we don't want to eat with Negroes, why do they want to eat with us?'" Nevertheless, The Group made a number of important advances toward securing greater civil rights. Grassroots activism in Lawton, as in thousands of communities across the United States, did something legislation alone could not accomplish—it quite literally set out to change one mind at a time through dialogue and interpersonal relationships. What made Lawton unique was not simply The Group but also the relationship that developed between Fort Sill and members of The Group.[22]

Just one month after the formation of The Group, its members confronted a "major challenge" when Fort Sill requested their assistance in conducting "an off-base equal opportunity inventory" of Lawton at the direction of the Department of the Army. According to The Group, "This comprehensive inventory reached into just about all areas in which segregation might exist." This joint effort by representatives from Fort Sill and The Group marked an important crossroads in the effort to integrate Lawton. It not only allowed The Group "to present a true picture of the community," but it also demonstrated the possibility of base personnel working with local activists to fight against discrimination. In fact, after a Lawton–Fort Sill conference on race relations in April of 1967, the Department of Defense praised The Group for its "untiring work and constant concern" in the area of civil rights. Regardless of numerous obstacles, The Group successfully employed "tactics of negotiation, persuasion, and indirect pressure" to facilitate a steady progression of integration in the city. Less than three years after the formation of The Group, Lawton's only black doctor, E. A. Owens, who served as the president of the Lawton NAACP chapter in addition to being a member of The Group, asserted that "by personal contact about 95% of the public accommodations were opened to all."[23]

Although The Group emphasized informal avenues of persuasion, Fort Sill had a more forceful course of action at its disposal—the base could put establishments off-limits to its personnel if officials deemed it necessary. Historically, military bases have taken this action with establishments in cases where soldiers faced discrimination, were cheated out of their money, or found themselves in too much trouble. A pawn shop where a couple of soldiers were beaten up or a bar frequented by prostitutes provide two common examples of situations in which base officials might intervene. In a city like Lawton, where businesses depended on patronage from the base, Fort Sill could cause a business to go under by forbidding its use by its personnel. It should be noted that such an action, though not uncommon, was not taken without significant justification on the part of the military. For business owners in Lawton, the mere possibility of having their establishments put off-limits often provided the nudge needed for them to integrate. Harris recalled members of the group telling local businesses that if they did not integrate, they would be put off-limits by Fort Sill. It is clear that "pressure from Fort Sill often played a significant role in breaking down barriers" because "the threat of being put off limits worried business owners."[24]

Ultimately, the struggle to achieve an integrated Lawton spanned many years and encompassed the efforts of numerous individuals, of whom Fred and LaDonna Harris were only two. While LaDonna worked with The Group, Fred served on Mayor Wayne Gilley's committee on integration and assisted civil rights proponents in trying to "force the city fathers" to support integration legislation. But by the time the city confronted its "most dramatic episode" in the integration effort, involving Lawton's only amusement park and swimming pool—the aptly named Doe Doe Park—Fred and LaDonna Harris had already entered into a much wider social and political arena in the nation's capital. The role played by Harris in the integration of Lawton and the way African Americans viewed her foreshadowed her later humanitarian efforts to protect the civil rights of people nationally and internationally.[25]

Ethnic Ambiguity

Harris's daughter Kathryn, who was a teenager during the Lawton integration effort, followed in her mother's footsteps with regard to civil rights. She too protested discrimination against blacks and even tried to convince her classmates to boycott a popular restaurant because it refused to serve African Americans. Unlike LaDonna, Kathryn has blond hair and light skin (both of which LaDonna ironically had as a child). Because she did not necessarily *look* Comanche, she found herself privy to a more overtly racist environment; one that directed racist sentiments at others but treated Kathryn as though she were white. Kathryn, however, never saw herself that way. She explains, "We weren't white. We were Comanche." Her sense of Comanche identity juxtaposed against the perception that she was white lent itself to a particular insight, one that differed from those of

her mother. As LaDonna—along with Fred—grew in prominence, LaDonna increasingly found herself in a position that
made her more aware of discrimination.[26]

Harris's ability to identify with others and to draw on her
own experience contributed significantly to her activism. One
African American who worked with her in the integration effort
recalled Harris's sympathy, feeling that she had a deeper understanding and compassion for their struggle because of the discrimination she had faced in her own life. When Fred decided
to run for the Oklahoma Senate in 1956—seven years before the
formation of The Group—his support for civil rights earned him
a number of minority votes. The relationship between the Harrises and the African American community in Lawton, however,
reflected a growing duality apparent in LaDonna Harris's Indian
ethnicity and the Harrises' position in white upper-middle-class
society and politics.[27]

Fred and LaDonna Harris's commitment to civil rights is obvi-
ous. Far more ambiguous, though, is the perception of their ethnicity. Some people thought Fred was Native American because of
his dark complexion and affinity for Comanche culture. At times
LaDonna Harris was clearly identified as "Comanche" or "half Comanche." Yet, in the context of African American struggles to gain
equal access to public facilities in Lawton, her ethnicity seems
conspicuously invisible at times. For instance, "a black business-
man in Lawton" said Fred and LaDonna "were among the first
white people to join" African Americans in the effort to integrate
Lawton. The man added that "LaDonna picketed with us. We trust
these two." Although these comments were intended to be com-
plimentary toward the Harrises, the words clearly designated Fred
and LaDonna as outsiders, albeit trustworthy outsiders. Similarly,
another African American, Betty Owens, who was at the center of
Lawton integration efforts, also remembered Fred and LaDonna as
"among the first white persons involved" with The Group. The
implication is not that these two African Americans were unaware
of her Comanche heritage but rather that juxtaposed against their
own racial identity amid the volatile civil rights movement, she
seemed white. Their own sense of "blackness" and "otherness"
clearly differentiated them from Harris.[28]

To further complicate the issue, by the early 1960s LaDonna Harris belonged to a white upper-middle-class "ethnicity" of sorts. As Fred's political career grew by leaps and bounds, both Fred and LaDonna increasingly became a part of the "whiteness" that so many African Americans found themselves defined against. At a time and place in which the very words "civil rights" and "equality" primarily signified the fight to end the oppression of black America, the light-skinned beauty from Comanche Country who grew up to marry a senator, live in the suburbs, and have three children was indeed caught between ethnicities. One of the most powerful contributions of the later American Indian movement came in the form of reinventing, redefining, and reasserting Indianness. Because this had yet to happen and because civil rights connoted a black struggle, the token status of Native Americans persisted. That Fred and LaDonna Harris were nicknamed "Freddie and the Indian" by one of his colleagues in the state legislature underscores the tokenism so indelicately apparent in the status of American Indians in the mid-twentieth century. Had Fred Harris been married to an African American woman instead of a Comanche woman, there can be little doubt that "Freddie and the Negro" or "Freddie and the Colored Woman" would have been viewed as neither quaint, charming, nor unthreatening.[29]

Expanding Gender Roles

Fred and LaDonna not only challenged the racial status quo; they also poked holes in traditional notions of appropriate gender roles. After Fred's election to the Oklahoma Senate, LaDonna frequently joined him on the floor of the legislature, sitting by his desk. Both were in their mid-twenties when Fred took office, making them considerably younger than the politicians with whom they interacted, and LaDonna felt that her assistance made Fred appear more mature. As the only senate wife present, however, it took people time to adjust to her unusual presence. For her part, Harris drew on her experience as a young girl in school when she learned how to read people to figure out how to fit in. Harris explained that she would watch people to determine what role she could play and how best to act, and in the state senate she solved this problem by serving as a hostess until eventually people grew accustomed to seeing her there. She poured drinks, emptied ashtrays, and ironically acquiesced to conventional assumptions about women's roles while simultaneously challenging them. Her very presence on the senate floor stood in stark contrast to perceptions of the proper role for women in general and political wives in particular. Yet acting as a hostess, she played a traditional female role in a nontraditional setting. She offered a further challenge to gender assumptions when photographed on the senate floor while very noticeably pregnant with her second child, Byron. When the picture appeared in the most widely circulated newspaper in the state, the *Daily Oklahoman,* Fred remembered it causing considerable grumbling about the inappropriateness of her being in the senate offices in such a delicate condition. Perhaps equally troubling to Fred's colleagues was when LaDonna joined them for after-hours socializing. She related an incident in which she accompanied Fred to a restaurant to meet several of his colleagues. The other men brought their mistresses making her presence— as the only wife—particularly disconcerting.[30]

Harris did, however, do more than simply spend time on the senate floor and play hostess to her husband's colleagues. She also actively campaigned for her husband in both the 1956 election and in his successful bid for reelection in 1960. In 1962, when Fred unsuccessfully ran for governor of Oklahoma, LaDonna figured prominently in the campaign literature. One Harris campaign brochure devoted an entire section to her accomplishments, describing her as "a working team-mate and companion of her husband" who "went to work, along with [Fred], to finance his college education." The brochure mentioned her membership in the Comanche tribe along with her commitment to "Indian progress." Because LaDonna had "personally toured many of the state mental institutions, hospitals and children's homes and schools," she could provide Fred with "the woman's view" on how such programs might be improved. Further described as a "devoted mother and housewife" as well as an "invaluable helpmate," Harris's visibility seems noteworthy—

not in and of itself, but because of the particular aspects of her life that were emphasized. Here was a woman who fulfilled both traditional female roles as a "devoted mother and housewife" as well as involved herself in supporting programs for "Indian progress" and provided "the woman's view" on a host of issues to her senator husband. The gendered imagery used to project both the public and private attributes of Harris seems significant in light of campaign literature's emphasis of precisely those qualities that were intended to give Harris and her husband the greatest appeal.[31]

Although it was not that unusual to see the wives of politicians campaigning for their husbands and acting as unofficial staff, Harris surpassed this sort of "helpmate" status relatively quickly. In fact, by the end of the decade Fred had become her helpmate in many respects. She used his staff, and on several occasions he responded to correspondence for her. The state senator made good use of his wife's talents as well. He received numerous invitations to serve on state committees and organizations and could not possibly accept them all. On occasion, Fred sent LaDonna in his place, and this arrangement opened the door for her to develop her own political identity. When Fred was unable to attend a week-long seminar on civil rights at the Southwest Center for Human Relations Studies at the University of Oklahoma, he asked LaDonna to attend in his place. He told the sponsors of the seminar that he would support whatever LaDonna said and that they would basically be getting two for one by having her in attendance.[32]

While attending the seminar on civil rights in Norman, Harris grew disturbed by the exclusive focus on discrimination against African Americans. Not once did she hear anything about Native American problems. She tried to raise this issue but could not find the words to express how she felt. Finally, she burst into tears of frustration at her failure to verbalize her concerns about Native Americans to the group. She and Fred had always worked so closely that they spoke as one; unfortunately for her, it was with Fred's voice. In his absence, she realized that if she wanted to make people understand Indian problems she would have to find a way to articulate her concerns. She still saw herself as a stoic Indian girl and had grown comfortable with Fred acting as their voice and she as their intuition. Over time and with a lot of practice, she became more comfortable speaking to groups of people. The emotion and frustration that caused LaDonna to burst into tears on more than one occasion ultimately became an asset after she learned to channel her strong feelings into action.[33]

The visibility of LaDonna in Fred's work, such as her attendance at the civil rights seminar, her presence on the senate floor, and her campaigning, continued to draw attention from supporters as well as critics. The criticism regarding her visibility in his career at the state level, however, paled in comparison to what they faced in his bid for the United States Senate. Some of the old guard from the Robert S. Kerr camp told Fred there was "too much LaDonna" in his campaign. When Fred gave speeches he typically said, "LaDonna and I did such and such" or "LaDonna and I think this or that." To him and LaDonna this seemed a logical outgrowth of their close relationship; they shared so much that it became second nature for Fred to include her in his speeches. The couple ignored the criticism and ultimately helped change the role of political wives in the United States. Despite the objection by some that she played too prominent a role in Fred's political career, others praised their teamwork. One newspaper commented, "Even in a town where husband and wife teams are no novelty, the young Fred Harrises (both only 34) stand out as one of the smoothest working combinations to come along."[34]

On the surface Harris did in many ways appear to be a traditional wife. Shortly after Fred became a United States senator, LaDonna criticized congressional wives who were absent from campaign functions: "If she's campaigning with him, if she's standing right back of him, if she's sharing with him, then she's being a real wife. That's what I am and am going to continue to be." Her daughters, Kathryn and Laura, were flabbergasted years later when they came across an old interview in which their mother said she did not help her husband make any decisions and that she just supported him. Laughingly, Harris explained, "I was smart enough to know what the general public expected of me at that time." Privately, however, she was anything but a traditional wife. Described as "serious and goal oriented" by one friend, it became apparent to many early on that she had no intention of being a stay-at-home wife and mother. In fact, some of her Lawton peers even wondered how the Harris children would turn out in light of their mother's flurry of political activity. What appeared to be the embodiment of the traditional role of homemaker as a wife and mother was only that, an appearance. Laura Harris explains that her mother was not a "milk and cookies" kind of mom. Both Fred and LaDonna Harris and those who knew them best in this critical period have described their marriage as a full partnership in every sense of the word. LaDonna became crucial to Fred's career, as he would to hers.[35]

In the Nation's Capital

When Fred and LaDonna moved from Lawton to Virginia to be near the nation's capital in the mid-1960s, they were catapulted into a very different world than the one they left behind. They abruptly found themselves socializing with President Lyndon B. Johnson and Lady Bird Johnson. They became good friends with their neighbors, Senator Robert Kennedy and his wife, Ethel, after LaDonna met Ethel at a Senate Ladies Club function. Right after they were introduced, Ethel said to Harris, "Kid, stay with me. I hardly know any of these people." Fred believed that her warm personality attracted Ethel and the two very quickly became good friends. Fred and LaDonna also made friends with Vice President Hubert Humphrey and his wife, Muriel, as well as Minnesota Senator Walter Mondale and his wife, Joan. Fred and LaDonna soon were socializing with a veritable "who's who" of Washington politics. One journalist described Fred Harris as "the only person in Washington who could have breakfast with Lyndon Johnson, lunch with Hubert Humphrey, and dinner with Robert Kennedy."[36]

Socializing aside, Fred faced many demands as he settled into his new job, and LaDonna confronted a new set of expectations as the wife of a junior senator. She had three children to raise and at times felt unprepared for the social expectations placed on congressional wives. She had no desire to become "a painted backdrop" as she described some of the senate wives. By this point in her life, Harris wanted to work on behalf of Native American rights, not attend social functions with other congressional wives. She still struggled to give voice to her passionate feelings about helping Native Americans as she and Fred adapted to their life in the nation's capital.[37]

Senator Harris began gaining a national reputation for his continued support of civil rights. As a state senator, Fred had supported adding an amendment to the U.S. Constitution banning the use of poll taxes and also introduced Senate Bill 273, which would establish the Oklahoma Human Rights Commission. After a series of race riots in the summer of 1967, the U.S. senator proposed the establishment of a commission on civil strife. President Lyndon Johnson liked the idea and decided to create such a commission and called Fred at home to give him the news just prior to making the announcement on national television. President Johnson told Fred that he had not only decided to create the commission, later known as the Kerner Commission, but also wanted Fred to serve on it. This afforded a considerable opportunity to the young junior senator. Recognizing this, the president recommended that Fred remember he was a "Johnson man." In the colorful fashion that made the outspoken Texan notorious, Johnson said that if Fred forgot their friendship he would take out his pocket knife and cut off Fred's "pecker." The president followed up his threat by saying that being from Oklahoma, he figured Fred understood that kind of language. Just a few years after arriving in the nation's capital, Fred and LaDonna had indeed come a long, long way from Walters, Oklahoma. Although President Johnson could be intimidating, Fred established a good relationship with him, and this, in turn, gave the Harrises a receptive audience to voice their concerns about providing more opportunities for Native Americans.[38]

As Senator Harris became increasingly well known for his work in the area of Native American issues, he drew enormously from the experiences of his wife. Early in their relationship Fred learned about Comanche culture and beliefs. He even learned to speak some of the language, which later became a way in which he and LaDonna could communicate privately in a public setting. One friend from Lawton recalled teasing Fred about being more Indian than LaDonna because he expressed such interest in Native Americans and would often break out in a Comanche song while driving. In fact, many people believed Fred Harris was Native American. They often asked LaDonna what tribe her husband belonged to, and when she replied that Fred was not Native American, some actually argued with her. Fred's olive complexion, coupled with his marriage to LaDonna and his knowledge of Native American cultures, contributed to the mistaken assumptions about his ethnicity throughout his public career. That said, Fred's relationship to Comanches and other Indians far surpassed a mere "interest" in their cultures. In 1955, the general council of the Kiowa, Comanche, and Apache tribes retained Fred as their attorney because of his "close association" with them and his sympathy and understanding of their situation.[39]

Comanche Separation

At the behest of LaDonna and many of her Comanche relatives, Fred embarked on a long journey to help secure the separation of the Comanche from the Kiowa and Apache tribes—first as their attorney and later as their state senator. According to Morris Foster, tensions over the proposed separation of the Comanches from the Kiowa and Apache produced two main groups: the "yes" people, who stressed the short-term economic benefits of a separation, and the "no" people, who argued that "the three tribes were politically stronger as a group than as separate entities." Part of the issue, argues Foster, is that the Kiowa, Comanche, and Apache tribe were expecting a large settlement from the Indian Claims Commission (which partially paid out in the sum of $2 million in 1958). Foster describes the "yes" people—who would include LaDonna Harris —as believing that the Kiowas and Apaches would "outvote Comanches and so obtain a disproportionate share of the land claim money." For Fred and LaDonna Harris and the Comanches who supported separation, the issue was actually far more complex.[40]

The separation debate, not insignificantly, began during the termination era. Termination, a policy laid out in the late 1940s and 1950s during the administrations of presidents Harry S. Truman and Dwight D. Eisenhower, set the tone for federal Indian policy that lasted until the 1970s. Both the Truman and Eisenhower administrations believed that getting rid of assistance programs, which contributed to the special status and lingering dependency of Indians, provided the best possibility for Native Americans to become full participants in dominant society. The federal government's effort to assimilate Native Americans into so-called mainstream white society resulted in the termination of numerous services (as well as dissolution of federal recognition of tribal status in many instances) and primarily accomplished the further marginalization of an already disaffected segment of the population. Largely hailed as one of the most destructive initiatives in the history of federal Indian policy, termination extended beyond the scope of mere law; it permeated the discourse on the rights and status of Native Americans for the next several decades, and it shaped the mind-set of millions of Indians and non-Indians across the country.[41] The underlying premise behind termination thinking was that progress equaled dominant white culture while tradition signified poverty and backward thinking. In other words, for Native Americans to succeed they had to abandon their traditional cultures—at least to some extent—to succeed economically, educationally, and even socially.

When Fred Harris described supporters of the Comanche separation effort in a 1957 letter to national policy makers as "mostly educated, self-sufficient people, who have to work for a living," he did so within the context of termination-era language. Despite a meeting on March 17, 1957, at the Fort Sill Indian School in which Comanches voted 262 to 142 in favor of separation, the matter only grew more controversial. Fred Harris accused "antiseparationists" of using "patently false" arguments to discredit the separation effort, including claims that separation would "end the trust period on individual land, would take the Comanches out from under supervision of the Bureau of Indian Affairs, would do away with their right to share in tribal benefits and claims, or receive welfare assistance." The Oklahoma state senator further described the people who opposed separation (who incidentally included some members of LaDonna's own family) as mostly consisting of welfare recipients "who mistakenly believe they will be cut off" and those "who are very dependent on the Indian Agency, many of who mistakenly believe that if separation is approved, they will have to fend for themselves." Others included in Fred Harris's list were "rehabilitation loan clients who are delinquent, and their families, who feel that their best chances for relief lie in the old organization." In spite of the sharp words used by Senator Harris to describe antiseparationists and his hope that the issue would reach a swift resolution, separation advocates did not prevail until the passage of a 1966 referendum approving the spilt. Three years later, in 1969, the Comanche Nation was established and "became an institutional means for Comanches to manage their own funds and programs, thus participating more actively in the politics of Indian affairs and in the Anglo economy."[42]

Economic Assimilation and Cultural Preservation

The battle over Comanche separation, and the support given it by Fred and LaDonna Harris, foreshadowed later tensions in the effort to promote both cultural preservation and new economic opportunities for Native Americans. By the mid-1960s, Harris had determined to enlighten policy makers, as well as the public, about the struggles of Native Americans. One of the most pressing questions remained the extent to which Native Americans could retain their traditional culture and still benefit from mainstream American opportunities. Harris in many ways represented this struggle: she was half white, and married to a white United States senator at that, but she had grown up in a home that stressed traditional Comanche values and culture along with American mores. Harris wanted Native Americans to maintain cultural autonomy and to have greater access to mainstream economic and social opportunities. The tension between preservation of heritage and opportunities in dominant society later manifested itself in the founding of Oklahomans for Indian Opportunity (OIO). In fact, people frequently asked Harris why

she wanted to "hold on to" her Indian culture (reporters in particular often assumed she was Cherokee). In a variation of this line
of questioning, one reporter quoted Harris as saying, "Everyone
says to me, Why can't you keep your culture? And my response to
that is, it's already lost." Despite the contents of this interview,
Harris has since maintained that her culture has been a vital part
of her life since childhood. She expressed frustration that in Oklahoma history classes discussion of Native Americans centered on
the Five Civilized Tribes. "I'm Comanche," Harris was fond of saying. "Not a Civilized tribe, I'm wild Comanche." Fred, knowing
that this overemphasis on the Five Tribes bothered her, occasionally teased her about taking her to meet some civilized Indians.[43]

The issue of Indian identity, embodied in the tension between
participation in mainstream society and cultural autonomy, permeated both government discourse on Indian assistance and the
manifestation and articulation of "Indianness" in society at
large. The seeming contradiction between maintaining Native
American traditions while functioning in dominant society
posed a considerable challenge to Indian rights advocates. Harris
dismissed the idea that a contradiction existed or that Native
Americans could not do both. Instead, she involved herself in
mainstream politics and community issues while identifying herself as a "wild Comanche" and working for Indian causes. Despite her own conviction that one could exist in both worlds, it
indeed posed a tremendous challenge for her to help others do
the same. "I was lucky," Harris recalled. "Somehow, I learned to
make it in both worlds—the white and the Indian."[44]

When President Johnson declared an "unconditional war on
poverty" in his 1964 inaugural address, he could not have
known the extent to which this war would ultimately shape and
complicate the dialogue on Indianness and the ability of Indians to access mainstream opportunities. In the months following his inaugural address, Johnson began articulating his vision
of building a "Great Society." In a commencement speech at the
University of Michigan, the president explained that "the Great
Society rests on abundance and liberty for all," adding that "it
demands an end to poverty and racial injustice." Johnson's
words linked together racism and poverty in a meaningful

recognition of their interconnectedness. The tensions identified and experienced by LaDonna Harris, then, reflected a wider national phenomenon in which poor people of color increasingly sought control over programs that directly impacted their lives. Furthermore, President Johnson provided the mechanism through which this could be pursued with the creation of the Office of Economic Opportunity (OEO) in August of 1964. OEO was to act as an umbrella agency to oversee Johnson's Community Action Programs (CAPs) in an effort to eradicate poverty, thus creating the "Great Society" envisioned by the president.[45]

Oklahomans for Indian Opportunity

The year after Johnson implemented his War on Poverty, Harris began making plans of her own to reach one of the poorest groups in the United States, Native Americans. Oklahoma Indians, in particular, faced a significant challenge in that they were not eligible to receive OEO funds because, technically speaking, Oklahoma is a nonreservation state. As a result, Oklahoma Indians were lumped in with whatever community in which they happened to reside. The fact that War on Poverty funds were not going to Oklahoma Indians, coupled with Harris's involvement with the Southwest Center for Human Relations Studies at the University of Oklahoma, led her to speak out about the problems facing Native Americans, including the highest rates of infant mortality, illiteracy, unemployment, and poverty of any group in the United States. Harris's determination led her to help organize a conference in the summer of 1965 on Indian opportunity at the University of Oklahoma. One product of this conference was OIO. Of approximately 1,500 Oklahomans, Indians and non-Indians alike, who were invited to participate in the initial meeting, about 500 were present.[46]

Backed from its inception by Senator Fred Harris, OIO eventually gained funding from the OEO and became a significant asset in the War on Poverty. Senator Harris's political position and LaDonna Harris's election as the first president of OIO lent a level of visibility to the organization that proved crucial to its success. Yet her husband's position alone did not enable her to emerge as a respected Indian rights advocate. John O'Hara, director of the Southwest Center for Human Relations Studies, wrote Harris, suggesting that she be appointed in her own right and paid a consulting fee as an expert on Indian problems in Oklahoma. O'Hara explained, "This arrangement would clearly differentiate between your role as an expert in Indian problems working for the OIO and your role as the wife of a United States Senator."[47]

While O'Hara voiced concern that LaDonna establish her role in OIO as separate from her position as Fred's wife, the publicity generated by the couple's involvement contributed a higher profile than OIO would have otherwise enjoyed. Moreover, the initial goals of OIO were in keeping with federal Indian policy, which encouraged Native Americans to avail themselves of the possibilities in society. The tension between integration and cultural autonomy that characterized the lives of many Native Americans also manifested itself from the beginning of OIO. The organization struggled to find how it could best serve Native Americans by helping them achieve greater access to mainstream opportunities, and it did so at a time when Great Society disciples across the country sought ways in which to elevate the poor and eliminate racism. Significantly, as Daniel M. Cobb has noted, "Through the involvement of Oklahoma's large, diverse Indian population, the politics of poverty and Indianness intertwined." At this critical juncture in poverty policy, community renewal efforts, and the struggle for civil rights, Native Americans in general and OIO staffers in particular found themselves caught in a dramatically shifting paradigm.[48]

Implicit from the very beginning in the goals of OIO were the competing impulses of cultural preservation and integration. The stated purpose for the creation of OIO was to "improve social and economic opportunities of Oklahoma and American Indians and draw them more fully into the Oklahoma and American economy and culture." At the same time, the organization sought to "preserve and perpetuate the history and heritage of Oklahoman and American Indians; and to promote brotherhood and harmonious human relations and communication among all Oklahomans and Americans." Although the constitution of OIO proclaimed a commitment to integrate Indians into the mainstream as well as to preserve Native American culture, the two objectives seemed difficult to reconcile. In its infancy OIO espoused an agenda that on the surface smacked of assimilation, and in the midst of a radical period of social change appeared quite conservative in doctrine and practice. To understand why LaDonna Harris and the organization she established seemed to embrace both assimilation and the retention of native culture, it is critical to consider the legacy of federal Indian policy.[49]

Assimilation, the cornerstone of federal Indian policy since the early nineteenth century, engendered tremendous problems for Native Americans. The 1887 Dawes Severalty Act, which ended the collective ownership of tribal land in an effort to turn Native Americans into yeoman farmers, created a cycle of poverty and a loss of community that shaped much of the twentieth-century Native American experience. The policy of termination, implemented after World War II, plunged Native Americans further into poverty as they lost numerous services that were vital to their survival. Relocation, another component of termination, provided federal money to help relocate poor Indians in rural areas to metropolitan areas where, in theory, they had greater job opportunities. Instead, it created a growing urban population of poor Native Americans who found themselves further alienated from their cultural traditions.

The tension between assimilation and a desire for cultural autonomy became stronger as dissatisfaction with termination policy grew, and by the mid-1960s it met with increasing criticism. Both Indians and non-Indians recognized that existing agencies failed to meet the needs of Native Americans. Self-determination, which has characterized federal Indian policy since the early 1970s, drew support because of the dawning awareness that Indians needed more control over programs and policies that directly affected them. Harris is a product of both termination and self-determination policies, and the growth of her activism can best be understood within the context of the shift in federal Indian policy from the former to the latter. The belief that Indians should be more directly involved in the agencies and programs designed to help them facilitated the founding of organizations such as OIO.

Although the OIO constitution stressed its commitment to drawing Indians "more fully into the Oklahoman and American economy," as well as "preserve and perpetuate" their culture, this proved a difficult task. Some Native Americans feared they faced more empty promises from whites and thought not enough was being done to preserve Indian identity, whereas others saw attempts at establishing "Indian" programs as detrimental to the goals of full participation in the mainstream. For instance, one letter to Fred Harris commented on LaDonna's efforts to help establish an Indian college and emphasized the need for Indians to assimilate into the mainstream: "We cannot afford the time to study dead languages." The letter added, "I have never regretted my grandfather's decision to discard an old culture for American. I am second generation with absolutely no vestige of the old culture. I have never felt any loss." The minutes from the initial meeting of OIO convey another aspect of this conflict. In the beginning the organization contemplated whether the Bureau of Indian Affairs (BIA) should be asked to oversee the running of OIO. One member said that if the program was to be successful, "We need the advice of these experts from the BIA." This person added that, if the BIA ran the program, it would "move faster because they know the Indians and their needs." Only a few years later Harris lambasted the BIA as "one of the major problems Indians have." Reflecting back on this period, she recalled that since childhood she had maintained a negative image of the BIA. When she first tried to articulate the problems facing Native Americans to a group at the Southwest Center for Human Relations, someone told her that there were no Indian problems in Oklahoma because the BIA took care of them. So frustrated that she burst into tears, Harris later explained that the BIA controlled everything from Indian housing to health care to education. OIO tried to change this so that Indians controlled their own lives.[50]

While Harris viewed the BIA as operating like a colonial government, others in the OIO organization took a very different view. Iola Taylor Hayden, one of the founding members of OIO and the organization's executive director, described the BIA in a more positive light. Hayden, who grew up in Lawton and attended the Fort Sill Indian School, taught at a BIA school before working for OIO. She said that despite problems of incompetence, which she added is something inherent in most bureaucracies and not limited to the BIA, her experiences were more positive than negative. Despite the poor education she received at the Fort Sill Indian School, she did not recall being mistreated. Instead she compared the experience to belonging to a large family.[51]

Although the OIO board ruled out asking the BIA for direct involvement, its members opted to reserve the right to consult the bureau when necessary. Significantly, the meeting then turned to a discussion of the most pressing problems among Indians that needed to be addressed. One member voiced a concern about Indians who had the opportunity to work but did not want to. He then asked, "What do we do about those who don't want to work but would rather live on welfare?" Harris replied, "You have to show them what an advancement it is to make money." This exchange goes to the heart of problems facing Native Americans and the implicit assumption that mainstream white culture is superior. The tension between the dominant society and Indian culture underscored much of the debate on Indian issues in this period. It proved a difficult balancing act to assess the extent to which Indians could both participate in the mainstream and maintain their traditional culture and customs.[52]

Because they did not live on reservations and the BIA largely failed to offer assistance to Indians not living on reservation land, Native Americans in Oklahoma continued to face an even more complicated situation than did many Indians living elsewhere. As Cobb noted, "Because neither the federal nor state government recognized reservations per se, Oklahoma Indians participated as minorities in county and city community action programs." Here, explained Cobb, "the social and political aspects of 'being Indian' in Oklahoman society collided." Ironically, the government's long-standing commitment to assimilation proved a double-edged sword to nonreservation Indians because it precluded them from partaking in many of the services offered by the BIA. In theory, the lack of reservations in Oklahoma furthered the ultimate goal of the government to integrate Indians into the mainstream and do away with the need for the bureau altogether. In 1966, Senator Harris articulated this dichotomy in his "American Indians—New Destiny" speech before Congress. He stressed the positive relationship between assimilation goals and the nonreservation status of Oklahoma Indians. He argued, "It has been much easier for Oklahoma Indians to become a part of the total community in Oklahoma than it has in reservation states." He supported his claim by pointing out that Oklahoma had in fact produced "Indian humorists, prima ballerinas, United States Senator's wives, and business executives." Despite his humor and optimism about the benefits of nonreservation status in relation to goals of integration, the ambiguous status of Indians in Oklahoma allowed many to slip through bureaucratic cracks into poverty and obscurity.[53]

In an attempt to reach these Indians, OIO organized CAPs to inform Indians about services available to them and encourage their active involvement in bettering their communities. Central to the philosophical approach behind these campaigns lay the recognition that the participation of Indians themselves was crucial to their success. As Harris pointed out, "We have been doing things *to* Indians and *for* Indians, rather than *with* Indians." A letter to Iola Taylor Hayden, executive director of OIO, from Virgil Harrington, the area director of the BIA, praised their work, saying, "Your organization is one that has moved into new fields of Indian participation that is contributing much progress toward the goal of full assimilation into the mainstream of society of our Oklahoma Indians."[54]

Yet just a few months later, in the summer of 1967, OIO found itself in a hotbed of controversy. Regardless of support for OIO's efforts to set up CAPs and encouragement from the Johnson administration, criticism erupted from a number of sources, as a growing tension emerged between tribal governments and OIO over control of funds and communities. One significant source of animosity toward OIO came after they began advocating that tribes elect their own leaders instead of having them appointed by the BIA. Not surprising, the bureau opposed this idea, but so too did tribal leaders, who themselves had been appointed by the BIA. At the heart of this tension lay fundamental issues about what constituted "Indianness" and who had jurisdiction over Indian governance. As a result of this struggle, some of the OIO board members called for Hayden's resignation, accusing her of hostility toward members of the staff, exerting unbridled power, and using arbitrary tactics in hiring and firing. They called her "anti-pow-wow, anti-church, anti-Indian, and anti-BIA."[55]

The fact that Hayden's critics characterized her in such contrasting terms provides insight into competing notions of Indian identity. In the end, Hayden remained in office, but concern over this tension lingered. According to Cobb, "The fear that power struggles might detract from OIO's successes in generating community action was well-founded." Although the organization had been praised for its efforts to draw Indians into the mainstream, competition over dispersal of funds and the CAPs led to an onslaught of bickering and criticism. The tension between assimilation and cultural autonomy, illustrated by conflicting notions of what constituted Indianness, further exacerbated these power struggles. Both tribal leaders and proponents of the BIA criticized OIO, fearing it had gained too much power.[56]

A 1967 report commissioned by OEO on OIO's efforts in Oklahoma revealed that by and large OIO was "well thought of" and considered "to be a legitimate action force within the state" but that there had also been "some adverse reactions from groups" that OIO "pressed" to "do more to help Indians." The report encouraged an "intensification of OIO's community organization efforts" and, at the same time, identified one of the fundamental problems in implementing CAPs in Native American communities: "intercounty jealousies" threatened CAP consolidation efforts and further complicated already heated debates over the jurisdiction of community, tribal, and outside organization officials. On the one hand, the problems encountered by OIO spoke to more generalized critiques of the War on Poverty's CAPs, but, on the other, the multilayered bureaucratic nature of tribal governance only widened the feasibility gap.[57]

Both the internal and external criticisms of OIO demonstrated the issues at stake on the larger scale of federal Indian policy. The wider movement underway to secure civil rights for minorities provided some benefits to Native Americans, but it also led many to see American Indians as just another minority, rather than as having a unique relationship to the federal government built upon centuries of treaty agreements. A further complication existed in competing notions of Indianness. As policy under the Johnson and Nixon administrations shifted toward self-determination, OIO had a significant role to play in Oklahoma. Yet divisions persisted over jurisdiction, identity, and organizational control. As controversy surrounding OIO continued, Harris became increasingly swept up in national politics. The day-to-day oversight of OIO fell to Iola Hayden, as did much of the criticism of the organization, while the Harrises found themselves operating in a wider political arena. Fred's career kept him in Washington much of the time, and LaDonna found new opportunities to work on behalf of Native Americans at the national level.[58]

Stereotyped Indianness

Stereotypes of Native Americans further aggravated the struggle to reconcile participation in dominant society with the preservation of cultural identity. At the same time the founder of OIO embraced her heritage and promoted the entrance of Indians into the mainstream, she also faced an interested, but often ill-informed, audience. For example, a representative from one of the best-respected museums in the United States, the Smithsonian Institution, met with Harris to discuss sponsoring a Native American heritage project and, in the course of the conversation, asked her whether Indians could vote.[59]

Ignorance about the status and culture of Native Americans posed a significant obstacle in the struggle to improve opportunities for Indians. In fact, Fred Harris often told people that when LaDonna first voiced her desire to interest people in Indian problems, even he responded out of ignorance: "What Indian problems? I've lived all my life among Indians and the only Indian problem I know of is the one I married." In fact, he made these comments in a speech to his fellow United States senators in 1966. Explaining the context of such remarks, the former senator said that this parodied a common response to his and LaDonna's raising the issue of problems facing Native Americans. For instance, a friend of the senator from Oklahoma once told him he had gone to school with lots of Indians and they did not seem to him to have any problems. When Fred asked his friend what had happened to those Indian classmates, his friend responded that he was not sure but that he did not think any of them had graduated from high school. Drawing on conversations such as this one, Fred used humor as a way to identify with people and put them at ease before turning to the sober facts surrounding the conditions of Native Americans. Moreover, Fred's characterization of LaDonna as "his Indian problem" mocked the very derogatory way in which many referred to "*the* Indian problem." Whereas today such a comment would likely be construed as racist and sexist, in the mid-1960s it allowed Senator Harris to identify with both his peers and his constituents by first relating to their ignorance before educating them on Indian issues. Still, the fact that employing stereotypes of Native Americans seemed a useful tool in educating Congress and the American public speaks volumes.[60]

This use of humor to combat ignorance helps explain why many of his peers in Congress considered Fred Harris to be an expert on Indian issues and why he characterized himself as a "self-admitted expert on Comanche Indian history and culture" while joking with the media about his wife's background. Fred commented at times that LaDonna was "fierce and warlike, but I domesticated her." He also told one reporter, "When a pretty Indian girl with brains leaves the reservation, watch out!" because "anything can happen." The fact that Harris never lived on a reservation and came from a nonreservation state did not prevent Fred from employing stereotypes of Native Americans as a public relations tool. He did, however, see such anecdotes as a way of poking fun at the general lack of knowledge about Native Americans rather than with the intention of simply perpetuating stereotypes and ignorance.[61]

Although this sort of lighthearted commentary may have inspired a few laughs, the ramifications were indeed more significant. These remarks evoked a vivid image in an era of social and political upheaval. The message seemed clear: Indians were not a threat. Moreover, they could be reformed and remade in the image of the white man. As long as assimilation, or more appropriately integration, of Native Americans into the mainstream remained the ultimate goal, the advocacy of Indian rights did not pose a threat. On the surface, Fred and LaDonna's relationship provided the ultimate metaphor for assimilation. She had married a white man and, as the wife of a United States senator, represented the epitome of the American dream, right down to their three children and suburban Virginia home located just a few doors down from Robert and Ethel Kennedy. Harris, however, strongly rejected the notion of assimilation, maintaining that her Comanche values defined both her and her life's work.[62]

Regardless of Harris's own feelings about assimilation in the United States, American society in the 1960s did not readily accept or even understand such sentiments. The media interest in Harris, the comments about her high cheekbones, the headlines that drew on stereotypes of Native Americans, and even to some extent the jokes made by Fred revealed that beneath the spirit of reform lay an uneasiness about race relations. In the 1960s reform generated conflict, and though the government paid lip service to improving the condition of Native Americans the assumption that improvement and assimilation were one and the same left little consideration for an alternative view of Native Americans. The "good" Indian or the "progressive" Indian was the one who entered into the mainstream, shedding his or her cultural baggage along the way. Moreover, as a politician from conservative Oklahoma, Fred's use of humor about LaDonna's heritage may have reassured the "good ole boys" network that neither he nor his wife was a threat to the existing power structure. Ultimately, both Fred and LaDonna Harris proved too liberal —indeed, too radical—for their Oklahoma constituents. Nevertheless, their success at the national level hinged, at least in part, on their insistence that Indians be encouraged to participate in the mainstream society and economy.

As a prominent interracial couple, the image put forth by Fred and LaDonna had significant implications for how society perceived them. Few Indians enjoyed both the high profile and unthreatening role that Harris held at the national level during the 1960s, and it is unlikely she would have reached the audience she did and met with such an enthusiastic response by government officials had her rhetoric not been in keeping with the federal government's ultimate goal to integrate Indians. As the epitome of the "good citizen Indian," she represented a number of positive attributes to the nation. First, she symbolized the beneficial aspects of assimilation as a Native American who had successfully become a part of mainstream society. Second, Harris acted as an advocate for Indians without appearing radical, especially in comparison to the young activists in the American Indian movement. The pictures of Harris that appeared in newspapers and magazines during this period very clearly identified her as belonging to the mainstream. Finally, in addition to being a "model" Indian, she also fulfilled the expectations of a congressional wife in a way that facilitated a positive image of both her and Fred.

To be sure, their public relationship had important ramifications both for their careers and the Indian advocacy they supported. Hailed early on as a great team, Fred and LaDonna Harris projected a united front that seemed impossible to top. One newspaper described her as a "unique Senatorial asset." She frequently drew praise for helping Fred with his career, enabling her to move forward with her own activism without appearing to threaten her husband. She represented both the ideal wife and a positive image of the assimilated Indian. As one reporter wrote, "Washington must be changing its mind about the Comanche Indian." Here again, although the message in the article paid a superficial compliment to Harris, its premise smacked of racially distorted stereotypes of Native Americans. Despite having to contend with such stereotypes, Harris managed to use socially constructed notions of both Indianness and femininity to her advantage. The image of Harris as a doting and supportive wife afforded a certain legitimacy to her own entrance into the political world in the unofficial, but ultimately highly effective, role of congressional wife. Furthermore, her public relationship with Fred and the way in which his prominence and her "Indianness" served to reinforce the status and effectiveness of the other facilitated their success in advocating for Native American rights. For example, in an address on Indian policy to Congress, Wyoming Congressman Alan Simpson complimented Fred on his marriage to LaDonna: "Although I cannot command a lovely Comanche wife, I can say that my Uncle Dick married a Shoshone Indian. So at least I can say that I have an Indian relative." While she helped legitimize his role as an expert on the problems of Native Americans, he provided "the muscle behind her convictions." In a period when race relations teetered precariously and radicalism permeated the mainstream, the rise of LaDonna Harris to national prominence illustrates the centrality of the image she projected to the success of her advocacy. She used her position to gain attention and support for her own work to better the conditions and opportunities of Indians.[63]

The language used by members of Congress and society at large revealed a growing awareness of cultural nationalism. Referring to Harris and other Indians as "being on the warpath," "putting on their warpaint," and "holding pow-wows" (instead of meetings) capitalized on stereotypes of Native Americans. Certainly racist by today's standards, it is important to point out that much of this vernacular signified an earnest effort by non-Indians to relate to Indians. Just as Fred Harris used humor to educate the public and his congressional peers about problems facing Native Americans, many newspapers nurtured a serious desire to educate as well. For instance, an article about Harris entitled "Warpaint for the Senator's Wife" recounted a litany of problems confronting Native Americans and praised Harris's efforts on their behalf. On the one hand, the language used smacks of racism and distorted views of Indians. On the other, the purpose does not seem to have been merely to mock Indians. Beneath headlines such as "Senator's Wife on Warpath" were stories promoting Indian issues rather than simply denigrating and dismissing them. In short, embedded in the use of racist stereotypes is also the effort to identify with Native Americans. That said, the racist imagery of such headlines cannot be ignored. The fact remains that the permissibility of depicting this image of Native Americans hinged on a comfortably ignorant fascination with the quaintness of Indians.[64]

That Native Americans were viewed as relics of the past rather than as a group in need of serious consideration explains some of the popular depictions of Harris and other Indians. Certainly it would have been unacceptable to see a comparable newspaper headline about African Americans, regardless of how supportive the story underneath might have been. Yet, because of the historically ambiguous status of Native Americans, a different standard existed for them. Both literally and figuratively, Native Americans held a mascot-like status in the United States. As Mary Ann Weston found in her study of media coverage of Native Americans, journalism has gone beyond simply reflecting "images and stereotypes prevalent in popular culture." Stereotyping, argues Weston, "does not depend only on the use of crude language or factual inaccuracies"; it also "comes from the choice of stories to report, the ways the stories are organized and written, [and] the phrases used in headlines." Ironically, many journalists no doubt viewed their depictions of the wife of a prominent senator as "going on the warpath" as merely a cute play on words.[65]

Despite having to contend with the continued stereotyping of Indians, in just a few years Harris became a nationally known and respected authority on Native Americans. One magazine article described Harris as "tough, smart, angry" and went on to say, "From that anger may grow a national realization that Indians should no longer be considered wards of the nation, but, instead, human beings with very human, basic problems." Articles in national magazines such as this one further propelled Harris into the national spotlight and brought the condition of Native Americans to the attention of those in power and the general public.[66]

The Third U.S. Senator

LaDonna Harris's status as a respected leader on Indian issues continued to grow, and in many ways she ultimately surpassed Fred in both prominence and effectiveness in advocating for reform of Indian rights and government legislation. Although Fred remained supportive of LaDonna's work, it rankled him when people begin referring to her as a senator. He told Myra McPherson that he could take everything "until they started calling LaDonna 'Senator.'" That, added Fred was "where the liberation stuff just stops." Sure enough, as she rose in national stature, LaDonna at times seemed the biggest competition Fred faced. There is no doubt that the senator's pride in his wife's work did not stem a sense of irritation when, in 1967, Ernest Woods, area coordinator of the Oklahoma CAP, wrote to him praising her: "Oklahoma is indeed fortunate to have Mrs. Harris, as a virtual *third United States Senator.*" Robert Kennedy also recognized LaDonna's contributions and characterized her as "one of the most ardent champions of justice for the American Indian."[67]

Because of her work and prominent status, she testified on July 13, 1967, before the Education and Labor Committee of the U.S. House of Representatives on the effectiveness of OEO in Oklahoma. She praised OEO, saying she could not overemphasize how important the organization had been in bettering the lives of Oklahoma Indians. Harris spoke highly of President Johnson's efforts, stating his War on Poverty "offers the poor the chance to win the struggle to overcome feelings of lack of self-confidence and the hopelessness of poverty." She described OEO as "truly the 'self reliance program'" adding that she was "unable to think of the War on Poverty in the abstract." Rather, she thought of all those whose lives were improved through the various programs funded by OEO.[68]

In fact, Fred Harris described this as the major difference between his and LaDonna's approach toward Native American problems. When he heard about a particular issue he tried to figure out what sort of legislation could be passed to remedy the situation. LaDonna, on the other hand, directly focused on helping individuals who suffered from the problem. Her compassion for people is one of the things that stands out in the minds of those who have known her. Her empathy for others lent a sincerity to her advocacy that was often lacking in the highly political and sometimes disingenuous world of Washington, D.C.[69]

In a relatively short amount of time Harris went from being a small-town girl from Walters, Oklahoma, to testifying before Congress as an expert on Native American problems in Oklahoma. This marked only the beginning, however, for the work that continued to define her. While friends from Lawton never saw Harris as a traditional housewife and Washington newspapers realized she was no "tea party congressional wife," she did in fact employ assumptions about traditional female roles to affect change for Native Americans as well as for women. When she and Fred first arrived in the capital, she remembered thinking she would go crazy folding bandages for the Red Cross along with other congressional wives, which was the type of civic service expected and encouraged for them. Within just a few short years no one would expect to see Harris folding bandages or organizing tea parties. She had become a respected leader in her own right. She accomplished this by expanding assumptions about the traditional role of women rather than directly challenging them, for the word "feminism" had not yet crept into Harris's vocabulary. That would come later.[70]

An Activist in

Her Own Right

While competing images of LaDonna Harris as a political wife, mother, activist, and Indian permeated the media, Fred Harris said that he "always saw LaDonna as a sort of Eleanor Roosevelt." His remark is revealing, in that Roosevelt was also a controversial woman married to a prominent politician whose activism and support of her spouse spanned a broad chasm between loyal wife and political lightning rod. Also like Roosevelt, Harris was a woman whose niche was difficult for critics and supporters alike to define. In this context, Ladonna Harris's ascent to activism at the national level continued in the late 1960s as she and Fred spent more and more of their time in Washington, D.C. They moved in high-profile social circles and became fixtures in capital politics. Yet, as 1968 rolled around, the nation as well as LaDonna Harris saw numerous changes. The year 1968 proved a volatile one in the United States. Support for the Vietnam War and President Johnson plummeted after the Tet Offensive, and the My Lai Massacre exposed the awful truth that the war was far from over and far from humane. In March 1968, Johnson decided not to seek reelection. The following month, on April 4, Reverend Martin Luther King, Jr., the most widely known and respected leader of the civil rights movement, was assassinated. Two months later, Fred and LaDonna Harris's good friend Robert Kennedy fell to the same fate as King, dying on the campaign trail during his bid for the Democratic nomination for president. In that same year the civil rights movement became more radical. A generation of young African Americans expressed disenchantment with the nonviolent approach to civil rights and instead stressed black power and black pride. Similarly, young Native Americans also began talking about red power and voiced profound disgust with the federal government's management of Indian affairs and, in response, started the American Indian Movement (AIM).[1]

A different type of change occurred for LaDonna Harris in 1968 as she moved further into mainstream national politics. The year witnessed two significant developments in the activism of Harris. First, she became more involved in women's issues through the War on Poverty. Second, her appointment to the National Council on Indian Opportunity (NCIO) brought national recognition for her work on behalf of Native Americans. These two aspects of Harris's activism for women and for Native Americans grew simultaneously during this period and converged, foreshadowing LaDonna's legacy as a human rights advocate rather than simply an exclusive advocate of one group. Although she at times employed elements of identity politics as a matter of political expediency, LaDonna Harris supported the betterment of all people who suffered from discrimination.

National Women's Advisory Council on the War on Poverty

Not knowing that Johnson would soon decide not to seek reelection, LaDonna resigned as president of Oklahomans for Indian Opportunity (OIO) in January 1968 to serve as chair of the National Women's Advisory Council on the War on Poverty. Although she had become a respected leader in the struggle to provide educational and economic opportunities for Indians, her work fit within the framework of women's roles in the War on Poverty, a logical extension of the role women have historically played in politics and social reform. Concern over education, poverty, and health care via community action programs remained acceptable goals for women reformers. As wives, mothers, and moral guardians of the home, it made sense for women to concern themselves with reform that affected the family. Despite the emergence of the feminist movement in the mid-1960s, the main focus of reform as it related to women in the Great Society continued to stress the gendered role women should play.[2]

The role of women in the War on Poverty became a valuable part of the Johnson administration's commitment to building the Great Society. One report suggested women could "be the representatives of the invisible poor" and argued that "women should use their particular sensitivity and particular expertise in bringing about changes between human beings in the problem of racism." It encouraged them to start in their hometowns and get out and see for themselves the destructiveness of poverty. The report admonished women against criticizing welfare mothers prematurely. Another publication urged them not to "indulge in idle gossip, not to pass along unverified rumor . . . to build up, not tare [sic] down." Issues that affected the well-being of families and communities, such as education, poverty, housing, health care, sanitation, the well-being of children, and even racism, came under the umbrella of "female concerns." Within this context, Harris exemplified the positive image of women's entrance into the world of reform and politics. Ultimately, it was because she embraced and expanded this role that she achieved such success as a nationally recognized advocate of Native American and women's rights.[3]

Harris's work with the National Women's Advisory Council on the War on Poverty brought her into contact with an aspect of reform that stressed the particular role women should play in government and society. The focus on what women could do *as women* yielded to a liberal feminist strategy that emphasized working within existing social and political structures. The idea that women possessed different sensibilities than men and thus engaged in politics and reform from a different perspective informed the kind of liberal feminism that characterized her activism. For instance, in one interview Harris expressed her belief that women were better qualified to deal with certain issues because of their gender: "It's easier for women to cross racial and political lines. We tend to see the woman first, then her color, and then her party." The notion that women shared certain attributes that uniquely qualified them to facilitate certain types of change heightened with the resurgence of feminism in the 1960s.[4]

Feminism and the Language of Equality

The feminist movement gained momentum and grew increasingly radical after 1968 and, in one way or another, permeated the consciousness of women such as Harris. The belief that women had historically been denied access to certain economic and educational opportunities because of their sex became a cornerstone of feminist ideology. Historians argue that the discourse of equality, embodied in the social movements of the 1960s, influenced many women who found themselves in subordinate roles within the very movements that espoused the rhetoric of equality. By no means a radical feminist, LaDonna Harris did not attempt to subvert the existing constructs of gender relations. She did, however, exemplify the attributes of liberal feminism in that she recognized the particular ways in which women could band together to effect change. To accomplish her goals, though, she made a conscious effort to play whatever role society expected of her. Harris grew progressively aware of social limitations placed on women, and, while she continued to mold her behavior and appearance to accommodate dominant social expectations, she grew less and less comfortable in this role as the decade progressed.[5]

One significant indication of LaDonna's growing commitment to improving opportunities for women came in 1971, when she along with such notable women as Betty Friedan, Gloria Steinem, Fannie Lou Hamer, Shirley Chisholm, and Bella Abzug came together to form the National Women's Political Caucus (NWPC). LaDonna credits her friendship with women like Friedan, whom she knew socially before becoming involved in the feminist movement, for drawing her into the organization. Described as a "bipartisan organization intended to increase female visibility and participation in the political arena," NWPC was not without its problems. On the one hand, the NWPC is largely credited for the increase in women who attended both the Democratic and Republican national party conventions—up 13 percent and 17 percent, respectively—from 1968 to 1972. On the other hand, issues concerning race, class, and ethnicity proved divisive. LaDonna recalls the difficulty of being one of the few women of color involved in the organization and the fact that many white women failed to appreciate the dual discrimination confronted by nonwhite women.[6]

Addressing a women's group in the early 1970s during Fred's bid for the presidency, LaDonna spoke about the aspirations of feminism and urged her listeners to recognize and respect their differences. At the same time, however, she also encouraged them to pull together, not just as women but as people, to find solutions to the problems facing the nation. Describing herself, she said, "These diverse things I am cannot be dismissed with a wave of a hand. My being an Indian in my forties born to a poor family and the wife of a candidate for President are as much a part of me as being a woman." She urged women to "become aware" of their "own divisions" and to "not change them but to fashion them into weapons" to meet their goals. She discussed women as a "secret-servant class" whose unpaid wages as homemakers enabled men to work in the marketplace. Urging women to make the nation's issues "women's issues," LaDonna concluded by admonishing, "If we are to reach out to our sisters and brothers who do not yet stand with us, we must understand and speak to *their* experiences, *their* problems, *their* aspirations."[7]

The language Harris employed in the early 1970s differed markedly from what she used when Fred first won election to the United States Senate in 1964. At that time, she characterized a wife's place as simply supporting her husband, asserting that she did not help Fred make decisions. Less than a decade later, she used phrases such as "secret-servant class" to describe housewives. There are two explanations for this rhetorical shift. First, as she herself explained, Harris repeatedly employed a tactic she learned as a shy young girl suffering from dyslexia: she figured out what to say and do to fit in and therefore consciously constructed a persona and language that afforded her acceptance into a given group. As the 1960s gave way to the 1970s it became more acceptable—and, in some circles, desirable—to condemn sexism and call for equal opportunities for women. In other words, her vocabulary changed in part because her audience did. Second, and more important, times were in fact changing with the expansion of the feminist movement, and LaDonna Harris changed as well. She was coming into her own and, by the end of the 1970s, would be both an activist in her own right and a feminist.[8]

The words chosen by Harris in her address to the women's group illustrate both the influence of feminism on women in politics in this period and her insight as a leader. Ultimately, the feminist movement splintered and the country moved into a more conservative era. Historians argue that the failure of women to address the differences among them largely contributed to the fate of the movement. It is interesting to note that the suggestions put forth by LaDonna Harris regarding the direction of the movement are perhaps the very ones that could have saved it. She reminded her listeners that the many components to her identity were as much a part of her as being a woman and urged them to embrace larger "human" issues. These were perhaps the two areas where feminism received the most criticism: diversity and commonality. The particular brand of liberal feminism Harris embraced illustrates her ability to reach a wide audience of women from all backgrounds. She recognized the importance of conceptualizing and working toward common goals rather than advancing the cause of any one group.[9]

In a speech to the United Steel Workers of America in the early 1970s Harris illustrated her ability to connect the particular struggles of one group to larger human issues. She cited the similarity between the "struggle for recognition and power that labor unions went through" in the early twentieth century and effort going on in the 1960s and 1970 "to secure full citizenship for black people, American Indians, Chicanos, Puerto Ricans, other Spanish-speaking Americans—and women." She went on to discuss the conditions of Native Americans and women, pointing out that Indians were "asserting the basic right to be different and still be entitled to the full promise of America" and that women were still "excluded from many jobs they can perform as well as, or better than, men." She ended her talk by pledging that "we must work together" and that "you need us, and we need you. The vested interests are our common adversary." LaDonna's address to the steelworkers offers insight into how she used a larger platform to speak out about problems facing both Indians and women. In many ways her speech demonstrated her own struggle to encourage Native Americans to reconcile participation in the mainstream and a desire to maintain cultural autonomy. She situated the tension within a broad context of the historical struggle of particular groups to maintain to their own identity while participating in the mainstream American economy and society.[10]

Harris's language, which conveyed the interconnectedness and universality of human struggles for recognition and acceptance, evolved over time. Her awareness of women's issues became more pronounced as did her sense of problems facing Native Americans. When she first began her work on behalf of Native Americans in the mid-1960s, the only voice she had was Fred's. It is quite significant that she searched for her own voice and her own language in the midst of the civil rights movement, the feminist movement, and the dawning of the Native American rights movement. Her exposure to the discrimination against African Americans in Norman and Lawton in the 1950s awakened her to the racism she had experienced in her own life. As she dealt with discrimination at an intimate level, her own sense of Indianness was heightened and clarified. Similarly, living in the nation's capital in the late 1960s and early 1970s, she could not help but be exposed to elements of feminism and instances of sexism, in very much the same way as she had become more aware of racism. The LaDonna Harris who cheerfully poured drinks and emptied ashtrays in the Oklahoma Senate in the late 1950s and early 1960s differed from the one who talked with steel workers about the shared struggle of women, Native Americans, and laborers in 1970. Her sense of self continued to evolve during this period just as her activism did.

National Council on Indian Opportunity

The year 1968 proved to be a meaningful year for Harris. It marked the beginning of her advocacy of women's rights and ultimately led to a deepening in her understanding of sexism, which paralleled her work on Indian rights in a notable way. As she strove to understand the extent to which Native Americans could integrate into the mainstream and still preserve their heritage, her experience as an Indian rights advocate blossomed. In 1968 Harris still seemed determined to work within government bureaucracy to effect change for Native Americans. According to R. C. Gordon-McCutchan, LaDonna and Fred Harris, along with Secretary of the Interior Stewart Udall and Assistant Commissioner of Indian Affairs Bill Carmack, convinced President Johnson to create a cabinet council designed to address Native American issues. As a result, on March 6, 1968, Johnson issued Executive Order 11399, which called for the creation of the NCIO. Chaired by the vice president of the United States, the establishment of the NCIO purported to give Native Americans a greater voice and ensure that programs designed to aid Indians did in fact work to their benefit. Harris accepted an appointment as one of six Indian members of the council. She recalled that all of the members of the council with the exception of herself had served in an elected capacity, again underscoring her success at utilizing the unofficial role of a congressional wife to affect changes to official policy. In fact, the brief description of Harris contained in the NCIO files on Indian members listed her principal occupation as "organizational official, housewife." Despite not being an elected official, she had considerable experience that she brought to the council. She, after all, had founded OIO and through Fred had been exposed to more upper echelon political wrangling than many Indian rights advocates.[11]

The Indian members of the council vocalized the sentiments of many Native Americans when they criticized the BIA and emphasized the desire for self-determination. "In short," the council explained, "the Indian people want more services, more self-determination and relief from the hovering specter of termination." The significance of this council in part stemmed from the fact that it was "the first agency of the Federal Government where Indian leaders sit as equals with the members of the President's Cabinet in overseeing Federal Indian policy." Yet the Indian members were quick to point out that "symbolism is not enough." They warned that unless the Indian members could report significant commitment from the government, "the distrust, the suspicion on the part of the Indians, which has dogged the Federal Government and has defeated its meager attempts to help the Indian people, will continue."[12]

In 1969 after the inauguration of Richard M. Nixon, the duties of presiding over the NCIO fell to the new vice president, Spiro Agnew. Even before becoming vice president, Agnew flirted with the idea of helping Native Americans and certainly paid lip service to the emerging concept of self-determination, which would give Indians greater control over administering their own programs. He voiced support of self-determination, saying it sounded "like a good old Republican philosophy." Shortly after taking office, the vice president wrote a letter to Harris, saying he was "looking forward" to his "responsibilities on the National Council on Indian Opportunity" and that he was "anxious to have a full meeting of the Council." Yet Agnew would prove slow to act and would eventually come under fire from Harris for that very reason.[13]

Despite Nixon and Agnew's promised support of Native Americans, direct action came too slowly for some. The initial excitement over the NCIO by Indians and non-Indians alike waned because the council did not convene again for some time. Harris grew frustrated with the inactivity of the council and Agnew's failure to call a meeting. According to an article in the *Washington Daily News* entitled "Agnew Better Watch Out for Those Comanches," "A war between the Comanches and Vice President Spiro T. Agnew may flare up any minute." The article went on to warn, "A pretty Comanche girl is already putting on her war paint." It described Harris as "ready to lead

the five other Indians on the council on the war path." The article made clear LaDonna's displeasure with the vice president
and quoted her saying that Agnew's indifference caused the
council to lose its operating funds in a House committee. To
that end, the *Washington Daily News* depicted her as a force to
be reckoned with, even when it came to the vice president. But
whether intending to or not, the paper's stereotyping of Native
Americans as warring savages trivialized the real issues at stake.
Harris's frustration with Agnew continued to deepen in the latter half of 1969 because the vice president still did not call a
meeting of the NCIO.[14]

Harris and Agnew did, however, end up on the same side in
one of the most poignant and significant victories for a Native
American tribe in the twentieth century: the return of the sacred Blue Lake to the Taos Pueblo Indians. The Taos Indians lost
possession of Blue Lake in 1906 during the administration of
President Theodore Roosevelt. Roosevelt established the Department of Forestry in 1902 and made conservation one of his top
priorities. He set aside millions of acres of land for national
parks and, in the midst of his conservation efforts, the Taos Indians were robbed of their sacred Blue Lake and thousands of
acres of land in what became the Carson National Forest in
New Mexico. This began a struggle that lasted for sixty-five
years as the Taos Indians fought for the restoration of their land
and their lake.[15]

In the late 1960s several factors converged that paved the
way for Taos victory. First, both President Nixon and Vice President Agnew supported greater self-determination for Native
Americans and voiced sympathy for the historic mistreatment
of Indian people. Second, Harris made sure the struggle of Blue
Lake got national attention as a human rights issue. Her friend
John Rainer, a Taos Pueblo activist, told her of his own people's
struggle for the return of their sacred lake. Taos representatives
also met with Fred Harris to discuss Blue Lake, and he was convinced that he should do something about it. The Harrises
worked together on the issue as they had done so often in the
past, Fred as a policy maker and LaDonna as an activist, though
this time the activist was also a member of the NCIO. Knowing

that Nixon had voiced support for Native Americans and self-determination in the 1968 election, Fred and LaDonna used that as an opportunity to seek White House support of House Resolution 471, which would return Blue Lake to the Taos Indians. U.S. Senator Clinton Anderson from New Mexico voiced serious objections to this effort, and LaDonna later recalled his anger at Fred over their perceived interference. Senator Anderson said, "By God, Fred, I don't mess with your Indians in Oklahoma and you shouldn't mess with mine in New Mexico." Anderson's statement is significant in part because of his objection to H.R. 471, but even more so because of his perception of Native Americans. Here again, the dependent and mascot-like status of Indian people influenced the thinking of policy makers like Anderson, as did the de facto state sovereignty exercised over Indians in each state.[16]

Nonetheless, the bipartisan effort to restore Blue Lake to the Taos Indians proceeded over Anderson's objections. LaDonna Harris worked to gain the support of African Americans and other groups in order to cast the Taos struggle as a civil and human rights issue. Her efforts moved forward on another front as well. She made sure the White House did not ignore or forget about Blue Lake. According to Gordon-McCutchan, Harris befriended Bobbie Green, a young Navajo woman who was a White House Fellow. Green assisted in the formulation of the Nixon Administration's policy on Native Americans and worked with Harris in connection with the NCIO. She and Green helped compile a report on the status of Native Americans. The report made a variety of recommendations about Indian housing and education and also called for the support of the return of Blue Lake to the Taos Indians. Gordon-McCutchan credits Harris and her friendship with John Rainer for the inclusion of the Blue Lake issue in the report. Once the issue made its way into the NCIO's report, it gained considerable publicity and ultimately support from key policy makers. Influential leaders such as Ted Kennedy, George McGovern, and even conservative Republican Barry Goldwater supported H.R. 471.[17]

In January 1970, when Agnew finally called a meeting of all the members of the council, Green and the Indian members of the NCIO submitted the findings of their report. This would be the first time the NCIO had met since Nixon and Agnew came to office a year earlier. There were two significant outcomes of this meeting. The first relates to H.R. 471. The effort to return Blue Lake to the Taos Indians gained substantial attention and support as a result of this meeting. In fact, Gordon-McCutchan argues that "the significance of this meeting cannot be over-stated." This seems a fair assessment of the meeting in terms of Blue Lake. Although political wrangling continued for several more months, this meeting marked a turning point, and on December 15, 1970, President Nixon signed a bill into law that restored Blue Lake and the surrounding 48,000 acres to the Taos Indians. Fred Harris called LaDonna's role in the return of Blue Lake "her biggest accomplishment," and Laura Harris pointed out that it was her mother's friendship with Bobbie Green that caused the issue to be brought to the attention of the White House. That John Rainer told his family to always remember Fred and LaDonna Harris in their prayers because of the role they played in the restoration of Blue Lake serves as a poignant testament to their significant contribution. Indeed, Blue Lake became a landmark restoration case that marked a significant shift in federal policy toward greater religious freedom and increased support for the rights of Native American people.[18]

The return of Blue Lake, however, did not happen immediately after the NCIO's meeting. The second significant, and more immediate, outcome of that January meeting had to do with the other recommendations in the report and LaDonna's subsequent disillusionment. The cabinet members on the council had thirty days to respond to the proposals in the report. When they failed to do so in the allotted time, LaDonna Harris's anger over the Nixon administration's seeming indifference reached a breaking point because virtually nothing came of the recommendations of Harris and the other Indian members of the council. LaDonna resolved to take action. In large part because of the inaction of the NCIO and Agnew, Harris founded a new national organization, Americans for Indian Opportunity (AIO), in the spring of 1970 to advocate for Native American rights.[19]

A New Advocacy Organization

A few months later, Harris, now president of the newly founded AIO, offered harsh words of criticism for Agnew's handling of the NCIO. In a *Washington Post* interview she unequivocally blamed Agnew for inaction. She said that the cabinet members on the council needed "knocking around by the vice president" and suggested he should criticize them and their staffs for doing a "crummy job." She expressed no interest in being reappointed to the council when her two-year term expired that same spring, saying that if she stayed she would inevitably clash with the vice president over his inaction. LaDonna indicated that the Nixon administration would not do anything unless someone stayed after them. Being the wife of a U.S. senator had opened a lot of doors to LaDonna Harris and likely contributed to President Johnson's decision to appoint her to the NCIO to begin with, but she had finally reached the limit afforded her by that role. She needed a new role and, in fact, a new organization. Explaining that "federal agencies were responding sluggishly to proposals to help Indians," it was clear that the time had come for Harris to work on Indian issues from another angle, one over which she could exercise greater control.[20]

The publicity generated by LaDonna Harris's anger over the failure by Agnew and NICO to take action illustrates both her growing prominence and her frustration with the slow pace at which bureaucracies move. Although Harris later acknowledged that Agnew's inaction likely had more to do with his own political and legal problems than simply a lack of interest in the NCIO, at the time his seeming apathy inspired her to form a national Indian rights advocacy organization. Her respected position among the political elite and her leadership role made her disillusionment with government claims of Indian advocacy all the more significant. Her criticism of the NCIO would later be vindicated. Two years after she left the NCIO a committee report from the New Directions Conference lent substantial support to her concerns. According to the committee, the NCIO had "failed in every major sense in its intended mission." The committee added that the NCIO had not been "truly representative" of the

Indian community, had not addressed the needs of the "total Indian community," and had failed to coordinate properly with other agencies to ensure implementation of goals.[21]

Both the annoyance expressed by Harris at the NCIO and the criticism of the council by others demonstrated the growing disenchantment with the effectiveness of government agencies in helping Indians. Criticism of federal management of Indian affairs was hardly novel. What was new was government's assertion that it would do more to work with Indian people directly. The slow pace at which this occurred made the criticism of the government more glaring. In the meantime, LaDonna's newly founded AIO afforded her an alternate route to advocate for Native American rights.

Harris used AIO to fill some of the gaps and said they "hoped to work with Indian tribes and groups not reached by existing agencies and programs." Geared toward similar goals as OIO's, this new organization seemed the best solution to Harris's dissatisfaction with both the BIA and other government programs. She hardly stood alone in her criticism of the federal government's handling of Native Americans. In fact, the same year Harris left the NCIO, President Nixon made similar criticisms in a speech on Indian affairs. Nixon's speech shaped the dialogue on federal Indian policy that continues to this day. He advocated a shift in BIA policy and embraced the concept of Native Americans shaping their own destiny and administering their own programs.[22]

A New Era

Nixon said changes in federal Indian policy were long overdue and argued, "The time has come to break decisively with the past and to create the conditions for a new era in which the Indian future is determined by Indian acts and Indian decisions." He laid out his administration's plans to make Indians more autonomous without undermining their relationship to, and their participation in, the wider community. The philosophy behind Nixon's plan resembled that of the founding members of OIO: the direct participation of Indians remained crucial to the success of government programs intended to aid them. Condemning termination as "morally and legally unacceptable," Nixon explained, "In my judgment, it should be up to the Indian tribe to determine whether it is willing and able to assume administrative responsibility for a service program which is presently administered by a federal agency."[23]

Nixon's articulation of the right of Native Americans to self-determination intensified the tension between assimilation and cultural preservation that shaped both the discourse on Indian affairs and the activism of LaDonna Harris. This tension must be understood within the context of the radicalism in the volatile period of the 1960s and early 1970s. Harris functioned as part of a movement that recognized the need for greater Indian autonomy. Her disillusionment with the BIA and with the government's handling of Native Americans in general only continued to grow. One interviewer related, "Perhaps the worst thing is the hopelessness and demoralization of these people, Mrs. Harris told me—'the result of spirit-destroying prejudice' and the 'slow, ineffective, paternalistic' handling of Indian problems by the United States Bureau of Indian Affairs." LaDonna Harris condemned the BIA and lamented that "generally BIA policy is to try to make white people out of Indians." Indeed, the federal government had repeatedly made the mistake of treating Native Americans as if they were all alike, while concurrently trying to assimilate them into mainstream white society.[24]

In April 1973, testifying before the House Subcommittee on Indian Affairs, LaDonna Harris articulated the disillusionment many Native Americans felt concerning the federal government's handling of Indian affairs. "We have come to this point in history along a trail of broken treaties. But over and over again we have believed in the basic sincerity of the government." She added, "Even now we are taking seriously the policy of self-determination as avowed by the last two administrations," even though "all our instincts—and much actual evidence—tells us that it is only rhetoric."[25] Harris did not stop her efforts to improve the conditions of Native Americans by working with policy makers, but her criticism grew increasingly harsh. She and other Native Americans remained emphatic in their demand that the government do more that simply pay lip service to the new policy of self-determination. Not everyone, however, agreed on the meaning and even implementation of self-determination. The basic issue of reconciling the preservation of native traditions and access to mainstream opportunities persisted.[26]

Along with the increasing emphasis on cultural autonomy and restoration came a changing dialogue on the nature of Indian identity. Harris dismissed the melting pot as a myth, citing as evidence the continued growth of the American Indian population. She added that with the increase in population had come a greater sense of national Indianness. She explained, "I am a Comanche first and an Indian second." The resurgence in Indian pride and identity exacerbated the demand for greater self-determination among Native Americans. The federal government had suppressed considerable knowledge of tribal languages and cultural beliefs as a part of Indian policy since the 1800s. With the shift toward a policy of self-determination, Indian rights advocates began efforts at preserving and revitalizing Indian heritage. A close connection developed between cultural restoration and the rising demand for self-governance among Indians.[27]

In many ways Harris and the two organizations she helped found, Oklahomans for Indian Opportunity and Americans for Indian Opportunity, foreshadowed the problems that President Nixon laid out and the problems with which Native American groups continued to struggle. Although Harris did not play a role in OIO after her resignation in 1968, her work with AIO remained a vital link between Native American tribes and the federal government. In the decade following the founding of AIO in 1970, the organization sponsored numerous symposiums on tribal issues and facilitated change that touched virtually every tribe in the United States.

AIO in Action

An analysis of AIO in the first decade of its existence provides a vehicle through which to understand both the advocacy and beliefs of LaDonna Harris and the changing nature of tribal needs, stemming from the shift in federal policy. Harris's own background and experience as both an activist and a politician's wife provided her with unique qualifications and insights to act as a liaison of sorts between Native Americans and the federal government. If Native Americans were in fact to exercise greater control over administering their own programs and if they were to attain any measure of sovereignty, tribal leaders would have to learn more about the government and their rights. Here is where AIO had a significant role to play. Explaining that AIO "is primarily concerned with governance issues," Harris said the organization was especially interested in helping Native American tribes "maintain their identities and cultural and political autonomy" within the larger system of the United States federal government. In addition, AIO addressed environmental problems, tribal leadership issues, education, and federal Indian law and policy.[28]

Although AIO accomplished a number of notable feats, the most important contribution of this organization came in the form of education. It played a tremendous role in educating Native American tribes, individuals, and organizations about their relationship to the federal government and the types of services available to them. AIO also tried to educate politicians about the status of Native Americans. Harris and her organization addressed leaders at every level of the political structure, from local lawmakers to governors, U.S. senators, and presidents. In fact, Harris remarked that each time a new president got elected she felt like she had to teach "Indian 101" all over again. Just when it seemed that the Nixon administration had demonstrated a serious commitment to Native Americans, scandal ensued. First, in late 1973, Agnew resigned under a cloud of suspicion resulting from allegations that he had accepted bribes while serving as governor of Maryland. Nixon resigned the following summer to avoid impeachment after the discovery of his role in covering up the notorious Watergate debacle. The next two administrations, under Gerald Ford and Jimmy Carter, provided new and not entirely welcome challenges to Harris and her organization. The inauguration of each marked a new task of explaining the same old issues all over again. A combination of persistence and knowledge provided the best weapon available to AIO.[29]

One innovative aspect of AIO's work to educate both Native Americans and government officials came in the form of emergency newsletters called "Red Alerts." Native Americans, including tribal leaders, were often ill informed when it came to national politics. AIO began sending out "Red Alerts" to notify Native American tribes and organizations about urgent national matters that directly affected them. AIO also sent "Red Alerts" to government officials and employees in an effort to inform them better about the needs and concerns facing Native Americans. For instance, in a letter to Albert Miller, the deputy undersecretary for field coordination for the Department of Housing and Urban Development, Harris explained her purpose in sending him a "Red Alert" describing the "distinction of tribes as *units* of government." She said that in many cases government agencies tended to treat tribal governments as minorities, failing to recognize the "governmental nature of tribes." In keeping with typical AIO emphasis on educating people, Harris included information on recent Supreme Court cases dealing with related Native American issues and responses from various government officials to AIO's "Red Alert."[30]

A further example of AIO's use of "Red Alerts" is evident in the newsletter announcing the use of population figures in the allocation of general revenue sharing funds. The "Red Alert" informed tribal governments what to do if they suspected inaccuracies in their population figures, including whom to contact for further information and how long they had to challenge the accuracy of population figures. Though perhaps unremarkable on the surface, the service provided by AIO bridged an important gap between federal policy of self-determination and the actual implementation of it by tribes themselves. Other "Red Alerts" brought to the attention of tribal leaders and government officials alike issues such as the Indian Child Welfare Act of 1978, the recruitment of Native American students by Ivy League universities, federal budget cuts, environmental legislation, and the *Oliphant* case in which the Supreme Court declared tribal courts do not have jurisdiction to try non-Indians for crimes committed on reservations. AIO sent these "Red Alerts" to tribes throughout the United States and often received praise from tribal communities for the timely and important information disseminated in them.[31]

In addition to "Red Alerts," AIO published numerous "Red Papers" (position papers) written by Harris and other AIO staff members. Here again, education of both Native Americans and policy makers in the federal government remained the primary goal. These "Red Papers" addressed a number of volatile and complex issues, including federal management of Indian forest lands, environmental hazards, and the relationship of Indian communities to federal policy. They are similar to the "Red Alerts" in the use of basic information but tend to be longer and somewhat more complex. For instance, "A Violation of Trust: Federal Management of Indian Forest Lands" described the failure of the federal government to oversee adequately and honestly the timber industry's use of Indian land.[32]

AIO helped establish the Native American Legal Defense and Education Fund to assist those most in need. The necessity of special legal assistance for Native Americans seemed particularly acute in light of the complex relationship between themselves and the federal government. According to one article profiling AIO's activities in the early 1970s, the lives of Native Americans were governed by "more than 2000 regulations, 389 treaties, 5000 statutes, 2000 Federal court decisions, 5000 Attorney Generals' opinions, and 33 volumes of the Indian Affairs Manual." The article explained that the primary role of the fund lay in making sure government programs responded to the needs of the Indian people as they were intended to do. The legal fund set up by AIO functioned in conjunction with other programs designed to promote overall social welfare and economic stimulation. For instance, the American Indian Investment Opportunities, Inc., jointly owned and operated by AIO and OIO, aided Native Americans in owning their own businesses.[33]

Being president of AIO afforded LaDonna Harris a bully pulpit from which to ensure that her message was heard. She brought prominence to AIO because of her past work and because of the Harris name. Although her primary focus centered on Indian advocacy, Harris continued to merge that advocacy with what she saw as larger human rights issues. She supported efforts to stop discrimination against aging Americans and women. She lent her whole-hearted support to Benjamin Rosenthal and Paul Findley in their effort to do away with mandatory retirement. While acknowledging that, as a nonprofit organization, AIO could not participate in the antidiscrimination legislation, she added that she personally would "be proud to be listed" in support of it. She lobbied for an extension on the time allocated for the passage of the Equal Rights Amendment as well. Although Congressman Manuel Lujan from New Mexico responded negatively to her request for his support by saying, "I feel that changing the rules can cause some serious problems with future Constitutional amendments," Harris continued to work in favor of the ERA. Her support for such varied causes demonstrates her lifelong commitment to bettering the conditions of all people.[34]

Benefits of Name Recognition

Although LaDonna Harris could not always effect change as quickly as she wanted, her prominent status contributed to countless gains for women, Native Americans, and other minorities. She explained that Fred's status had a lot to do with her voice being heard: "They could not ignore me because of Fred." The prominence of both Fred and LaDonna Harris aided in accomplishing gains for Native Americans, but, as the decade wore on, it became increasingly clear that policy makers could not ignore her either, because of her own status and accomplishments. In fact, the mere linking of her name to an issue involving Native Americans brought it considerable attention and credibility.[35]

Harris recalled a friend telling her that she accomplished more by accident than on purpose simply because of her high profile. She related an experience that took place several years earlier in which she and two associates had a meeting scheduled with the commissioner of Indian Affairs. She and her associates were so busy chatting at lunch that they forgot to put together their presentation for the meeting. As they walked into the meeting with the commissioner of Indian Affairs, Harris tried to figure out what she would say, but the commissioner never gave her the chance. He told her he knew why she was there and explained that they had reversed their plan to treat Indian lands like public lands on mining regulation. Harris laughingly said that, to this day, she cannot remember why they had scheduled that meeting. Still, the national reputation of LaDonna Harris reflected the extent to which her very presence facilitated the protection of rights for Native Americans.[36]

It is clear that Harris's ability to reach such a wide audience stemmed in part from her focus on issues that united rather than separated people. Ever conscious of the bigger picture, her commitment to human rights enabled her to transform both "Indian issues" and "women's issues" into human issues. The implicit liberalism in her activism informed both her articulation of issues and the avenues through which she sought to effect change. By the beginning of the 1970s, after her disillusioning experience with Agnew and the NCIO, she became outspoken in her criticism of the federal government's handling of Indian policy and programs. The Department of the Interior, in particular, disgusted Harris because of its treatment of Native Americans as property, as if they were no different than the trees and land the department managed. In spite of Harris's critique of the Department of Interior and her description of it as a "good old boys network," she still worked to effect change within the existing legal, social, and political structure. Without attacking the fundamental principles of its existence, she advocated reforming the system. By the end of that decade she had indeed come into her own as one of the leading advocates of Native American rights.[37]

Harris continued to serve as the head of AIO, testify before Congress on Indian issues, and work with government agencies to better the conditions and opportunities for Native Americans. She actively supported the preservation and perpetuation of Indian heritage as well. Both her identity and image, along with how she changed over time, is indicative of larger tensions in the movement to protect the rights of Native Americans. Harris played a crucial role at a very critical stage in federal Indian policy. She helped define the changing dialectic of both what it meant to be an Indian and how that concept pertained to the relationship and responsibilities of the federal government to Native Americans.

When Congress established the Indian Policy Review Commission in 1975 in response to growing criticism of the BIA and federal Indian policy, Harris wrote to Speaker of the House Carl Albert, also from Oklahoma, enthusiastically describing it as "the most important thing [that is] going to happen in Indian country for years to come." Although the Indian Policy Review Commission did not report its findings until 1977, that the government recognized a need for such a commission indicated the impact of Indian rights advocates like Harris on affecting federal policy. While Nixon laid the foundation for the era of self-determination in his 1970 speech, the findings of the Indian Policy Review Commission provided the context needed to implement policy in keeping with Indian autonomy.[38]

The decade of the 1970s did indeed constitute a period of both great change and growth for LaDonna Harris. She founded AIO in 1970. Fred ran for president in both 1972 and 1976, though the latter of the two elections was the more serious attempt. Harris's 1976 presidential campaign marked his last bid for elected office. It also exemplified the political partnership that had defined the Harrises' careers and their lives. In fact, this idea that people got a sort of two-for-one deal when Fred held office is further reflected in the campaign buttons that said "LaDonna Harris for First Lady." She had mastered the delicate balancing act of appearing strong but not domineering. Barbara Blum, who served as the deputy director of Jimmy Carter's 1976 presidential campaign, first met Fred and LaDonna Harris during that campaign. She recalled being amazed by LaDonna because she "was so charming, outgoing and self-effacing." Blum added that she never perceived "just Fred" as running for president, but rather Fred *and* LaDonna as seeking the office. "They have always been a team," explained Blum. Nevertheless, even though Fred included LaDonna and they both projected an image of partnership and teamwork, LaDonna remained the candidate's wife, not the candidate.[39]

End of a Partnership

When his second bid for the presidency failed, Fred Harris was ready to retreat from the hectic world of politics and move away from Washington, D.C. LaDonna, on the other hand, wanted to remain in Washington and continue the work of AIO in the exciting and volatile climate of the nation's capital. As one friend described it, Fred wanted to can tomatoes and LaDonna wanted to lobby for Native American rights. As his political career came to an end, hers had really just begun. Fred left the United States Senate in January of 1973, and his unsuccessful campaign for the presidency marked his official retreat from national politics in 1976. No longer the wife of a leading politician, LaDonna Harris instead presided over her own nationally renowned organization and had earned a reputation as a respected activist in her own right.[40]

The Harrises attempted to accommodate the changes in both of their lives, but it proved an arduous challenge. They moved to Albuquerque, New Mexico, in 1976, where Fred taught in the political science department at the University of New Mexico. Shortly after moving to Albuquerque, Fred wrote an "anecdotal account" of the twelve years he and LaDonna spent in Washington, D.C. In the introduction to *Potomac Fever,* Fred Harris indicated that both he and LaDonna were ready to "trade the steamy banks of the Potomac River for the cottonwood shade of the Rio Grande" and said that they "felt it was time to move on to a new phase" in their lives. They were nearing new phases in their lives, but not the one described by Fred. LaDonna had little time to spend "in the shade." Their children had reached adulthood, her commitments as a senator's wife had ended, and she wanted to focus her energies on activism rather than having a relaxed, semiretired lifestyle. She continued to run AIO but moved the offices to New Mexico. Ultimately, LaDonna went from being the wife of a mainstream politician to being a candidate outside the two-party system. In 1980, she made her own bid for elected office by running as the vice presidential candidate for the newly founded Citizen's Party. Among other positions, the Citizen's Party criticized the similarities between the

Republican and Democratic parties and called for "the creation of a safer environment." LaDonna described this experience as "one of the best and worst things that ever happened" to her because, while tremendously demanding, it also pushed her out on her own in a way she had not experienced before. During the election, LaDonna's oldest daughter, Kathryn, pointed out that her mother was being treated like a candidate's wife, to which a friend and AIO staff member added that Harris acted like a candidate's wife. Harris realized that she had reverted back to that role because of the comfort and familiarity it afforded.[41]

Even though Harris and her running mate, Barry Commoner, did not have a realistic chance of winning the election, the experience proved a turning point for her. For the first time in her life, she was the candidate and she had to learn how to talk about herself, her beliefs, her accomplishments, and her goals and not simply those of someone else. She viewed her nomination for vice president as "an additional opportunity to do more" for what she believed in. Although her experience with the election aided her in coming in to her own politically, it also came at the expense of her marriage. Regardless of the efforts the Harrises made to accommodate each other's changing needs, the strain caused by their lives moving in two different directions finally resulted in divorce in 1980, just four years after moving to Albuquerque. They remained close friends, but not before going through a strenuous and awkward period of adjustment. She recalled this difficult time in her life: "Somewhere I couldn't let go and stop my work and pay attention to my marriage." During this time she was "very much involved in the women's movement and was helping to start the Women's Political Caucus" and said "I was just moving into my own world. Still, when the end came, I was surprised."[42]

After her divorce, Harris moved AIO back to Washington, D.C., where she ran the organization for the next decade. In 1990 she, along with AIO, returned to New Mexico. She faced a difficult transition after being married for more than thirty years. Their divorce marked a turning point in not just her own personal identity but also in her life's work. She now faced a greater challenge because her work had been tied so closely to her marriage to Fred. Her advocacy on behalf of Native Americans and other groups grew and matured just as she did. Feminism also resonated with her to a greater degree after her marriage ended. One friend said Harris did not appear to be a feminist until her divorce, and Harris herself remembered becoming more aware of the women's movement around this time.[43]

Harris not only came into her own as a leader but also found herself on her own quite literally for the first time in her life. In an interview with Rusty Brown from the *Albuquerque Tribune*, she admitted to being scared about the big change in her life but described her divorce as amicable. Brown captured the sentiment of many friends of Fred and LaDonna Harris: "Thus comes to an end one of the best husband-wife political teams ever to stump the Oklahoma cornfields or crack the Washington power structure." Indeed, many expressed surprise and sadness at the split between Fred and LaDonna Harris but said that the fact that the two remained close illustrated the strength and depth of the bond they shared. Ironically, as Laura Harris explained, "Dad actually became more politically active rather than less after their divorce." Nevertheless, the decade of the 1970s saw LaDonna Harris become an activist in her own right. She became more confident and sure of herself. Her work, which so neatly dovetailed with Fred's while he served in the Senate, evolved and took on a life of its own. By the end of the decade he was a former senator and she a former wife. Her activism transcended and surpassed both roles. She had indeed found her own voice.[44]

◀◀◀ MANKILLER ▶▶▶

II

Beloved

Woman

Politicized

Wilma Mankiller's path to political prominence could hardly be described as inevitable. In fact, becoming a political figure of any kind, much less the head of the second-largest Native American tribe in the United States, was never a goal to which the young Mankiller aspired. As she explained, "I couldn't imagine myself in a political office and having to go out and sell myself like a tube of toothpaste or something." Yet Mankiller's heritage, her awakening political consciousness, and her community development work with the Cherokee Nation all played a part in preparing her for a role on the national and international stage and demonstrate how her particular background proved invaluable in training her for a career in politics. Two central themes emerge in an analysis of Mankiller's career: the first concerns her identity or self-image, which formed over time and was influenced by her heritage and experience, and the second pertains to the image Mankiller projected to society as a political figure. To understand the many influences on the image that Wilma later projected as a Cherokee tribal leader, it is first necessary to examine the critical experiences of her youth and her social activism. As a feminist and an outspoken proponent of Native American rights, these two components of her identity held significant ramifications both for the image that she projected to mainstream society as well as within Cherokee politics.[1]

Mankiller's exposure to both Cherokee traditions and discrimination against people of color greatly influenced and shaped the person she would later become. She was born to a Cherokee father, Charley Mankiller, and Dutch-Irish mother, Clara Irene Sitton Mankiller, in the W. W. Hastings Indian Hospital on November 18, 1945, in Tahlequah, Oklahoma. Wilma was the sixth of eleven children born to Charley and Irene Mankiller. Her birth came shortly after the end of World War II and in the early stages of the baby boom. Although the twenty-five years following the end of the war ushered in an unprecedented level of prosperity in the United States, that prosperity did not touch all Americans. In fact, one-fifth of Americans continued to live below the poverty line, and Wilma Mankiller came from just such a family. Mankiller spent the first decade of her life living in rural northeastern Oklahoma on her grandfather's Dawes allotment called Mankiller Flats in Adair County, just east of Tahlequah. The family hunted and grew what food they could in addition to cutting railroad ties to help make ends meet. Her father and her oldest brother, Don, also worked each year in Colorado to help harvest broom corn and earn extra money for the family.[2]

The family struggled financially, but Mankiller recalled her family being close and affectionate and surrounded by other Cherokees. Mankiller said she used to hide when she saw white people because she did not like the way some of them looked down on her and other Cherokees. Although she did not grow up learning to speak Cherokee, she knew some words because her father, who was fluent, often spoke the language. Even though her mother was not Cherokee, she too learned to speak and understand some of the language, though never fluently. Mankiller also learned about Cherokee history and culture in that first decade of her life. She credited both her parents and other Cherokees in her community for instilling in her a love of traditional stories and knowledge of Cherokee history.[3]

Relocation to San Francisco

Although Mankiller recalled the early years of her childhood with fondness and a sense of security, the financial burden of caring for a large family on a limited and unstable income finally forced the family to take drastic measures. They moved to San Francisco in October 1956 as part of the federal government's relocation program—an extension of termination policy. This program helped Native Americans move to urban areas where, at least in theory, they could find better employment opportunities. Though relocation was voluntary—unlike the implementation of many federal Indian policies—the element of coercion and the exploitation of desperation cannot be ignored. As one piece of relocation propaganda told Indian parents, "If you won't do this much for yourself, at least do it for the sake of your children." Many families who took part in relocation felt they had no other option but to seek opportunities in large cities. Upon arrival, however, they often discovered the "tragic realities" of a program that "was inherently biased toward the lowest-status careers."[4]

Mankiller's harsh introduction to the large, noisy—and altogether foreign—city, which she later described as her own personal trail of tears, resembled that of numerous Indian youths. It is, however, difficult at best to fully ascertain when this connection emerged. Her autobiography, which provides the best insight into her life and identity to date, was written from the perspective of a grown woman whose Cherokee identity may in fact have become more pronounced than when she actually had the experiences. That said, she recalled feeling sad as her family drove to the train that would take them to San Francisco. She tried to memorize the landscape she would not return to for another twenty years: her school, the trees, and even her grandfather's yard. As Susan Lobo explains, "For many, the move into the city was lonely and frightening, like stepping off into the unknown, and the actual arrival was often a sudden jolt of urban reality." Peggy Berryhill, who also moved with her family from Oklahoma to California in the 1950s, recalled a "harrowing and hilarious experience" when she accompanied her mother across a drawbridge on their way to a store. She explained that after making it "about halfway across the drawbridge, the alarm signal went off" and, she added, "so did I!" The young girl continued running until her mother caught up to her. Although Berryhill eventually developed a fondness for the bridge, her initial fear illustrates the disconcerting nature of making the transition from rural to urban life that caused difficulty for so many Indian children.[5]

Wilma and the other members of the Mankiller family struggled to adjust to San Francisco. As one article described it, "They may as well have landed on another planet." Everything seemed so different from the small rural community that she had known all her life. They no longer found themselves surrounded by other Cherokees. As did other relocation children, Mankiller and her siblings grappled with new experiences, such as hearing sirens for the first time and learning to "dial telephones, roller skate, and ride bicycles."[6]

Like LaDonna Harris and other people of color, Wilma Mankiller encountered racism at a young age. She recalled a woman in San Francisco calling her and her siblings "nigger children" and her mother a "nigger lover." It is notable that this slur racialized Wilma in a context of "blackness," thereby erasing her Indianness in this particular instance. Whereas Harris often found herself racialized as white within the framework of a black/white struggle over civil rights, Wilma Mankiller experienced a sort of generalized "blackness" in the signification of otherness. She felt alienated from other children, saying, "I was uncomfortable. I felt stigmatized." Rosalie McKay-Want, who later became Mankiller's friend, also identified the discrimination against Indians in California as she recounted how her mother would hide her and her siblings when social workers visited their home. Whites "have always had so much control in our lives," explained McKay-Want, which caused a tremendous amount of fear.[7]

Mankiller shared a similar sense of disenchantment with the treatment of Indians, and, although she eventually adjusted to life in San Francisco, much of that had to do with her becoming connected to other Indians whose families had also been relocated. Like many Native Americans in urban areas, Mankiller confronted the difficult process of trying to fit into mainstream America while maintaining her heritage and cultural traditions. That she compared her family's move to San Francisco to the Cherokee Trail of Tears shows that she made sense of the world around her through her tribe's history.

The experience of the Mankiller children coincided with that of a number of Indian children. One scholar noted that 54 percent of Native American children living in San Francisco in the 1970s said that they learned native traditions in their homes. The Bay Area Indian community—of which Mankiller and her family became a part—provided "a wide range of circumstances and symbols that foster[ed] 'Indian' relationships at the family and community levels."[8]

Not long after their relocation, the Mankiller family became acquainted with people at the San Francisco American Indian Center. The appeal of native traditions and the desire to be around other Indians led Wilma to spend a significant amount of time at the Indian Center, where some of her fondest memories of her San Francisco youth were made. In fact, Mankiller said that after her family moved to California, the center helped them "adjust to urban living." And when Wilma later lived in Oakland, she said that the Intertribal Friendship House offered a "sanctuary," adding that it "was the heart of a vibrant tribal community." The San Francisco American Indian Center and the Intertribal Friendship House of Oakland were among the many Indian centers established in the 1950s and 1960s to meet the cultural needs of the growing population of urban Indians. They provided a haven and a sense of cultural connectivity for Indians who came from tribes all over the country to urban relocation centers. The relocation of thousands of Indians from all different tribes to large urban areas helped lay the groundwork for the pan-Indian movement of the 1960s and 1970s. As a young adult Mankiller clearly identified heavily with other minority groups and felt alienated, and ultimately those feelings informed the way she experienced San Francisco in the 1960s.[9]

After finishing high school in 1963, Wilma began dating Hugo Olaya, a young Ecuadorian man four years her elder. They married that fall just a few days before her eighteenth birthday. Her parents voiced some objection because of her young age, but she had a job and no one expected her to go to college. After they married, both she and Hugo continued to work while he finished taking college courses. After giving birth to her first child, Felicia, at nineteen, Wilma stayed home and took care of her. Less than two years later, she had a second child, Gina, to care for as well. They continued living in San Francisco and were engulfed in the swirling changes that characterized that decade. Mankiller in particular found herself caught up in the idealism and activism of the 1960s. She cheered for Cesar Chavez when she heard about his efforts with the National Farm Workers Association and even attended several events in support of his work. She also related to the issues raised by the Black Panthers and admired the way in which they stood up for the rights of African Americans. And like Harris, she ultimately came to relate discrimination against other people of color with the discrimination she encountered.[10]

Red Power Movement

By the late 1960s, Mankiller began taking college courses and grew more and more interested in the activism around her. Then in 1969, two events occurred which altered her life. The first involved the San Francisco American Indian Center where she spent a substantial amount of time as a youth and even after her marriage. Much of her exposure to Indian activists took place at this center. It was there where she met Mohawk activist Richard Oakes and became deeply influenced by him. In October 1969 the center caught fire and burned to the ground. Mankiller was devastated by the fire and described the center as a home away from home for thousands of Native Americans. Others shared her sentiments, and the fire quite literally fueled a desire to make a public stand in support of greater tribal sovereignty. Plans were already underway to seize Alcatraz Island, the former federal prison, in the name of Indian sovereignty, but the fire that destroyed the center lent even more urgency to the cause. Finally on November 20, 1969, they made their move.[11]

Oakes led a group of seventy-eight Native Americans through the cold waters of San Francisco Bay and headed for Alcatraz. The occupation lasted nineteen months and brought considerable attention from the media. The new occupants of Alcatraz likened the former federal prison to an Indian reservation. They condemned the treatment of Indians at the hands of the white government and called for greater self-determination. In effect, the Indian occupation of Alcatraz represented a reassertion of tribal sovereignty.[12]

The occupation certainly saw its share of problems, including unsafe conditions and intense divisions in the leadership, but it was what Alcatraz represented to thousands of Native Americans that made it so significant. Donald Fixico described the occupation as igniting a greater critique of white society by Indians living in San Francisco as their group sense of Indianness became more heightened. The occupation also deeply affected Mankiller's life and her own perception of Indianness. In fact, Mankiller had never voted prior to the occupation, which she credited for awakening her to the importance of politics. Her characterization of Alcatraz mirrored that of other Indian activists who felt the impact of Alcatraz on shaping both their activism and their sense of Indianness. The occupation came to an end in June 1971, but the Indian-led movement for greater sovereignty and self-determination continued, as did Mankiller's activism.[13]

Mankiller began doing volunteer work with the Pit River tribe in Northern California after watching a story about them on the news regarding their efforts to regain their land from the Pacific Gas and Electric Company. Mankiller recalled being struck by how much the Pit River people reminded her of people back home in Oklahoma. The Pit River Indians' struggle to regain their land began in earnest in August 1970, with the occupation of Alcatraz still underway. Six members of the Pit River tribal council wrote to President Nixon, saying they hoped his words in support of Indian rights were "true in [his] heart and were not for political reasons." They asked the president to support them in the effort to regain land that had been taken from them in violation of the Fifth Amendment guarantee of due process of law. Raymond Coulter, from the Office of the Solicitor in the Department of the Interior, responded on Nixon's behalf, saying that their claim to 3,386,00 acres had previously been resolved by the Indian Claims Commission, "which found that while the Pit River Indians at one time had Indian title to the land, the title had been extinguished by the Act of March 3, 1853, 10 Stat. 244." This, coupled with the 1964 cash payment of $29,100,000 to California Indians (including the Pit Rivers), concluded Coulter, brought an end to the matter.[14]

The letter from the Department of the Interior failed to persuade the Pit River Indians that their claims lacked merit. Close to sixty Pit Rivers had already reoccupied their land and were told by the U.S. Forest Service that they had to leave. On October 27 about 150 federal agents appeared to remove them. A fight between the natives and federal agents ensued and resulted in the arrest of about thirty Pit Rivers. In the early part of their efforts, Oakes tried to help the Pit Rivers in their struggle. Others from Alcatraz rushed to their aid as well because their struggle represented both a condemnation of the federal government's treatment of Native Americans and a reassertion of tribal sovereignty. Through Mankiller's work with the Pit River Indians and their legal defense fund, she learned about treaty rights, law, and sovereignty issues. This experience further nurtured her commitment to activism on behalf of Native Americans, but the significance of her contact with the Pit Rivers goes beyond learning about treaty rights. In fact, Vine Deloria argued that the whole sense of Indianness during this period was judged by whether people participated in events such as Alcatraz and Pit River. In short, the significance of Wilma's contact with other activists and her own activism in support of Alcatraz and Pit River shaped her understanding of Indianness, just as it did for the other Indian activists in California and around the country. Events such as the occupation of Alcatraz and the Pit River struggle cannot be overstated in terms of their impact on shaping Wilma's understanding of Indian identity and self-determination.[15]

Mankiller also worked as the acting director of the Native American Youth Center in East Oakland. She and the other employees sought to instill a knowledge and appreciation of native cultures in the children with whom they worked. Wilma recalled learning about the importance of self-help while working at the youth center, a lesson that guided her later work with the Cherokee Nation.[16]

Fighting the Feminine Mystique

Living in the San Francisco area during the 1960s and early 1970s, Mankiller continually found her life inundated with the spirit of activism that defined the era, which eventually contributed to her marital problems. Wilma recalled feeling tension in her marriage after about three years. She and Hugo wanted different things and increasingly moved in opposing directions. In addition to her budding political consciousness, or perhaps because of it, Mankiller found herself struggling with her role as a woman and her own sort of "feminine mystique." Mankiller wanted to continue her work on behalf of Native Americans and to keep taking college classes. She criticized suburbia and the lifestyle it represented, saying, "I knew I did not want to live like that." She added, "I had no wish to become the kind of woman who would later be called a 'Stepford wife.'" She felt an increasing tension between her desire to be involved as an activist for Indian issues and her role as a wife and mother.[17]

Despite the strain her activism put on her marriage, Mankiller explained, "I wanted to set my own limits and control my destiny." Mankiller and her husband separated and then divorced in 1974. "There was this contrast between staid sort of marriage and home and then this world of change and activism swirling around me." She wanted "to be a part of that world and that change," and ultimately "that world and that change won out." Prior to her exposure to feminism, Mankiller felt that something must be wrong with her because she did not find being a housewife fully satisfying. After her divorce, Mankiller struggled to find autonomy and her own sense of self.[18]

The second-wave feminism of the late 1960s and early 1970s continued to shape Mankiller's attitudes about women's issues throughout her political career. She described her exposure to second-wave feminism while living in San Francisco, writing, "I eventually discovered that many of those women were wives, mothers, students, bright dropouts, and others who met to discuss" their shared problems and experiences. She further described the movement as having a tremendous impact on both her life and the lives of other women. Ultimately, Mankiller's own feminism played a key role in defining how she thought about women and politics.[19]

Return to Oklahoma

Mankiller's decision to return to Oklahoma after living in San Francisco for two decades seemed the right thing to do for a variety of reasons. She feared her ex-husband would take one or both of her daughters. He had kept Gina away from her for an entire year, and even after Gina returned home Mankiller worried that Hugo would make good on his threats to separate her from her daughters. She and her two daughters visited Oklahoma in the summer of 1976 and moved there permanently the following summer. By the time Mankiller returned to Oklahoma, her father had passed away and her mother was again living in Adair County, not far from where the family lived before moving to San Francisco. Many of her brothers and sisters also moved back to Oklahoma. As natural as this move may have seemed to her, Mankiller's two daughters had a very different experience. Ironically, they faced a degree of culture shock because of their own "relocation" not unlike what their mother went through as a child. Gina and Felicia were children of the city. They knew how to navigate the public transportation system in San Francisco and were unaccustomed to isolation of rural living. They talked and dressed differently than other children at school, and, though they eventually adjusted to life in Oklahoma, Gina remembered hoping her mother would change her mind and take them back to San Francisco.[20]

Mankiller's decision to return to her family's home in Oklahoma began a new phase in her life. She took with her the lessons she learned during the time she spent in San Francisco and returned as a veteran of 1960s urban activism. Mankiller also decided to finish her bachelor's degree in social work and then went on to take graduate course work at the University of Arkansas in Fayetteville. While Mankiller continued her college education, she also worked for the Cherokee Nation. She served as the economic stimulus coordinator, then moved up to the central planning department and eventually oversaw the Bell Community Revitalization Project, which Chief Ross Swimmer initiated. This project played a definitive role in shaping Mankiller's outlook on community development and propelling her into Cherokee politics. Tremendously successful, in addition to building and remodeling dozens of homes, it laid sixteen miles of water line. Cherokees living in the Bell community did the work themselves, and, if families did not show up to work, they faced being dropped from the project. According to a letter sent to the families in Bell, only 5 of 103 families had failed to do any work by March 1983. By the time those in Bell completed the project in mid-1984, some families had been dropped from the project for not working on the water line or for not putting in the required 350 hours on housing construction. Mankiller said, "Some people did not think they really had to work." Nevertheless, a vast majority participated in improving their community and "had a lot to be proud of."[21]

Bell served as a model for Mankiller and the Cherokee Nation in a number of other communities. Mankiller's experience with the people in Bell deepened her desire to help Cherokees in other poor communities, such as Kenwood. This, in part, inspired her involvement in Cherokee politics. Bell, which many described as the Harlem of eastern Oklahoma, was one of the poorest communities in the state. This project brought considerable attention to Mankiller and opened the door to her political involvement. Swimmer, the principal chief of the Cherokee Nation, brought in people to train Mankiller in community development. He also created the new department of community development and asked Mankiller to serve as the first director, which she did until she resigned to run for deputy chief in 1983.[22]

Introduction to Tribal Politics

By 1982 it became clear that Swimmer's deputy chief, Perry Wheeler, intended to challenge Swimmer for the position of principal chief in the 1983 election. Swimmer, who was battling cancer, had not planned to run for reelection in 1983 but changed his mind because of apprehension over the type of leadership he feared Wheeler would bring to the tribe. Swimmer consulted with friends and colleagues for advice on a running mate, to little avail. He wanted someone active in the community who would take on the responsibilities of deputy chief as a full-time job. His attention turned to Mankiller because of her success with the Bell project and her work as director of community development for the tribe. Thus began Mankiller's entry into tribal politics. Although she had not been engaged in politics herself until she agreed to run for deputy chief, her childhood experience of relocation, the activism of the 1960s, and her work in the area of community development converged in the formation of her political persona. Moreover, the feminist understanding through which she came to identify and articulate her experience in tribal politics added another layer to that persona.[23]

Wilma Mankiller's transition from being an activist to working for the Cherokee government and leading community development projects to being a key player in contentious tribal politics is noteworthy. No doubt a substantial connection existed between her identity and her budding public image, but the latter evolved to fit a particular set of political circumstances. An evaluation of both underscores the path Mankiller took from becoming an activist to holding elected office. Her bids for election in 1983 and in 1987 have been described as fraught with gender bias. From the very beginning, it seems, Mankiller faced opposition from certain factions within the Cherokee Nation.

When Swimmer asked Wilma to run as his deputy chief in 1983, he faced criticism by some of his associates who questioned the wisdom of such a decision. A number of people had hoped he would select Gary Chapman, a member of the tribal council and longtime friend of Swimmer; they were more than a little surprised when he did not. Mankiller explained that people assumed Swimmer "by-passed all the male executives to ask me to take on a few more responsibilities during this period because of his admiration for me." She admitted that this may have been the case, but added, "perhaps he had little choice" because he needed someone he could trust. Although trust certainly factored into his decision, he also believed that he and Mankiller would compliment each other well. Swimmer spent a lot of time traveling to Washington and wanted a deputy chief who would go out into the communities and work with those who most needed help. He felt that Mankiller had already demonstrated her ability to do this type of work.[24]

Nevertheless, Mankiller recalled her reluctance when Swimmer approached her about being his running mate. "When he first asked me to run for Deputy Chief, I was very flattered but I also thought it was a ridiculous idea." She saw herself as an activist, not a politician. For Gina, the decision of her mother to get involved in politics had a more personal impact. She recalled that, although she felt proud of her mother, the biggest drawback was that there was no longer time to take "spontaneous weekend trips to Eureka Springs, Arkansas," and that "there was no more dancing in the kitchen to Aretha Franklin songs."[25]

Despite her family's reaction and her own misgivings, Mankiller decided to run for office because it offered her a greater opportunity to battle the poverty she saw among the Cherokee. Ultimately, her assent to office proved to be anything but smooth. The early criticism of Swimmer's selection of Mankiller as his deputy chief only intensified as the campaign progressed. According to Mankiller, all fifteen council members on Swimmer's slate opposed her candidacy and even threatened to withdraw their support for him if he did not drop her as his deputy chief candidate. Mankiller said that, though "they all opposed my candidacy," no one did so more than the Swimmer campaign manager, Councilman Gary Chapman. She discovered that Chapman spread false rumors about her "campaigning in bars" and that members of the Swimmer campaign team were even handing out campaign literature for an opponent, J. B. Dreadfulwater. Opposition to Mankiller did not stop with council members and

Swimmer campaign staffers. When they went out on the campaign trail, Mankiller remarked, "[Swimmer] would introduce me and people would virtually ignore me."[26]

Layers of Opposition

Mankiller explained the extent of the criticism against her: "People complained to [Swimmer] because I am female, because I am a Democrat, because they didn't like the way I dressed, because I had not paid my political dues by serving on council [or] something first." She concluded, "But the big issue seemed to be my being a woman." Both in her autobiography and in speeches, Mankiller described herself as encountering a great deal of opposition because of her gender during and after the 1983 election. She explained that by the time of the 1983 election the Cherokee history "of balance between men and women seemed to be long forgotten." Mankiller said she had been prepared to debate whatever issues came up except the one over whether or not women should hold office. Mankiller did not consider it an issue: "The thing that was a surprise to me was the number of people who opposed me simply because I am female." Expressing shock and frustration, she said, "In my entire life I had gotten through all these things without having that kind of overt in-your-face kind of opposition simply because of my gender." One article described Mankiller's experience, stating, "By far the greatest prejudice she encountered as a rising political force among the Cherokee was because she was a woman."[27]

Despite the contention that sexism constituted one of the most significant campaign issues Mankiller faced, her opponents for deputy chief were a man, J. B. Dreadfulwater, and a woman, Agnes Cowen. Dreadfulwater openly opposed the idea of women in leadership positions but was soundly defeated in the July election. Of the total 11,069 votes cast for the office of deputy chief, Dreadfulwater received only 2,785, while Cowen received 3,157, and Mankiller pulled in the most, with 5,127. Though not enough to give Mankiller the 50 percent majority needed to win the election outright, the election made it clear that sexism did not inform the decision of a vast majority of the voters. The defeat of Dreadfulwater in the July election left Mankiller in a runoff election with Agnes Cowen. Dreadfulwater refused to support either candidate, again citing his belief that women should not hold the position.[28]

When Michael Wallis asked Mankiller whether Cowen encountered the same sexism, she speculated that there were probably some who objected to Cowen because of her gender but said she doubted as many people confronted her because of the kind of demeanor she possessed. Mankiller explained, "She was politically savvy." Cowen was also in her fifties while Mankiller was only thirty-seven. Cowen had far more experience in politics and with the Cherokee Nation than did Wilma, which raises the question as to what other factors influenced the opposition against Mankiller.[29]

Certainly some tribal members opposed Mankiller because she was a woman. Similarly, there were those who also opposed Cowen because of her gender. Mankiller suggested that on the day of the runoff election, those voters simply stayed home. Although each woman likely experienced individual acts of sexism, it did not constitute systemic or institutionalized sexism. Further, the characterization of the election as one in which gender served as the most significant issue seems implausible given that Mankiller's biggest competition was another woman. Another factor bearing consideration is that, in addition to Mankiller and Cowen, seven other Cherokee women ran for tribal office in 1983, three of whom won election to the tribal council. Two of these women, Barbara Starr Scott and Wathene Young, ran campaigns that emphasized their gender as a positive attribute. They ran a political advertisement in which the following quotation appeared beneath their pictures: "Historically Cherokee women have had a strong voice in the direction of our peoples' lives. Allow women this opportunity once again." In spite of Scott and Young's use of gender identity politics, neither woman supported Mankiller in her bid for deputy chief. It should also be noted that in the 1983 election council members ran for office at large as opposed to running from a particular district or county. In light of this approach, which has since changed, the top fifteen vote getters became council members. In that election, Barbara Starr Scott received the second-highest number of votes, a fact that offers a further challenge to the notion that gender bias acted as any meaningful barrier for the Cherokee women running for office.[30]

That said, both Cowen and Dreadfulwater, as well as other Cherokees, criticized Mankiller for reasons unrelated to gender. They took her to task for having been involved with the Cherokee Nation for only a short time and for her relative inexperience in Cherokee politics. In fact, Cowen became the first woman elected to the tribal council in 1975 and then ran for deputy chief in 1979. By the time of the 1983 election, she had already been through two campaigns. And, if a few more votes had gone the other way, it would have been she and not Mankiller who became the first female deputy chief in 1983. Cowen, who died on August 27, 1999, has been described by those who knew her as tough and no nonsense. She apparently rubbed many people the wrong way. Cowen never hesitated to tell someone when she disagreed with them. Her daughters remember her as a strong-willed feminist with a big heart who had little tolerance for excuses. To those who found themselves at odds with her, Cowen could seem domineering and harsh. Here, Swimmer's support of Mankiller proved vital to her winning because he remained strongly opposed to having Cowen as his deputy chief, because the two had found themselves at odds in the past.[31]

One issue with which Mankiller had to contend and Cowen did not was Mankiller's twenty years spent outside Oklahoma. According to Mankiller, a number of people, particularly tribal executives and council members, viewed her as something of an outsider and perhaps even a young radical because of her connection to Alcatraz and California Indians. When she first went to work for the tribe as the economic stimulus coordinator, Mankiller said people viewed her as an upstart. One tribal member, Leo Fishinghawk, even told her, "You know, you're pretty smart. You'll do ok here in Oklahoma as long as you stay out of politics." The point here is not to dismiss sexism as an issue, but rather to suggest that other factors figured into the opposition

to Mankiller, thereby creating a much more complicated portrait of opposition than a strictly legalistic definition of sexism
implies. Cowen and Mankiller experienced sex discrimination
differently and to varying degrees. Perhaps the fact that Cowen
had more experience in the tribe and came across as more "politically savvy" than Mankiller also played a role in why people
viewed them differently. As Mankiller explained, "The conventional wisdom was that if a woman was going to win it was going to be Agnes because she had been on the council and directed the Bilingual Cultural Center, [she] had been there all her
life, that sort of thing."[32]

Indeed, Mankiller's political inexperience, the way she
dressed, the years she spent away from Oklahoma, her outspo-
kenness, and membership in the Democratic Party all factored
into the opposition against her. Although the will of Cherokee
voters failed to support the contention made by Dreadfulwater
and others that the tribe did not want a female leader, Mankiller
nonetheless felt the sting of sex-based criticism. Perhaps one
reason behind this opposition stood out to Mankiller was because it seemed the least fair, the least relevant, and the most
impossible for her to change. Other issues, such as criticism of
how she dressed, also seemed to center on her being a woman.
Because of the type of work Mankiller had done prior to running for deputy chief, she often wore jeans and cowboy boots.
Though appropriate for working out in the rural Cherokee communities, she felt pressure to dress more professionally when
she campaigned for office. Some people, including Swimmer's
supporters, thought that she needed to dress up more if she
were going to run for the second-most-powerful position in the
tribe. In a letter to Swimmer at the beginning of the campaign,
Mankiller wrote that she would try to take more care with her
appearance, adding, "I will try to look like I have at least considered the question of whether certain colors go well together."
One the one hand, some of the criticism of Mankiller's attire
may be attributable to the professional dress required of political leaders in general. On the other hand, female politicians
have often had to be more conscious of their appearance than
their male counterparts.[33]

Grassroots Campaign

Appearance aside, Mankiller ran a campaign that emphasized grassroots democracy in the form of community development and economic renewal, and she did so very successfully. She enlisted the help of family members and a "small crew of volunteers" with Charlie Soap at the helm to forge a campaign separate from that of the Swimmer team, whose members largely opposed her. Mankiller had also developed a relationship with many rural Cherokees during her community development work. This group, as well as some older Cherokees and those who voted for her because of Swimmer's personal support, proved crucial in her election. Despite of the criticisms against her, Mankiller won the runoff election, becoming the first female deputy chief of the Cherokee Nation.[34]

Once she began settling into the office of deputy chief, the difficulties Mankiller faced in the election did not entirely subside. She continued to experience a turbulent relationship with several members of the tribal council, which she presided over as deputy chief. Mankiller related an instance from her first meeting in which a male council member kept interrupting her and saying she was in violation of various regulations that she had never even heard of. Before the next council meeting she had the microphones rewired so that she could control whose voice was heard. This was a maneuver of a skilled politician and not simply a triumph over sexism. What is missing from this story is that three women were members of the tribal council, none of whom supported Mankiller.[35]

The three women on the tribal council elected in 1983 neither supported Mankiller in the election nor extended their support to her when she became deputy chief. Barbara Starr Scott, Wathene Young, and Patsy Morton instead allied themselves with Gary Chapman, who strongly opposed Mankiller. Although Mankiller's interaction with the tribal council often remained strained, she did establish herself as a strong deputy chief over the next few years. Early on, though, he voiced concern about her role: "I have mixed emotions about my new position." Mankiller, it seems, feared that she would get bogged down in the bureaucracy of tribal affairs and not be able to focus on the initiatives most important to her. This did prove a struggle, but she worked hard as deputy chief to continue community development projects.[36]

The community development that meant so much to Mankiller and that helped her get elected also changed her life in another way. She and Charlie Soap got to know each other while working on the Bell project and then he became one of her strongest supporters in the 1983 election. Soap divorced his wife in 1983 and took over as director of community development when Mankiller stepped down. He worked as the director until October of 1985, when he and Mankiller were married. According to Cherokee nepotism laws, no relative of an elected official of the tribe can work for the Cherokee Nation, so Soap had to resign from his job after their marriage. He remained a vital presence, though, in the work on community development and strongly supported his wife's role in Cherokee politics.[37]

Becoming Chief

Later that same year, Swimmer told Mankiller that he planned to resign as chief to assume the position of assistant secretary of the interior for Indian affairs. Although his announcement left little time for the two of them to discuss the transition, Swimmer maintained that he would not have taken the job unless he could be certain that Mankiller would stay and accept her constitutional duty to become principal chief upon his resignation. When Swimmer did resign in December 1985, just two months after Mankiller and Soap were married, she became principal chief and later described herself as unprepared for assuming her new role and for the "hardball politics" that went along with it.[38]

Because this now left a vacancy, the tribal council began searching for someone to elect as deputy chief. While in Washington, D.C., Mankiller received a telephone call from a friend who told her that some members of the council planned to select Gary Chapman, one of her harshest critics, as the deputy chief. At first, Mankiller thought this was only a rumor, but she soon discovered that, despite Chapman's earlier statements to the contrary, he planned to seek the position. Mankiller said, "I knew that if he obtained the position, he would oppose me at every opportunity." Sexism may have motivated some council members, but, significantly, Chapman enjoyed the support of the female council members.[39]

In response to these plans, Wilma asked first-term council member John Ketcher, who was one of the candidates for deputy chief, to stay in the race. Mankiller thought she would be able to work well with Ketcher and knew his election offered her the best hope of maintaining control over a difficult situation in which so many on the council openly expressed hostility to her and had since the beginning. Mankiller recalled that the future of her leadership "came down to that one critical moment." As the selection process got underway for a new deputy chief from within the ranks of the tribal council, the December 14 council meeting took on greater significance. Initially, five of the fifteen council members submitted their names for consideration. After the fourth round of votes was cast, a deadlock remained between Ketcher and Chapman. At that point the council asked Mankiller to comment and she lent her full support to Ketcher. Chapman then requested his name be withdrawn and made a motion that Ketcher be named deputy chief. The potential crisis passed and Mankiller had the deputy chief she wanted.[40]

Gender and the 1987 Election

As Mankiller prepared to run for the 1987 election, the political climate became particularly nasty. Looking back, she described it as "by far the worst election," explaining that even after her recent introduction to the underbelly of politics, she was surprised by what she encountered in the 1987 election. Mankiller learned a valuable lesson about the negative side of politics, commenting, "I am no longer the young social activist who couldn't find her way around Washington and was shocked that my own team would betray me." Mankiller faced three opponents in the 1987 election—Perry Wheeler, Dave Whitekiller, and Bill McGee. Whitekiller apparently did his best to make

Mankiller's gender an issue in the election. She recalled him saying to her "on numerous occasions that he didn't think women should be in leadership positions." Whitekiller told at least one reporter that Mankiller's "being a woman was a drawback that caused other Indian tribes in America to lose respect for the Cherokee Nation."[41]

Whitekiller also criticized Mankiller for not using her husband's last name. He even went so far as to file a complaint with the tribal election committee to try to force Mankiller to use "Soap." His reason, at least according to the letter he wrote to the commission, was that he thought "Whitekiller" and "Mankiller" sounded too similar and would confuse voters on the ballots. He based his request on the gendered assumption that, because of Mankiller's marriage to Charlie Soap, she had automatically taken her husband's last name. In fact, Mankiller had opted not to change her name and had never gone by the last name Soap. Ironically, if anyone had something to gain by voter confusion of the two names, it was Whitekiller because Chief Wilma Mankiller enjoyed far greater popularity than did he. Mankiller viewed the event as a gender-based attack and in many ways it was; certainly, a male politician would not be vulnerable to such an assumption. The complaint, however, stemmed mainly from ignorance—albeit ignorance rooted in sexism. Whitekiller believed that Soap actually was Mankiller's legal last name by virtue of her marriage and, on those grounds, petitioned the council, not because he felt that she should have to change her legal name. He even suggested she go by "Wilma Pearl Mankiller Soap." The election committee, with three women and two men in attendance, unanimously voted to deny Whitekiller's request after a brief discussion of its frivolity, and subsequently the issue was dropped.[42]

Although the controversy over her last name subsided, it left Mankiller with a sense of unease about gender-based attacks against her. In an interview shortly before the election, Mankiller said, "The central issue is whether or not gender has anything to do with leadership." Statements such as this led one writer to proclaim, "Sexism was the *only* issue of the '87 campaign, not roads, schools, jobs, health care, sobriety programs, improving housing, or even Indian sovereignty." On the one hand, Mankiller's gender was central to some of the campaign attacks against her. People such as Whitekiller clearly made sexist remarks about female leadership in general and Mankiller's in particular. On the other, Mankiller was by no means the only prominent female in Cherokee politics. In fact, her strongest competition in the 1987 election came from Perry Wheeler, who had as his deputy chief running mate Barbara Starr Scott. In short, although a minority of tribal members did not want any women holding important leadership roles, there is no evidence to suggest that sexism guided the bulk of opposition to Mankiller.[43]

Sexism, it seems, provided an easy way to attack Wilma and certainly got the most amount of attention. That Mankiller appeared to experience a greater degree of sexism than other Cherokee women who held office is perhaps not surprising. With a few exceptions, it appears that most of the attacks against her came not because she was a woman but because of the particular woman that she was. The sexism directed at Mankiller underscores the complexity of sex discrimination in the context of socially constructed gender roles. Her experience reflects the way in which women who more obviously deviate from traditional constructs of femininity have been more likely to experience sexism. In essence, opposition to Mankiller took on a conveniently gendered tone. Moreover, as a feminist with a fundamental understanding of female oppression, she was more likely to view attacks against her as gender-based than perhaps were other more conservative women. Regardless of the degree of situational sexism Mankiller encountered, the fact remained that many Cherokee politicians opposed her for one reason or another. Indeed, Swimmer repeatedly cautioned Wilma against running for office in 1987 because she did not have the council's support.[44]

Despite the council's hostility, the issue of sexism, and Swimmer's warnings, Mankiller continued on in the 1987 election. John Ketcher ran as her deputy chief, and, although both were forced into a runoff election, each prevailed in the end. In the July 18 runoff, Mankiller faced Perry Wheeler, who had served as Swimmer's deputy chief before challenging Swimmer in the 1983 election. John Ketcher faced Barbara Starr Scott, whom he beat 5,819 to 4,714, and Mankiller defeated Wheeler 5,914 to 4,670. Saying, "It was a sweet victory," Mankiller added, "Finally, I felt the question of gender had been put to rest." She quickly pointed out that because of her election to the most powerful office in the tribe, "some people erroneously conclude that the role of native women has changed in *every* tribe." This, she went on to say, "is not so." After her election in 1987, however, the issue of sexism seemed to be dismissed. In the introduction to her autobiography, Michael Wallis wrote, "In the beginning there were many problems and obstacles. There were some Cherokee who didn't wish to be governed by a female." He concluded by placing that sentiment firmly in the past: "Now when disagreements occur, they are based on issues rather than gender."[45]

Agency and Identity Politics

The contentions of Mankiller and her autobiography coauthor raise a number of significant issues about the politics of identity. Published two years before the end of her last term in office, her autobiography at times reads (perhaps not surprisingly) like a propaganda effort to show that, although problems and sexism existed in the past, her election as chief demonstrated an increase in gender equity within the tribe. In light of her election, Mankiller pronounced, "We are also returning the balance to the role of women in our tribe." Furthermore, she came to characterize sexism as a decidedly "un-Indian" phenomenon. Just six months after being subjected to sexism at the hands of her own tribe during the election, Mankiller told an audience at Harvard, "Contrary to what you've probably read in history books, not all tribes were controlled by men." She explained, "Sexism was one of the many white influences on Cherokee culture." She continued this theme in her autobiography, writing, "Europeans brought with them the view that men were the absolute heads of households, and women were to be subordinate to them." Certain that sexism "was not a Cherokee concept," Mankiller could then dismiss the gender biases she experienced in the 1983 and 1987 elections as another detrimental aspect of acculturation.[46]

Mankiller's autobiography also told her personal story within the context of Cherokee history. At times the result is a static and ahistorical depiction of white/Indian interaction. In response to a Bureau of Indian Affairs official pointing out a few minor factual errors in her book, Mankiller reiterated that it was, in fact, an autobiography and added that she would "be very much surprised if anyone mistook it for a definitive book on Indian policy." Nevertheless, an analytical problem emerges in the commingling of her personal story and historical imagery. Nonetheless, the arguments made by Mankiller offer a revealing glimpse into her use of identity politics, both in terms of feminism and Indianness.[47]

In recent years, scholars have attempted to restore agency to Native American women and debunk the notion that females exercised little or no power within their communities. As a part of this effort, increasing attention to the status of Cherokee women prior to Euro-American influence revealed that Cherokee women did in fact enjoy a greater degree of freedom than did many other women. Cherokee women experienced relative sexual freedom, they could attain a divorce as easily as men, and they had a women's council. The most powerful role afforded to Cherokee women was the status of "war woman" or "beloved woman." In *Cherokee Women,* Theda Perdue notes that at times the two terms appear interchangeable in sources, though it seems likely that war women became beloved women after menopause. War women attained an elevated status in the tribe by distinguishing themselves in battle and consequently exercised authority over the fate of war captives and other matters of import to the tribe. Nancy Ward, the last known beloved woman of the Cherokee, died in 1824, and since that time the status of women among the Cherokee increasingly resembled that of American women.[48]

Perdue emphasizes the harmonious nature of gender relations among the Cherokee, despite the changes their culture underwent in the eighteenth and nineteenth centuries. She argues that, although Cherokee women maintained "considerably more autonomy than elite Anglo-American women, they usually did not approach any sort of gender equity." Even so, Perdue explains that Cherokee men and women continued to adhere to a traditional worldview that "sanctioned the autonomy, complementarity, prestige, and even power of women." She describes the traditionally gendered division of work among the Cherokee and states that "native men and women lived remarkably separate lives," but this did not lead to sexism because of the belief in balance and harmony. In other words, men and women filled different roles, but their roles complimented each other. Perdue chronicles the impact of change on Cherokee society and maintains that, despite the influence of white culture, many Cherokees adapted to this change while maintaining their traditional beliefs. The election of Mankiller as chief of the Cherokee Nation, concludes Perdue, further illustrates the endurance of a culture in which women played a vital role. "The story of Cherokee women, therefore, is not one of declining status and lost culture, but one of persistence and change, conservatism and adaption, tragedy and survival."[49]

Mankiller's election brought with it considerable attention to and interest in the historic role of women, not only in Cherokee society but also among other native societies. Scholarship reveals that women in many native societies, including the Cherokee, enjoyed more autonomy than in European cultures. Some writers, however, romanticized Indian femininity and rejected historical accuracy in favor of glorifying indigenous gender roles. For instance, one writer emphasized the harmony of gender relations among Indian tribes, stating, "In many communities, particularly among the Iroquois, women and men enjoyed mutual respect, sharing of power and balance in the social life of the community." The author went on to explain, "Since there was no evidence for the subordination of women, there was no basis for even the conceptualization of feminism." The essay concluded with a suggestion that perhaps now all cultures can learn from the sort of implicit feminism apparent in the gender equity of indigenous tribal cultures.[50]

The depiction of sexism as a European import is not new. Yet it seems dubious to suggest that although both Europeans and

Native Americans (and most other cultures for that matter) divided work by sex—thereby *constructing* gender—it was the Europeans who introduced sexism to otherwise equitable and harmonious gender relations among Indians. It is clear that a danger exists in applying modern notions about what signifies sexism and oppression to cultures that judged power relations by different criteria, especially since the word "sexism" did not exist at the point of contact between Native Americans and Europeans. It is a modern construction that reveals more about the period in which it came into use than the time preceding it. Division of labor based on sex does not necessarily reflect an inherent denigration of women. The argument that sexism did not exist among Indians until contact with whites obscures and distorts more than it illuminates. The debate over sexism is, however, important to the extent that it shapes a modern native understanding of gender roles and balance. The belief that native women historically enjoyed greater balance and equity provides an affirmative justification—and indeed a powerful political tool—for Indian women who transgress mainstream white gender roles by wielding public power. In that context, it also offers insight into how Mankiller viewed herself, her career, her relationship to society, and her understanding of Cherokee culture. For she ultimately described her election victories as "a step forward for women and a step into the Cherokee tradition of balance between men and women."[51]

A Story of Great Triumph

The belief that women in Cherokee culture enjoyed gender equity and a greater degree of autonomy than did many Euro-American women helped justify Mankiller's assent to the highest elected office in the Cherokee Nation. Here the historical validity of such a claim became obscured by the politics involved on all sides of the issue. Mankiller's role in Cherokee politics received significant media attention. In fact, her communications staff had difficulty keeping up with the multitude of requests for interviews with the chief and were not entirely prepared for how extensive the media interest in Mankiller became.

The image of Wilma Mankiller triumphing over sexism to become the first female chief of a major Native American tribe is
one that appeared in countless newspaper articles, magazines,
and even children's stories. Indeed, it makes for a compelling
story. Her last name alone sparked considerable interest among
non-Indians. Add to that her being a feminist, a Cherokee (the
tribe most readily recognized by most Americans), and someone
who overcame tremendous health problems, and all the ingredients converged in a story of great triumph. Moreover, as a
woman, Mankiller did not conform to the stereotypical image
of a male chief wearing a headdress. The phrase "first female
chief of a *major* Native American tribe" appeared in print repeatedly in reference to Mankiller. Cherokee Nation communications director Lynn Howard recalled that many journalists mistakenly wanted to refer to Mankiller as the first female chief of
any tribe, which necessitated the clarification of "major" Native
American tribe. This is because she was by no means the first female chief of *a* tribe. She was not even the first female chief of
an Indian tribe in Oklahoma or the second for that matter.[52]

The Sac and Fox Indian tribe of Oklahoma, for example,
chose a female chief almost a decade before Mankiller began her
political career. Aside from mention in a few local newspapers,
Dora Schexnider got very little publicity for her role as a female
chief. Her sister, Mary McCormick, also served as chief but received no more publicity than did Schexnider. Perhaps this happened because the chief headed a tribe that only boasted a
membership of 2,000 or perhaps it just did not make for as good
a story. When McCormick became chief in December 1975, she
reported having "mixed emotions" about her new position.
"Probably I would rather have seen a man chosen," she explained. McCormick's tenure as chief lacked the magical ingredients of Mankiller's story. And so, even though she did not become the first female chief of a Native American tribe, the name
Wilma Mankiller is the one that resonates with people when
they think of female chiefs. Fond of telling people that she
earned her name, Mankiller quite obviously enjoyed enormous
success in gaining the interest of the media as well as writers of
children's stories.[53]

Although children's books can hardly be held to the same standards of scholarship as historical monographs, the children's stories written about Mankiller provide a useful lens through which to view the public consumption and articulation of the Mankiller story. One book in particular, which followed a format similar to that of her autobiography, explained the difficulty Mankiller faced when she agreed to run for deputy chief. After making her decision to run in 1983, the story describes people being "unfriendly" to her. "Something was very wrong. Wilma could feel it. Soon the truth came out. People were talking behind Wilma's back. 'We Cherokees never had a woman as deputy chief,' they said. 'It's a job for a man' they said." This book did not go on to explain any other reasons why Wilma encountered criticism, or the contentious atmosphere of tribal politics.[54]

Still another story, this one targeted at slightly older children, delved even further into emphasizing gender-based opposition to Mankiller's decision to run for deputy chief: "Fellow Cherokees were not greeting her with open arms. And their disapproval was not of her stand on issues. Nor was it of her running mate. The problem they had was with Wilma's gender." The story then described some of the bad things that happened to Mankiller in the 1983 election, including slashed tires, destruction of campaign posters, and threatening phone calls. The only context given to explain why such things happened to her implied opposition to female leadership. No mention was given to the other female candidate for deputy chief or the fact that Mankiller's experiences in that election often mirrored those of male candidates in tribal elections. Ironically, this came from a book in *The Library of Famous Women* series. Why not a story about an election in which the leading contenders were both women? One in which the male opponent, who said women should not be chief, got less than 25 percent of the vote? If the purpose of these children's stories had been to provide a lesson for their young readers by demonstrating a meaningful triumph over sexism, both for women and the Cherokee, the actual story was better than the one perpetuated in these books.[55]

The November 1999 issue of *Oklahoma Woman* contained an

interview with Mankiller, who at the time was recovering from radiation treatments for breast cancer. In the interview, Mankiller said she did not plan to get involved in politics again. She described herself as "a very ordinary woman . . . who happened to be exposed to a very extraordinary set of circumstances." Her understated characterization of her life and role in politics left researchers with the task of placing Mankiller in historical context. Though lacking political experience when she first ran for office in 1983, she indeed became a skilled politician. In fact, her autobiography can be understood, in part, as a manifestation of her skills as a politician; she used the public interest in her life to talk about Cherokee history. The story Mankiller told depicted adversity and hardship followed by triumph and restoration, for both herself and her tribe. One cannot understand Wilma Mankiller or her contribution to history without first examining the way in which feminism and Indianness shaped her sense of self, her perceptions of the 1983 and 1987 elections, and her career in politics.[56]

The role of image and identity in politics signifies a great deal about both society and political leaders. Mankiller clearly considered—and continues to consider—herself a feminist. In the 1983 and 1987 campaigns, she reacted to sexism by refusing to entertain the notion that women should not run for office. She firmly remarked, "Gender is not related to leadership, leadership is not related to gender," and she refused to acknowledge gender-based attacks. After she was elected principal chief in 1987, however, she seemed to downplay the problem of sexism, at least among the Cherokee. Did she abandon the tenets of feminism for political power? Or did the sexism she claimed to encounter really decline upon her election? One early male critic of Mankiller changed his attitude, consenting, "I had negative thoughts [about women leading the tribe] before. But I have had the opportunity to work with her. I have been impressed with her leadership." Some critics changed their minds about Mankiller's ability to govern as a woman as she gained popularity and brought national attention to the Cherokee tribe. Nevertheless, feminism and Indianness at times seem in competition in the manifestations of her political image.[57]

The relationship between feminism and Indianness, manifested in both Mankiller's political rhetoric and popular interpretations of her experience with sexism, should not be examined in a vacuum. In fact, historians argue that perhaps the greatest limitation of second-wave feminism stemmed from the movement's failure to allow for and accommodate the differences that exist between women. Issues of class, race, ethnicity, and sexuality led to a great deal of division within the movement. The fundamental premise of the feminist movement in the 1960s and 1970s, which erupted while Mankiller lived in San Francisco, consisted of the belief that above all else women were united by their gender and that everything else remained secondary to this one commonality. Although Mankiller did not directly participate in the movement, she did credit it with having a significant impact on her. The point, then, is not that she experienced the tension within the feminist movement per se, but rather that the tension between feminism and Indianness in her own image should be understood within the larger context of challenges to feminism. Mankiller herself did not articulate feeling torn between being a feminist and an Indian, to the extent that she utilized identity politics in her political career, but this tension emerges in an examination of her rhetoric. She claimed that no sexism existed among Cherokees until contact and thus described the gender discrimination she encountered in the 1983 and 1987 elections as un-Indian. Once she won election in her own right, she and her coauthor seemed to downplay the issue by emphasizing a restoration of gender equity. Here it seems Mankiller acted as a skilled politician in her use of gendered imagery.[58]

Sexism as a Political Tool

The assertion that Mankiller's political career and her election as chief in 1987 marked a return to Cherokee tradition is clearly an oversimplification. The exact nature and extent of sexism in Cherokee society remains unclear. Although the allegations of sexism were inconsistent and at times unsubstantiated by the evidence, they can best be understood as political tools. An analysis of the elections in 1983 and 1987 does not reveal widespread gender hostility toward Mankiller or any of the other candidates. Other Cherokee women, most notably Cowen, were politically active before Mankiller ran for office. Men did not constitute her only competition and not all women supported her. If the 1983 election revealed anything about opposition to women running for political office it was that those people were clearly a small minority. J. B. Dreadfulwater's elimination left Mankiller and Cowen vying for deputy chief. His attempt to make the gender of his opponents a meaningful issue patently failed. In both elections, in which Mankiller's gender has been described as a major issue, there were politically prominent tribal women involved in the opposition to her.

The role of rumor and historical memory also complicates any attempt to identify the exact nature of sexism in the 1983 and 1987 campaigns. Mankiller's deputy chief, John Ketcher, recalled hearing that Mankiller had encountered sexism when running for office, but he had no direct knowledge of it. Saying he had nothing but the utmost respect for the work of Mankiller, Ketcher described her as a remarkable woman who has overcome many obstacles in her life. Similarly, Lynn Howard did not recall sexism being a particularly significant issue for Chief Mankiller. In a 1986 interview, however, an article in *Mother Jones* quoted Howard as saying, "there was plenty of sexism" when Swimmer left office and Mankiller became chief. Howard added, "This area is very rural, very inbred, and full of a lot of good Baptists who think God doesn't want a woman in charge of anything." It is noteworthy that, shortly after she replaced Swimmer as chief, Mankiller conducted an informal poll of twenty people to gauge the reaction of Cherokees to female leadership. On the basis of the poll results, Mankiller said the "support was overwhelming" and "so the myth that people have worries about a woman is indeed a myth." By and large, the sexism Mankiller encountered came from only a handful of people who were looking for any reason to discredit her politically. Both her own popularity among the tribe and the role of other Cherokee women in politics further supports such a conclusion. Yet the struggle to overcome sexism presented a national platform for her story, and this is where Chief Mankiller, the politician, made use of the forum available to her.[59]

When Mankiller ran for her final term of office in 1991, she won by an astonishing 82.5 percent of the vote. Her margin of victory would be considered a landslide for any political race, but it was especially remarkable in light of the contentious nature of tribal politics. She once told an audience of college students that she did not yet believe that women had achieved equality in politics because a woman needs a resume twice as long as a man's. Mankiller went on to add that only when mediocre women begin to be elected to high offices will equality truly be achieved. It is in that spirit that the emphasis on sex-based attacks against Mankiller should be understood. As long as a woman's triumph over sexism is viewed as a necessary precursor to political participation and there is an eager reception to stories that celebrate this triumph, gender will be privileged over substance. Indeed, as long as this is the case, women in politics will remain an anomaly, an oddity, an out-of-the-ordinary success to be alternately scrutinized and venerated, instead of women being remembered for where they stood on the issues.[60]

Tribal

Governance and

Indian Identity

"It's not just that she has led a new world interest in the Cherokee Nation and shared the story of the Cherokee Nation around the world," said Congressman Mike Synar. "[Wilma Mankiller has] made a difference with people—white, black, red, young and old, rich and poor." Indeed, Mankiller's prominence on the national scene continued to grow after she became chief in her own right. With the 1987 election behind her, Mankiller finally felt she had the support of her tribe and a mandate to govern the Cherokee Nation. Although she had accomplished some gains for the tribe when she filled the last two years of Ross Swimmer's term as chief, it would not be until elected in her own right that she finally felt secure in her position and could wholeheartedly devote herself to running the Cherokee Nation. In the ten years that she served as chief, Mankiller accomplished a great deal for her tribe and helped the Cherokee build several million dollars worth of new facilities.[1]

As the head of the second-largest Indian tribe in the country, Mankiller's jurisdiction in Cherokee country covered approximately 7,000 square miles and she managed an annual budget of more than $75 million. The tribe employed over 1,200 people, and according to Mankiller's autobiography, her job responsibilities were "the same as a head of state and chief executive officer of a major corporation." Membership soared, tribal revenues increased, the tribal government was revitalized, new health-care and educational facilities were built, and a tribal police force was established, along with a host of other improvements. To understand the impact Mankiller had on the Cherokee Nation, it is essential to examine both her accomplishments and the ways in which others viewed her: part of what made her so successful and brought such attention to the Cherokees stemmed from her ability and willingness to use media interest in her to stimulate tribal development. She granted countless interviews and involved herself in national lobbying efforts to better conditions for the Cherokees and other Indians. Mankiller also used her membership in numerous national Indian organizations and her autobiography as a means to enhance and bring attention to the Cherokee Nation.[2]

Community Development and Health Care

Mankiller's work with community development helped her get elected and continued to be one of the most important issues in her administration. A Cherokee Nation profile of Mankiller described her philosophy as "empowerment of people at the local level." She "strongly encourages the tribal membership to become more self-reliant in outlook," the profile explained. From her early days of working with the Cherokee Nation, first as the economic stimulus coordinator and later as the director of community development, Mankiller maintained a strong desire to help those who needed it the most. For Mankiller, "creating community based change—getting health care, children's services, [and] housing"—to people took priority over ideology and politics. In fact, her community development work transformed her attitude on the use of federal funding. According to Mankiller, she "went from being a purist (no federal funds, etc.) to a master of garnering federal support for everything from rural water lines to a youth shelter."[3]

The emphasis on community development among the Cherokee earned both Chief Mankiller and the tribe considerable attention. U.S. Senator David Boren, also an Oklahoma Democrat, praised Mankiller and said that, because of her efforts, the Cherokee Nation "has the most outstanding community development effort of any Tribe in our country." He hailed the Cherokee Nation as a "model for others to emulate." Boren cited the most significant outcome of the community development work as the increase in standard of living that many Cherokees enjoyed. After becoming involved in community development work, Mankiller discovered a "national interest in self-help." She speculated that the interest in self-help for Native Americans came from the challenge it offered to "the old stereotypes of American Indians as lazy and dependent" or because "it is extremely unusual for a community of people to build their own water system and housing." As chief, Mankiller worked to continue development in Cherokee communities by getting the people involved at every level of the process.[4]

The fact that Mankiller herself came from a large, poor, rural family afforded her an empathy for Cherokees living in abject conditions. And, in light of the personal trauma she felt when her family moved to California because they could not make a living in eastern Oklahoma, it comes as no surprise that helping poor Cherokees become economically self-sufficient remained one of Mankiller's most personally gratifying goals. She did not want other Cherokee families to have to make the same decision that hers had. In many ways, Wilma embodied the role of a woman of the people. She identified with poor rural Cherokees because of the similarity to her own childhood and has spent a considerable amount of her time and energy seeking to improve the conditions of poor Indians. Mankiller did not want others to share in her family's experience of having to move away from their ancestral home to make a living, so she encouraged Cherokee people to take charge of their own communities and become more politically active.

Health care constituted another significant issue for Mankiller—one that bore a similarity to community development in that it was close to her heart because of her own experiences with illness. Over the course of her life, Mankiller has endured a staggering number of medical problems. After a head-on car collision in 1979, in which the driver of the other car was a friend who did not survive the accident, Mankiller went through a painful recovery only to find out the following year that she had myasthenia gravis, a debilitating neuromuscular disease. Her condition worsened to the point where she struggled just to hold a hairbrush, had trouble swallowing, and spent time confined to a wheelchair. After undergoing a successful surgical procedure in which the doctors removed her thymus gland, Mankiller again recovered but suffered from the side effects of her medication. She gained fifty pounds in a short amount of time and has since struggled to control her weight. She has had breast cancer and colon cancer and has received two kidney transplants.[5]

Her health represented a major campaign issue in both the 1987 and 1991 elections, when she constantly had to reassure both supporters and critics that her health would not jeopardize her performance as chief. She even had to hold a press conference from a hospital bed in 1987 to convince her constituents that she had not died, despite rumors to the contrary. According to the Cherokee Nation communications director, Lynn Howard, one small-town newspaper obtained copies of her medical charts which contained a misdiagnosis and used it to further challenge Mankiller's medical status. When asked what the worst thing someone had done to her politically, she described this 1987 experience. While hospitalized shortly before the election, Mankiller learned that an opponent had launched a telephone campaign falsely informing voters that her doctors expected her to die very soon. In light of her health problems and the publicity they generated, it comes as no surprise that tribal health care drew considerable interest from Mankiller. Certainly no stranger to hospitals and fully aware of the need for competent health-care providers in Indian country, Chief Mankiller made it a top priority to improve health care for Cherokees. One new Cherokee medical clinic located in Stilwell, Oklahoma, and built under Mankiller's leadership bears her name in recognition of her efforts. Although her own health problems gave her a greater empathy for others, they also provided ammunition against her in campaigns.[6]

Mankiller's health had implications for those outside the Cherokee Nation as well. A transplant recipient who saw her as a role model wrote a particularly poignant letter to Mankiller, seeking her advice about another transplant. The man had already undergone one heart transplant but discovered that he needed a second to survive. This father of four sought Mankiller's advice because he had done something that made him ashamed and felt that he did not deserve another chance at life. While this man solicited Mankiller's advice because he felt she had made good use of her own transplant by helping others, some people with health problems responded differently. One angry and desperate woman wrote to Chief Mankiller asking for financial help for her medical problems. The woman wrote, "When you had your medical emergency no money was cut. There was plenty of everything that you needed." The woman concluded by writing, "I realize that I am a nobody but I plead for your assistance. Please cut the red tape and let me enjoy my life and my girls." This woman was not even Cherokee but somehow, in her distraught state, believed that Mankiller was in a position to help her. Beyond fielding letters such as this, Mankiller also lent her name to a variety of organizations relating to transplantation and other health-related issues.[7]

Education and Business Affairs

Aside from community development and health care, education constituted one of the most important issues to Chief Mankiller. Believing education essential to any sustained prosperity and self-sufficiency, Mankiller devoted considerable efforts to improving educational opportunities at every level for Cherokees. She helped improve Head Start facilities and worked to strengthen the management of Sequoyah High School. Thus, Mankiller became involved in the most basic issues concerning the running of the tribe. Both her involvement and her sense of humor emerged in a memo she wrote in response to complaints about the uncleanliness of the Sequoyah High School bathrooms: "I have lots of things to do in my daily schedule but I have never had an occasion to write a memorandum about toilets."[8]

On a more serious note, the chief also revived the Talking Leaves Job Corps, which provided training to Cherokee young people. Housed in an old section of dorms at Northeastern State University in Tahlequah until its lease expired in November of 1987, the Talking Leaves Job Corps came very close to being shut down because of the difficulty involved in finding a new location for the center. Roger Webb, the president of Northeastern, informed Mankiller that the expanding university needed the space occupied by the job corps so the lease would not be renewed. In May 1986 Mankiller testified before Congress in an effort to save Talking Leaves. She said that only two such facilities in the United States emphasized reaching the Indian population and indicated that it would hurt both the Cherokee and Oklahoma economies to lose the corps. The following month she received a scathing letter from Roger Semerad, the assistant secretary of labor, in which he blasted the entire operation of Talking Leaves. He accused the "top leadership of the Cherokee Nation" of paying "little attention to its responsibility" of running the job corps. This particularly disturbed him, he said, because of the $248,774 the Cherokee Nation received annually to operate the facility. Semerad vehemently disagreed with the criticism of the Department of Labor's evaluation criteria as "biased and inequitable." He concluded that "the logic employed is weak and tortuous, and further handicapped by the inaccuracies" in the analysis offered by the Cherokee Nation.[9]

Despite this withering critique and considerable opposition from the tribal council, Mankiller saved Talking Leaves from being closed. In the midst of the chief's efforts to keep the job corps open, a number of people phoned the Cherokee Nation to oppose the continued operation of Talking Leaves. Some people who called or sent petitions argued that the Cherokee Nation "had no business operating a program for white youth or black youth or Latin youth" because "they would burglarize the homes in Cherokee county." Others argued that a new center would hurt the Tahlequah economy because fewer people would retire there and more interracial marriages would also occur. Mankiller eventually convinced the tribal council to close the Tsa-la-gi Lodge and Restaurant, which then afforded a temporary place to house the program. She described her struggle to get a new Talking Leaves Job Corps center built as "the biggest political fight I ever had." She did, however, prevail in this effort, and a new $11,000,000 center now houses Talking Leaves. Lynn Howard described this as by far one of Mankiller's greatest accomplishments as chief.[10]

Another aspect of Mankiller's interest in education manifested itself in her devotion to bilingual programs. She played a key role in making Cherokee language classes available to both children and adults and increased the number of college and graduate scholarships available to Cherokees. Oklahoma State Superintendent of Public Instruction Sandy Garret recognized Mankiller's work on education and wrote to the chief, saying, "You are to be commended for your continued support of education of Oklahoma's Indian children." Mankiller's concern for education and young people in the Cherokee Nation took on other forms as well. Her administration established a youth shelter and sought to better the condition of Cherokee children in foster care. Mankiller praised Phyllis Wheeler, the executive director of Tahlequah Project Inc., for her efforts to provide safe activities for teenagers in the community. Mankiller wrote to Wheeler, "I am delighted that someone is making a serious effort to serve Tahlequah youth," adding, "Be assured that I fully support your efforts." In the same letter, Chief Mankiller expressed concerns about gang activity and the need for teenagers to have safe activities that kept them from being unduly influenced by college students from nearby Northeastern State University.[11]

Community development and improving education and health care held a special place in Mankiller's administration, but she also had to manage the business affairs of the tribe. Her activist background and her community development work prepared her for these responsibilities, but not for dealing with the business side of Cherokee affairs. During Mankiller's tenure in office, the Cherokee Nation operated numerous facilities, including schools, health-care clinics, a nursery, a hotel, a restaurant, a museum, and a manufacturing plant called Cherokee Nation Industries. Howard attributed some of Mankiller's success as chief to her willingness to listen to the advice of others and the way in which Mankiller surrounded herself with qualified and knowledgeable staffers. On several occasions Mankiller described the role of chief as "something like running a big corporation and a little country at the same time." She characterized the Cherokee Nation as "more of a republic than a reservation." From her involvement in community development to the handling of personnel matters and the business management of the tribe, Mankiller undertook an enormous task in governing and expanding the Cherokee Nation.[12]

Self-Governance and Political Infighting

One significant accomplishment for the Cherokee Nation came in 1990, when Chief Mankiller negotiated a self-governance compact with the federal government. The 1975 Indian Self-Determination Act, which gave Native American tribes greater autonomy in administering a variety of government-funded programs, laid the foundation for agreements such as this one. According to the compact, the assistant secretary of the interior agreed to "conduct the relations of the U.S. on a government to government basis" with the Cherokee Nation. The agreement stipulated that the secretary "pledges to the maximum extent to honor the laws of the Cherokee Nation and any decisions of the Cherokee Nation's court or tribunal." This historic agreement indeed opened the door for the Cherokees to exercise more power over a host of programs, including health care and education, than they had in more than a century. Mankiller summed up the significance of such an agreement by saying that, although she could not get very excited over the tribe using its power to issue Cherokee license plates, she could get excited when "the Cherokee Nation uses its authority to buy back some of our land base, to build and operate our own health systems or to sign a government to government agreement."[13]

In view of the contentious nature of politics in general and tribal politics in particular, it hardly comes as a surprise that Mankiller could not please everyone all of the time. She drew criticism throughout the duration of her time in office. On the eve of her bid for reelection in 1991, Mankiller described Cherokee elections as "full of blood-letting" and said that "if one blinks during this period, the penalty is to get behind." Furthermore, "If one sleeps during this period, one is liable to lose the entire election." A few months prior to the election, Swimmer wrote to the chief to explain some comments attributed to him in a recent interview. He told her that she was "doing a great job" and added, "I think you might have even exceeded George Bush's popularity ranking—something I could never achieve." Swimmer's predictions about Mankiller's popularity proved accurate. Despite her concern that her health would be a big issue in the election, she won reelection by a staggering 82 percent of the vote and went on to lead her tribe for another four years. Nevertheless, Mankiller's concern demonstrates the nasty side of tribal politics.[14]

Policing Claims of Indianness

Because the Cherokee name is familiar to people around the world and because people often recall vague stories of Indian ancestry in their family tree, the Cherokee Nation has had to confront problems with various groups using the Cherokee name without permission. Mankiller finally became so frustrated by innumerable complaints about groups and individuals who falsely claimed to represent the Cherokee Nation or who misused the Cherokee name that she circulated a list of unacknowledged groups claiming to be Cherokee to governors and other state and federal officials around the United States. Her efforts to curb these illegal and fraudulent activities unfortunately earned her harsh criticism from a number of individuals as well as from some groups that perhaps failed to understand the events necessitating her actions. The Pan American Indian Association blasted Mankiller, saying that although some of their individual members may identify themselves as Cherokee, the organization itself had never done so. The concluding comments of Day Flower, the educational director of the organization, captured the overall tone of the letter: "You must realize that Great Spirit and the federal government throw maize to the whole flock not just one old hen and her biddies." Another member of the Pan American Indian Association, Chief Walking Bear of the Amonsoquath Tribe, also condemned Chief Mankiller's actions. He asked what gave her the "power to refuse anyone the right to use the Cherokee name" and then described his tribe's Cherokee history. He argued that Mankiller's jurisdiction was "only good in Eastern Oklahoma and nowhere else." This emotionally charged letter accused her of "disgracing the Cherokee name" and went so far as to call her "an ugly person."[15]

While uncommon, such attacks on Mankiller demonstrate an unintended consequence of her battle against fraud as many of those who criticized her seemed to view the list as an assault against their personal identity. In fact, this issue reveals the bitter and contentious nature of one aspect of Indian identity and the "right" of individuals to identify with a given tribe, even if that tribe and/or the federal government fails to recognize a person as a member of the tribe. The response to Mankiller's actions indicates that some clearly (though perhaps incorrectly) viewed it as an attack on individual identity. Luis Zapata of the D.C. Native Peoples Network wrote to Chief Mankiller in regard to the misuse of the Cherokee name. He said many in his organization were "perplexed" by her actions because they viewed Mankiller as "one of the few [national] champions of *real Indians*" and therefore could not understand why she wrote the letter to state governors that seemed "to delegate *sole* discretionary power of deciding who is Native American and who is not to a non-Indian bureaucracy in Washington, D.C." In essence, he argued that a contradiction existed in Mankiller's recognition of people with legitimate but undocumented Cherokee descent and her circulating a list of unrecognized groups claiming to be Cherokee. Here again, this issue goes to the heart of the politicization of Indian identity. Identity is by nature a personal issue and often evokes powerful emotions, yet the legal status of Native Americans creates tremendous complexity for those without documentation.[16]

Strong resentment emerged from those not able to document adequately their Indian heritage, as evidenced by some of the letters written to Mankiller. "Not all Cherokees were receptive to the roll system," admonished one angry person who stated that the rolls "should not judge whether I am Native American or not." He claimed that he and others who lacked documentation simply wanted to be "acknowledged and respected." Describing Mankiller's actions as "unfair," another critic asked her how she knew whether the people she accused of pretending to be Cherokee had any Cherokee blood in them or not. This writer concluded by stating that "a lot of us just want to be accepted as Cherokee when we are, and not for the Government money." Here the issue of federal recognition of Native American tribes ran headlong into individual issues of identity. People with stories of Cherokee ancestry in their families who had opted not to sign the Dawes Roll had no legal claim to Cherokee ancestry. Condemning Mankiller's "blacklist" of people claiming to be Cherokee, one woman said, "I have always been proud of my Native American ancestry," but she felt "sad and angry" at reading about Mankiller's list. The woman asked Mankiller, "Who are you to say who is who?" As she explained, "The Great Spirit or Maker of Breath is the one that put me here at this time in history with mixed heritage."[17]

Although the issue seemed very clear to those who wrote such letters, the process of federal recognition of Native American tribes and the implications of that recognition are anything but simple. And in fact, the phrases used to criticize Mankiller's "list" reveal the disjunction between the right of individuals to express their identity and the unique legal status of quite literally being a card-carrying Indian in the United States. There is no small irony in seeing Mankiller, in her capacity as the chief of the Cherokee Nation, criticized for a recognition process necessitated by policy implemented by the federal government. Granted, the Cherokee Nation has jurisdiction over defining its own membership criteria, but the ramifications of tribal membership/recognition were established by the federal government. Chief Mankiller could not stand idly by while people falsely claimed to represent the Cherokee Nation. If the Cherokee Nation suddenly began recognizing everyone as Cherokee who wanted to be Cherokee, thought they had been Cherokee in a past life, or, in the more serious cases, were Cherokee but lacked documentation, it would have dire consequences for the enrolled members of the tribe and for federal money allocated to the tribe.

Federal recognition of Native Americans indeed remains one of the most volatile concerns among Indian groups. Angered by the Georgia legislature's decision to recognize three groups as tribes, two of which identified themselves as Cherokee, Mankiller wrote a letter to Georgia Governor Zell Miller, saying she "was shocked and dismayed" over the decision. According to Mankiller, Jonathan Taylor, the principal chief of the Eastern Band of Cherokee, had also urged the governor not to sign the bill into law. Mankiller explained that they were concerned over states deciding to recognize or create Indian tribes "without specific recognition criteria." She reminded the governor that the United States government "has a complex set of criteria and a federal acknowledgment process each tribal organization must undergo to determine recognition eligibility." Mankiller laid out the complexity of recognition status and added that the groups recognized in Georgia would apply for federal recognition, costing both the Cherokee Nation and the Eastern Band significant time and energy to oppose their efforts.[18]

Mankiller recognized and had sympathy for those of Cherokee heritage who lacked proof. In legal terms, however, Native Americans occupy a unique situation that brings legal and economic ramifications to claims of Indian ancestry. Mankiller did not begrudge those with undocumented Cherokee ancestry, but the use of the Cherokee name by both groups not legally recognized by the federal government and those individuals not recognized by the Cherokee Nation brought negative consequences for the tribe. As chief, she had a responsibility to uphold the law. Although the federal government, not Wilma Mankiller, set the criteria for federal recognition of tribes, each tribe set the criteria for individual membership within the tribe. Nevertheless, Mankiller had an obligation to the enrolled members of the Cherokee Nation to maintain the integrity of the process and protect the tribe against cases of fraud. That fact, however, appears to have been lost on some. Both the issue of establishing individual claims to Indian ancestry and attempts by groups to gain the status of federally recognized Indian tribes brought tremendous division and emotional responses on both sides. Here Mankiller found herself caught between the proverbial rock and a hard place.

A further manifestation of the minefield involved in tribal identity emerged in the relationship of the Cherokee Nation to the Delaware tribe. The Delaware and the Cherokee Nation have inhabited the same Oklahoma land since their 1867 agreement, which allowed the Delaware to relocate within the Cherokee Nation. According to the agreement, each Delaware who participated received 160 acres and became members of the Cherokee Nation. The agreement stipulated that the children of those Delaware "shall in all respects be regarded as native Cherokees." In 1985 the Cherokee Nation passed a resolution allowing the Delaware to take control of their tribal affairs and essentially function as a "tribe within a tribe." In 1992, however, the Delaware proposed a separation from the Cherokee Nation. The significance of the debate that followed stems from the centrality of identity and the role of Mankiller, who strongly supported the separation of the Delaware, in mitigating the contentious ordeal.[19]

One of the clearest articulations of identity came from a Delaware woman who vehemently desired separation from the Cherokee Nation. In a letter to Mankiller regarding this proposed separation of the Delaware from the Cherokee Nation, the woman described the Cherokee Nation as being "as bad as the federal government" and accused the Cherokee of denying the Delaware their identity. She described Mankiller as a symbol of oppression to the Delaware and called on her to support their quest for independence. The woman asked Mankiller how hard she would work if someone told her that her tribe was not Cherokee but instead was Seminole or Navajo and ended the letter by writing, "What would you do if another tribe had jurisdiction over yours and considered your people to be their property? You would fight. And so will we." Here again, the issue over the federally recognized status of a tribe versus tribal or individual identity emerges. The characterization of the Cherokee as oppressors of the Delaware seems both unfair and inaccurate. What the woman who wrote the letter failed to consider is that if the Cherokee severed their relationship with the Delaware, no guarantee existed that the federal government would in fact recognize the Delaware as an independent tribe.[20]

Tobacco Compact Controversy

Aside from the flack Mankiller received over Indian identity, she also encountered tremendous criticism from some Oklahoma tribes for negotiating a compact with the state in which the Cherokee Nation agreed to pay a 25 percent tax on all tobacco purchased from manufactures for the purpose of resale. The agreement came in response to a U.S. Supreme Court ruling in the case of *Oklahoma Tax Commission v. Citizen Band Pottawatomi Indian Tribe of Oklahoma* stating that Oklahoma could collect state taxes on cigarettes and other tobacco products sold by tribes or members of tribes to non-Indians. As a result of this ruling, tribes had two options: they could agree to a compact as the Cherokee had, which provided for a flat tax paid up front on all tobacco purchased from the manufactures, or they could collect the taxes themselves from tobacco products sold to nontribal members. The second option was fraught with complications and for most tribes more trouble than it was worth. By law, the compact recognized the right of tribes to sell tobacco products to its own members "free from state taxation." In practice, however, the agreement meant that tribes that signed the compact paid a state tax on the tobacco regardless of who purchased it from the smoke shops.[21]

The Supreme Court ruling left tribes with very little room to maneuver on the taxation issue, which makes the harsh criticism of Mankiller all the more intriguing. Mankiller and leaders from the Chickasaw, Choctaw, and Seminole Nations who signed identical compacts with the state (as most of the tribes in Oklahoma would eventually do) used the compact for expediency and also as an expression of self-government. The wording of the compact made clear that the tribes had "sovereign powers of self-government," and this language ran throughout the agreement. Other tribes, most notably the Wyandotte and the Wichita and Affiliated Tribes, saw the compact quite differently, fearing it would undermine tribal sovereignty. Leaford Bearskin, chief of the Wyandotte tribe, cautioned Mankiller that "the actions taken by the Cherokee will have a great impact on the entire Indian world." When Mankiller failed to heed his warnings, he became particularly nasty. He accused her of pursuing her "own selfish interests" and added that by negotiating the compact she had "usurped the power and authority" of all the other tribes in Oklahoma. Chief Bearskin said that he would never again seek her council. He accused her of selling the other tribes of Oklahoma down the river and closed by saying, "I view your despicable actions with complete disgust and contempt." One member of the Wyandotte tribe even drew a cartoon depicting Mankiller as both figuratively and literally being in bed with the Oklahoma Tax Commission. Although her sex did not constitute the reason for Wyandotte criticism of her, her critics did not hesitate to use it in their attempt to discredit her leadership. The cartoon showed Mankiller in a clinging nightgown sitting in bed with a man from the Oklahoma Tax Commission who was smoking a cigarette. When a member of the Wyandotte tribe walked in on them, the caption above the gendered caricature of Chief Mankiller said, "Oh! Well ... UH ... None of this is as bad as it looks!!!"[22]

Mankiller calmly but firmly responded to Chief Bearskin's attacks. She rejected the argument that the compact with the state of Oklahoma undermined the authority and the sovereignty of tribes, characterizing it as "pure nonsense." She explained that the Cherokee Nation, as well as other tribes in numerous states, had entered into a variety of similar agreements, all of which were "exercises of tribal sovereignty." Mankiller dismissed Bearskin's "scurrilous personal attacks" and said she disagreed that the tribes in Oklahoma should "conduct business through some kind of state-wide consensus." Instead, she argued "the very essence of tribal self-determination and sovereignty is for each tribe to chart its own course." Mankiller concluded by saying that she happily pled guilty to his charge that she had acted in the selfish interest of the Cherokee Nation and added that she would continue to do so. Chief Mankiller made it clear that she had no interest in any sort of intertribal consensus governing and, in fact, viewed it as the antithesis of sovereignty and true self-determination.[23]

Despite Mankiller's defense of her actions, she still faced hostility. Gary McAdams, president of the Wichita and Affiliated Tribes, reinforced the criticism voiced by Chief Bearskin. He acknowledged the right of the Cherokee Nation to "determine its own destiny" but said that Mankiller "owed an explanation to all of Indian Country" for her support of the tobacco compact with the state of Oklahoma. McAdams accused her of "arbitrarily and erroneously" speaking for the other tribes in Oklahoma and argued "we cannot think of any more damaging action to tribal unity than your recent decision to assist in the drafting of this legislation." George Wickliffe, a Cherokee and vocal opponent of Mankiller, later accused her of being "willing to negotiate away our sovereignty" because of her support for the compact.[24]

On the one hand, the Cherokee Nation had no choice but to comply with the state tobacco tax on nontribal members. Both Mankiller's participation in drafting the legislation and her signing of the agreement reinforced the government-to-government basis on which Native American tribes exercising sovereignty wished to act. On the other hand, Mankiller herself worried about the implications of the tax compact for tribal sovereignty. Certainly there existed a danger of tribal sovereignty being undercut by the right of state governments to collect the tax. This incident reveals a strange and complicated dialogue regarding the connection between tribal unity and tribal sovereignty. Different leaders and tribes interpreted tribal sovereignty in contrasting terms. To some, entering into a legal agreement with Oklahoma constituted an expression of tribal sovereignty, but to others it seemed an erosion of tribal power.

Fixation on Indianness

While issues of unity, sovereignty, and identity often underscored the volatile nature of tribal politics, the increasing national and popular interest in all things Indian added a further element of complexity. Americans have a long history of embracing equally romantic and denigrating images of Native Americans, but the final decades of the twentieth century wit-

nessed an increasing fascination with Indianness. Tribal membership increased drastically during the ten years Wilma Mankiller
served as chief. Part of the reason stemmed from the overall increase in the number of Americans claiming Indian ancestry. As
Joan Nagel argues, "Widespread ethnic renewal is the only way
to account for the extraordinary eightfold increase in the Indian
population in the twentieth century." The Cherokee Nation witnessed a substantial growth in membership during Mankiller's
time in office as a part of this trend. According to an article in
the *Cherokee Phoenix,* between 1987 and 1991 membership increased from 77,043 to 116,053 and continued to increase every
year thereafter. In fact, the prominence Mankiller brought to being Native American, especially to the Cherokee, also played a
significant role in generating Native American ancestral self-
pride. As a man who described himself as a conservative Republican put it, "I have never been ashamed of my Native American
heritage, but I never took pride in it." He then proclaimed that
Mankiller had "changed that forever!" The story Mankiller told
in her autobiography affected people in many ways and very often made people feel better about themselves because they could
relate to her story. The struggle she went through trying to adapt
to life in San Francisco as a child, her deepening sense of Indianness that came though her exposure to Alcatraz and the Pit River
struggle, and her homecoming to Oklahoma and subsequent involvement with the Cherokee Nation resonated with many of
her readers. One Cherokee woman described herself as feeling
like "an ex-patriot and a member of an endangered species" until
reading Mankiller's book.[25]

For some, proof of their Cherokee ancestry seemed a last-
ditch effort to validate their identity. The "extreme importance"
of "heritage pride" coupled with the desire to "become officially
a member of the Cherokee tribe" led one woman to lash out at
Mankiller when writing for the third time about her efforts. It is
interesting to note that when the writer failed to receive the information she wanted, she criticized Mankiller, stating, "Upon
first hearing that a woman was Chief, I felt great pride in my
gender." She quickly added, "Methinks this job is perhaps more
suited to the male gender." The desire to trace and legitimize

Cherokee heritage inspired many to write very personal letters to Mankiller explaining how important their heritage was to them. "You have truly been an inspiration at this time in my life," said a fan of Mankiller's, who described her "only goal" as finding her "Cherokee roots" and claiming her heritage.[26]

Establishing Indian ancestry held deep significance to the identity of many who wrote to Wilma Mankiller, but for others personal profit seemed the main goal. In fact, according to James Clifton, "Every time the value of being Indian increases, the number of persons of marginal or ambiguous ancestry who claim to be Indian increases." Although the value of Indianness meant different things to different people, to a small minority seeking to establish their Indian heritage it came as a monetary incentive. One person wrote succinctly to Mankiller, "I would like to find out if I have enough Indian in me to draw any money." Another asked Mankiller for claim forms to fill out in expectation of receiving money. "Please send me information on what qualifies me to receive payment because of my heritage." Most who wrote to Mankiller in an attempt to trace their ancestry did not do so for money, but those who did serve as a reminder of the complexity of Indianness when ethnic identity becomes juxtaposed with the political and legal status of *being Indian*.[27]

Aside from letters she received from people wishing to establish their Cherokee heritage, Mankiller received numerous letters from both Indians and non-Indians who felt compelled simply to share their stories with her. Such letters should be understood, to some extent, as a part of a wider social trend venerating all things Indian that, while not new, increased the 1980s and 1990s. Nevertheless, Mankiller exuded a quality that encouraged a familiarity from people. The sentiments expressed by one fan mirrored that of many others: "After reading her autobiography I know her well and almost feel she is a friend who lives just up the road." Her communications staff grew during her tenure in office as they struggled to keep up with all the fan mail and requests for interviews she received. Letters from a wide array of people made their way to Mankiller's staff as media coverage fed an ever-greater interest in her. She received requests for everything from buffalo skulls and tobacco to her favorite squash recipes and even requests for her to perform "Indian weddings" and give people Indian names. These inquiries came from Indians and non-Indians, men and women, from all over the world.[28]

An examination of some of the letters written to Mankiller reveals both the fascination people have with Indians and the use of Indian imagery to satisfy something otherwise lacking in their lives. One letter from a woman asking Mankiller to give her an Indian name explained, "I feel as though my life would be altered significantly with some meaning attached to it." The letter concluded with a plea to please help her "sad spirit." On one hand, some of the letters sent to Mankiller can simply be dismissed as the handiwork of lonely people looking for attention. On the other, even the strangest letters provide insight into the larger tendency of new age spiritualists and self-help gurus seeking to find some sort of universal truth through romanticized notions of Indianness. The preoccupation with a kind of modern noble savagery revealed in many of the letters written to Mankiller reinforces a static and ultimately racist view of Indians. The fact that Mankiller felt the brunt of some of this attention is not surprising in light of the high visibility of the Cherokee Nation and Mankiller herself. A man wrote to Mankiller, asking her to put him in touch with "any young Cherokee women" who would start a friendship with him that would hopefully lead to marriage. Saying that he had always thought of himself as Indian, he turned to an idealized version of Indians to bring meaning to his life. Two factors were at work in this letter. First, the man simply wanted a date. But second, and more important, he wanted a particular type of date. Specifically, he preferred someone who knew about "the old ways, traditions and customs" and could teach them to him. Drawing on a romanticized notion of Indianness—and indeed a modern extension of noble savagery—he believed that a Cherokee woman could put him in touch with tradition and meaning, qualities seemingly absent from his world.[29]

Confronting Stereotypes

Fixation on romanticized Indianness exacerbated stereotyping of Native Americans. Because of her visibility, Mankiller, like LaDonna Harris, often confronted those stereotypes. Wilma criticized the image she believed many people had of Native Americans. In an interview, she said, "We need to get Oklahoma to not just see us as a people that dances and makes nice baskets." She indeed saw herself as combating a variety of stereotypes. In fact, when she left office in 1995 and taught as a visiting scholar at Dartmouth, she described her duties as in part to "interact with as many people as possible to dispel stereotypes about Native people." One newspaper described her as "helping erase the Western movie stereotype of the drunken Indian on a horse, chasing wagon trains across the prairie and pillaging white settlements." Still, the use of stereotypes took on varied forms. Just as some in the media regaled their readers in the 1960s with physical descriptions of Harris, Mankiller received similar treatment by at least one journalist more than twenty years later. A reporter for the *Chicago Tribune* painted a vivid, albeit stereotypical, picture of Mankiller for his readers. He described her as having "the features that identify her people" and said, "Her high cheekbones frame large soft eyes that look into a man as much as at him." In a single sentence, he captured the stereotype of Native Americans as having high cheekbones *and* possessing an intuitive spirituality. Each depicts a static and often highly romanticized and unrealistic image of Indians. The journalist even described her hands as "clasped in front of her, her thick fingers appear as though they would be at ease shucking corn or clutching a pen to authorize an act of office." It seems highly unlikely that a white male politician would receive similar treatment, and yet the writer no doubt viewed his description as flattering.[30]

Ignorance about Native Americans manifested itself in more ways than one. Saying he had been a fan of Mankiller for some time, a man wrote to ask her whether it was true that Indians were the best kind of people because they did not want to own land. He did not intend to be insulting in the letter but wrote to her because he had heard conflicting information about Native Americans and wanted a more accurate understanding of them. Some people's lack of understanding of Native Americans manifested itself in a misguided desire to help them. After praying about what she could do "to help make the Native American again a strong and proud person," one woman explained her concerns to Mankiller and said that she "struggled within" to "read, live, and see the alcohol deteriorating a once brave, strong, wise, and noble people." Mankiller responded brusquely to the letter saying, "It is not true that Native people have been almost destroyed by alcohol" and concluded that she could not think of anything the woman could do.[31]

The perpetuation of stereotypes by organizations meant to help Indians offered a further irritant to Chief Mankiller. The Native American Children's Fund incurred the wrath of the chief after circulating fliers that grossly distorted the situation of Native Americans. Drawing on stereotypes of an alcoholic father and poverty-stricken family living in a broken-down automobile with nothing to eat but an old biscuit or sweet potato, a newsletter circulated by this organization sought to raise money to help Indian children. Mankiller chastised the man responsible. Calling this newsletter "one of the worst examples of stereotyping" of Native Americans she had ever read, she added that the newsletter evoked "powerful images of pathetic, helpless people." Mankiller informed him that she planned to ask for an investigation into his organization and warned him that he would not get away with exploiting children for the purpose of fund-raising.[32]

The desire to help Native Americans took on a number of different forms among those who wrote letters to Wilma Mankiller. Ironically, often little or no difference existed between letters from Indians and non-Indians, as both struggled for meaning and a sense of belonging. A man with some Cherokee ancestry wrote, "My heart is all Cherokee" and stated that he felt "the need to help—make a difference—protect—educate . . . my spirit cries out for this." Another person, who identified himself as a "half-breed," described the difficulties he had experienced living in the "outside world." He offered to give the Cherokee Nation all of his possessions if he could live there. "I ask nothing in return; not even living quarters or food, *just to come home!*" This man from Tennessee clearly hoped that the Cherokee could restore something missing from his life. Letters such as these, as misguided as some were, illustrate that Mankiller's own struggles provided a symbol of hope to those who read about her.[33]

Along with letters containing misconceptions about Native Americans and the Cherokee tribe in particular, Mankiller also received numerous "white guilt" letters. These letters provide useful insight into the general public's perception of Native Americans in the final decades of the twentieth century. Further, such perceptions illustrate why a ready-made audience existed for the story of triumph over tragedy that characterized Mankiller's own life. As Lynn Howard explained, Mankiller's time in office "came in the middle of a growing awareness of Indianness" and indeed coincided "with the height of the Indian wannabe period." This upsurge in fascination with Native Americans translated into an even greater interest in Wilma Mankiller.[34]

A number of people wrote to the chief to express their concern for the treatment of Native Americans. Her autobiography prompted one person to write that prior to reading Mankiller's autobiography, she "had little first-hand knowledge about the terrible injustices committed by my people against your wonderful race." After watching a television show about the atrocities whites committed against Native Americans, a former naval officer wrote to Mankiller, "I must tell you of the shame I feel because of what my ancestors did to yours." Similarly, another letter to Mankiller also addressed the issue of guilt: "It's difficult to say why I feel the need to write other than to express the feeling of anger, outrage, and guilt at the terrible things done by my people to yours." Still another person, describing herself as an "American of European ancestry," voiced her shame over the "systemic [sic] genocide of Native Peoples in the United States" but added that Mankiller's autobiography gave her hope. Similar letters came to Mankiller from around the United States and from all over the world. A woman from Germany expressed her "rage and sorrow" after reading about Mankiller's life as well as the treatment of other Native Americans. She said she had always been interested in Indian culture and that she wanted to express her "solidarity" with Mankiller. This type of letter often came across Mankiller's desk as a part of the desire of some to right past wrongs. Both her national visibility and her autobiography contributed to the large amount of mail she received.[35]

Inspiration and National Acclaim

In fact, many people expressed profound awe at the story Mankiller told in her autobiography. The most common response came from those describing how she had inspired them to do things they had not been able to in the past. She appealed not only to Cherokees and other Native Americans but also to women and people with health problems. A person with a physical handicap thanked Mankiller after hearing her speak and said, "Your lecture gave me the courage to return to the University of Michigan and get my Master's." Several letters to Mankiller simply thanked her for sharing her story and for giving them hope that they too could overcome difficult obstacles in their lives. One writer who had been going through a stressful period in her life said how much better she felt after reading about Mankiller's difficult experiences. "I needed to hear how brave you've been and how far you've come," she said and added, "I find strength in you." Another person described Mankiller as "a woman to be reckoned with" and called her a role model for Indian leaders. She applauded Mankiller for standing up "without pretense, without glamor and selfish ambition" in her work for all Native Americans.[36]

As many of the issues and letters examined here demonstrate, Wilma Mankiller had become a national figure. As chief of the Cherokee Nation she made tremendous contributions to the betterment of the tribe in health care, education, membership, revenue, and certainly in visibility. After announcing that she would not seek reelection in 1995, Mankiller described her experience with the Cherokee Nation, saying, "I've been here seventeen years. I've grown up and become a grandmother. I've met with three presidents, lobbied Congress for everything from job corps to head start and been given more awards and honors than any one person deserves." Mankiller closed by explaining, "The thing I have appreciated most is when a group of male Cherokee elders still tells me they respect me and asks me to sit and talk with them." Many Cherokees expressed disappointment with Mankiller's decision not to seek reelection. After describing Mankiller as a "fabulous leader and friend," Ross

Swimmer said, "I am very disappointed, but I feel like she is just changing her role of leadership."[37]

Believing it necessary to serve on national committees and engage in national politics, Mankiller played a vital role in shaping the Cherokee tribe of Oklahoma and in shaping federal Indian policy. Her visibility at the national level brought forth worldwide interest in the Cherokee Nation and in her personally. Howard commented that, although she did not see Mankiller as seeking out media attention, she certainly learned how to use the forum it provided her. Howard maintained that, contrary to what some believed, nothing special went into the press releases about Mankiller put together by the Cherokee Nation communications department. The fascination many had for Mankiller took on a life of its own and lent itself to a ready-made audience eager for any news surrounding her role as chief. That fascination with Wilma Mankiller led many to praise her efforts as a national figure. Indeed, just a year before she left office, Oklahoma Lieutenant Governor Jack Mildren wrote to Mankiller, praising her work and stating that her "commitment to leadership of the Cherokee Nation and its great traditions continues to bring national and international attention to your state and its heritage." Mildren said that he "sincerely appreciated" her and the work she had done "for all Oklahomans."[38]

As chief, Mankiller no doubt made sizable contributions to her tribe. What is most striking, however, remains the fact that so many people identified with her and saw her as a source of inspiration. Those who wrote to Mankiller felt as if they knew her regardless of whether they had ever met her or seen her in a public appearance. Although her work often had state and national implications, she acted first and foremost in the interest of the tribe that elected her chief. She made it clear through a variety of actions, including the tax compact she made with the state of Oklahoma, that her first loyalty and devotion was to the Cherokee Nation. Even as she pursued the self-interest of the tribe that elected her, she became increasingly aware of the need to be involved nationally to best serve the Cherokee. Because of that national visibility, Mankiller took on a significance that extended far beyond the borders of the Cherokee Nation.

◄◄◄ COMPARISON ►►►

III

LaDonna Harris manning the phone during Fred Harris's bid for the U.S. Senate in 1964.

Courtesy of LaDonna Harris, Americans for Indian Opportunity.

above—Left to right, Laura Harris, Fred
Harris, LaDonna Harris, Kathryn Harris
(Tijerina), and Byron Harris in 1967.
Courtesy of LaDonna Harris, Americans for
Indian Opportunity.

right—LaDonna Harris in 1974.
Courtesy of the Lawton Constitution.

Original members of the National Council on Indian Opportunity with Vice President Hubert Humphrey in 1968. Left to right, Cato Valandra (Rosebud Sioux tribe), Wendell Chino (chairman of the Mescalero Apache Tribal Council), LaDonna Harris (Comanche), Humphrey, Roger Jourdain (chairman of the Red Lake Chippewa Tribal Council), Raymond Naki (chairman of the Navajo Tribal Council), and William Hensley (Eskimo member of the Alaska State Legislature). Record Group 220, National Council on Indian Opportunity Papers. *Courtesy of the National Archives and Records Administration, College Park, Maryland.*

left—LaDonna Harris marching in an Indian Day parade in Marquette, Michigan, in 1971. *Courtesy of LaDonna Harris, Americans for Indian Opportunity.*

below—LaDonna Harris during Fred Harris's campaign for president in 1976. *Courtesy of LaDonna Harris, Americans for Indian Opportunity.*

above—Chief Wilma Mankiller speaking
at Cherokee National Capitol Building
Rededication, Tahlequah, Oklahoma,
1991. *Courtesy of the Research Division of the
Oklahoma Historical Society.*

right—Wilma Mankiller in 1987.
Courtesy of the Oklahoman, *copyright 1987,
the Oklahoma Publishing Company.*

Wilma Mankiller autographing her book for Sue Wieldner of Edmond, Oklahoma, in 1993. *Courtesy of the* Oklahoman, *copyright 1993, the Oklahoma Publishing Company.*

Portrait of Wilma Mankiller in 1996. *Courtesy of the* Oklahoman, *copyright 1996, the Oklahoma Publishing Company.*

Politics and

Policy

5

"A leader," explained LaDonna Harris, "does not ask, 'what can I control?' but 'what am I responsible for?' Not 'what do I get' but 'what can I contribute?'" This "ancient way of being" described by Harris sums up Native criticism of the federal government's consistent mishandling of Indian affairs. The latter half of the twentieth century gave rise to two of the most significant changes in federal Indian policy in the history of the relationship between the United States government and Native American tribes. Both the termination policy carried out by presidents Harry S. Truman and Dwight D. Eisenhower in the 1940s and 1950s and the shift to a policy of self-determination in the 1970s during the presidency of Richard M. Nixon characterized a sharp federal policy shift and played a defining role in the lives and activism of both Harris and Wilma Mankiller. Termination policy sought to assimilate Native Americans into the mainstream by doing away with services provided to them by the federal government. Both the role of about 25,000 Native Americans in World War II and the push toward conformity that defined the decade of the 1950s contributed to the implementation of this policy. Here again, the federal government treated all Native Americans alike and failed to take into account their varied cultures and needs. Alison Bernstein and Donald Fixico have argued that termination ultimately proved highly detrimental to Native Americans. Although some supported the policy as a way to achieve autonomy, "for the most part Termination frightened Native Americans."[1]

Living Termination Policy

Harris, who grew up during the Great Depression and Collier's Indian New Deal, was a young adult before the enactment of termination policy began. She had already become active in civil rights issues and, along with her husband, became engaged in mainstream politics with his 1956 election to the Oklahoma State Senate. Harris took a dim view of termination and characterized it as one of the worst things that had ever happened to Native Americans. She saw termination policy as an attempt by the federal government to erase native cultures and traditions, which is why she also described assimilation as meaning "to no longer exist." In school, the message she received was blunt: "If you give up your Indianness and become educated like us—be like us—then you will be accepted in our society." Harris rejected the notion that it had to be an all-or-nothing approach—either the complete abandonment of Indian culture to join the mainstream or the retention of that culture to the exclusion of "fitting into" dominant society.[2]

In fact, most of Harris's work can best be understood as an effort to counter the effects of termination policy and convince Native Americans that they could retain their traditional beliefs and values while simultaneously participating in the mainstream society and economy. She also sought to help Native American tribes that were terminated, such as the Menominee, regain federal recognition. In a letter lending AIO's support to the Ramapuogh Mountain Indian tribe's restoration efforts, Harris said she hoped "justice will prevail" and that termination would cease. This would, Harris said, finally end "one of the ugliest and most hurtful chapters in the history of Federal/Indian relations."[3]

Mankiller, fifteen years Harris's junior, felt the direct impact of termination in her early life. She too depicted termination as a very dark period in federal Indian policy. Her condemnation of it comes, in part, from her personal experience as she herself grew up as a product of this policy. It had, after all, been the federal Indian relocation program that grew out of termination policy that had uprooted her family from their home in eastern Oklahoma and moved them to the big city of San Francisco. Mankiller described termination and the relocation program as "another direct assault on Native American rights and tribal identities." Here, Mankiller and Harris certainly agreed about the detrimental aspects of termination policy, each viewing it as an attempt at cultural genocide. Whereas some policy makers in the 1950s believed termination provided the best way to aid Native Americans in participating in the mainstream, it came at a heavy price. Many in Mankiller's generation suffered from a loss of cultural knowledge but would later challenge termination policy and reassert pride as a part of the red power movement.[4]

Push for Self-Determination

This emphasis on termination and its erosion of native cultures and traditions is most apparent in the sharp critique of federal Indian policy that emerged in the 1960s. At the heart of this critique lay the desire of Native Americans to reassert tribal sovereignty and celebrate cultural pride. This push for self-determination and greater sovereignty emerged in conjunction with a number of other social changes. The struggle of minority groups for civil rights, the Community Action Programs (CAPs) of Lyndon B. Johnson, the increased public awareness of government mismanagement of Indian affairs, Richard Nixon's support of greater autonomy for Native Americans, and the articulate leadership of young Indian radicals, as well as more mainstream figures such as Harris, all played a role in ushering in the era of self-determination. Thus, a variety of factors converged to create a climate conducive to a shift in federal Indian policy. The life work of Harris and Mankiller, the images they projected at a given time, and the manifestations of Indianness in their politics demonstrate the larger shift in policy that transpired.[5]

While termination policy began to ebb in the late 1960s, Congress waited until 1988 to formally repeal House Concurrent Resolution 108, otherwise known as termination. Hawaii Democrat Daniel K. Inouye, chairman of the Senate Select Committee on Indian Affairs, stated that alterations to the trust relationship between Native American tribes and the federal government "must never again be considered without the consent of the tribes involved." He called termination "both morally and legally indefensible," which ironically bore a striking similarity to Richard Nixon's condemnation of it eighteen years earlier, when he characterized termination as "morally and legally unacceptable." It was no doubt gratifying to leaders such as Harris to see the formal repeal of termination policy; however, the fact that President Nixon and Senator Inouye uttered basically the same criticism of termination two decades apart as a rallying cry for change reveals the limited amount of progress that actually took place. It is small wonder that Harris voiced frustration at having to reeducate policy makers at every level with each new election.[6]

Harris had come to national attention with the termination period still underway. The founding of Oklahomans for Indian Opportunity (OIO) in 1965 in the midst of President Johnson's CAPs initiative marked both the beginnings of a greater emphasis on self-determination and a carryover of termination-type language in which OIO articulated its goal as helping Indians participate more fully in the social, economic, and political mainstream of Oklahoma. Herein lies the fundamental transformation of federal Indian policy and the activism that went along with it. Johnson's CAPs, which he intended as a "hand up, not a hand out," brought significant ramifications for Native Americans and indeed for those who acted as advocates for them.

Community Development and Sovereignty

As Harris and Mankiller found themselves affected in one way or another by the shift in federal Indian policy, one of the most significant elements to emerge in a study of the two women lies in the work each did in the area of community development, which provided a vital link in the transformation of the larger policy toward Indians. The work of Harris and OIO predated that of Mankiller and certainly provided a useful model for others to follow. Harris became involved in community development through the Johnson administration's Great Society and community action initiatives. She became convinced that if Native Americans were ever to break out of the cycle of poverty, they must gain autonomy over the programs and agencies designed to help them. Her criticism of the Bureau of Indian Affairs (BIA) helps explain why she first saw community development as essential. She described the BIA as a "controlling institution that keeps people from doing what they could do." Moreover, nonreservation Native Americans got even less assistance from the BIA than did others. Harris also criticized what she termed the "BIA old Catch-22 runaround," which she outlined as follows: "I don't have enough information to make a decision, and I won't tell you what information I need." She called this attitude of the BIA "exasperating but also humiliating." In light of the slow and ineffective movement of the BIA on any number of issues, Harris felt that this lent even greater urgency to the need for a reassertion of tribal sovereignty. If Native Americans and their tribal leaders could exercise greater control over their own programs and within their own communities, they would gain optimal possibilities for economic and cultural self-sufficiency. Harris's work with community development is what brought her to the national political spotlight. In fact, the first time she testified before Congress she addressed the impact of the Office of Economic Opportunity, which funded OIO and other such efforts in Oklahoma.[7]

Nearly two decades after Harris founded OIO and became involved in community development, Mankiller's work with community development also served as a catalyst for her own involvement in politics with the Cherokee Nation. Whereas OIO had worked on a number of projects with the Cherokee Nation, there appears to be no direct link between the organization founded by Harris and the community development project in the Bell community that brought Mankiller to the attention of Chief Ross Swimmer in the early 1980s. Regardless, the work Mankiller did in Bell and other communities secured her election to deputy chief in 1983 and chief in 1987. She appealed to Swimmer because he

wanted someone who would spend time in the Cherokee communities, and she also developed a strong support base from those
rural Cherokees she had helped.[8]

In short, community development provided a venue in which
both Harris and Mankiller could stand out and affect change at a
very rudimentary level. They continued to emphasize the centrality of community development to economic stability for Native
Americans. The main difference between Harris and Mankiller regarding community development lay in the role each played. As
president first of OIO, then AIO, Harris put together literally thousands of proposals and held workshops for tribes across the
United States to provide leaders with the skills they needed and
with information on how to access federal money for community
development projects. Mankiller, on the other hand, worked in a
more hands-on fashion, first as director of community development for the Cherokee Nation and then as deputy chief and principal chief. Still, both women viewed self-help as essential to any
long-term success in improving the lives of Native Americans.
Economic self-sufficiency clearly remains a necessary ingredient
in ensuring any meaningful degree of tribal sovereignty.

Two Paths to Self-Governance

Their insistence on greater self-governance for Native American
tribes reinforced the emphasis each placed on community development. The shift of federal Indian policy to self-determination
made possible a resurgence in tribal self-governance. Harris, in
particular, played a prominent role at the national level in promoting tribal self-governance. One of the greatest obstacles facing tribes in this quest has been a lack of information and understanding of federal Indian law. Once the federal government
agreed that Native American tribes should have greater control
over tribal affairs and programs, the next step did not automatically become clear. Here, Harris proved a vital asset to numerous
tribes. She wrote countless letters to government officials on behalf of tribes and worked closely with tribal leaders in the pursuit of economic independence and self-governance. Reuben
Snake Jr., tribal chairman of the Winnebago Tribe of Nebraska,

wrote to Harris, "Our tribe owes much of our long range planning and development efforts to your wisdom and to AIO for its continued, invaluable help in many areas." Harris also testified for tribes as an expert on various issues. The tribal chairman of the Ute Mountain Tribal Council, Ernest House Sr., expressed his "sincere appreciation" for LaDonna's testimony in support of his tribe's water rights settlement legislation and for her "past and continued support."[9]

AIO spearheaded self-governance workshops and sent letters to tribal leaders across the United States inviting them to attend. In some cases AIO provided funding for tribal representatives to attend such workshops. The workshops were run by experts who understood the highly complex and ever-changing body of federal Indian law, as well as by grant writers and government officials from Indian agencies. Although self-governance became a key goal for many tribes, by no means did all tribal leaders view it in the same way or as being beneficial to the tribes. Harris remained a staunch proponent of self-governance, but, at the same time, she and AIO helped bring to light some of the problems that emerged from the shift toward greater self-governance and sovereignty. After conducting a two-year project with three tribes, Harris revealed their "most frightening conclusion," which dealt with the heavy economic burden of tribes taking over the administration of various federal programs. She described possible bankruptcy for tribes "in the name of self-determination." Harris not only played a role in facilitating self-governance but also followed through by identifying problems resulting from the actual implementation of self-determination policy.[10]

In a Red Paper, AIO addressed the language used by Ronald Reagan regarding self-determination in his 1980 presidential campaign. In "New Federalism: The Role of the Indian Community," AIO incorporated several quotations from Reagan about his support for more local control and for Indian sovereignty. In so doing, Harris and her staff members conveyed to their readers the issues at stake. Although President Reagan stated that he supported self-determination, AIO pointed out the inconsistencies between his rhetoric and his actions, as he also advocated a cut in the funding of Indian programs.[11]

AIO provided a vital service to many Native American tribes and organizations by holding information symposiums and workshops related to self-determination and governance. In an effort to help tribal leaders cultivate skills useful to governing their communities and in working with the federal government, AIO often sent material to leaders and organizations across the United States about their workshops. Here again, Harris and AIO found a vital role to play. Harris's position and reputation enabled her to see firsthand where Indian leadership lacked skills and information and to work with policy makers in the Washington power structure.

One of the most successful symposiums put together by Harris grew out of the Governance Project. The "To Govern and to be Governed: American Indian Tribal Governments at the Crossroads" symposium took place in Washington, D.C., and included leaders from seven different tribes, scholars, and various representatives from all levels of government. Acting as a broker between federal and state governments and Native American leaders, AIO helped create a comprehensive dialogue on tribal governance. After the symposium, AIO published a fifty-eight-page booklet about the issues discussed and the possible solutions to problems in tribal governance.[12]

Wilma Mankiller played a different role in the process of reasserting self-governance. As chief of the Cherokee Nation, her first obligation went to her constituents. She assumed a vital role in the reassertion of self-governance for the Cherokee. Mankiller not only entered into the self-governance compact with the state of Oklahoma; she also negotiated agreements with the state of Oklahoma, such as the cigarette tax compact, on a government-to-government basis as an expression of self-determination. The criticism Mankiller encountered from some of the other tribal leaders in Oklahoma over the Cherokee Nation entering into contracts with the state reveals the contentious and contradictory nature of the self-governance issue. Not all tribes viewed the meaning of self-governance the same.[13]

In short, although Harris and Mankiller played different roles in the return to self-governance, both supported the policy despite the problems they encountered with it. Similarly, both viewed self-governance as critical to the survival of Native Americans in the twenty-first century. Shortly before Mankiller left office in 1995, she testified before the House Interior Appropriations Subcommittee, directly addressing the need for greater self-governance and self-determination among Native Americans. She outlined the components necessary for improving the conditions confronted by Native communities, citing the need to "advance self-determination through tribal self-government, continue to empower adults with real economic opportunities and job training," and "ensure that children are given every chance to succeed through proper schooling and preventative health care."[14]

Lobbying Policy Makers

Harris and Mankiller spent considerable efforts lobbying Congress and others in powerful positions. While Harris initially drew on her husband's role and connections to make her voice heard, it was ultimately her natural ability to form friendships—such as the one with White House intern Bobbie Green—that opened even more possibilities. In fact, Laura Harris, who now serves as the executive director of AIO, credits her mother's friendship with Green and others in influential positions for getting things accomplished that would otherwise get lost in the bureaucratic shuffle. Similarly, Barbara Blum, who served as President Jimmy Carter's deputy administrator of the Environmental Protection Agency (EPA), credits her friendship with Harris for awakening her to the grave environmental hazards on Indian reservations, which in turn led the Carter administration to award AIO a grant to study those problems. Mankiller, on the other hand, skillfully capitalized on the media interest in her election and the size and notoriety of the Cherokee to use as leverage with both state and national policy makers. Each woman made remarkable efforts in lobbying Congress, and, at times, each sought the opinions of members of Congress on issues relating to Native Americans.[15]

Hawaii Senator Inouye from the Select Committee on Indian Affairs asked Harris for her input on a piece of legislation he introduced called the Indian Development Finance Act, or S. 721. He wanted her to review the bill and offer her expert opinion on the ramifications of it if passed. The senator also asked Harris to pass along information to tribes or individuals who might be interested. With these requests, Harris's reputation for acting as a liaison between the Indian community and policy makers in Washington, D.C., was clearly demonstrated. In fact, Harris described AIO's role as bringing people and information together. Harris also actively opposed H.R. 4162, which would have amended the Alaska Claims Settlement Act. In her efforts to protect the rights of Indian people from encroachment by lawmakers, Harris took up a number of such issues. She wrote to New Mexico Democratic Senator Jeff Bingaman to voice her objection to a recommendation under consideration by the Department of Justice that would potentially privilege state law over tribal laws in the operation of tribal bingo facilities. She explained the importance of bingo to numerous tribal economies and concluded by stating that "it is not the job of the Department of Justice to make Indian policy and law." Instead, she added, "that is the job of the President, the Bureau and the Congress in careful consultation with the tribes." Such correspondence between Harris and lawmakers illustrates the breadth of Indian policy issues addressed by AIO. In fact, Assistant Secretary of the Interior Kevin Grover described AIO as being "at the forefront of every major national native initiative" and said that AIO had also "provided better cross cultural understanding."[16]

Similarly, Mankiller engaged in numerous letter-writing campaigns to policy makers and testified before Congress. She wrote to Oklahoma Senator Don Nickles and others asking for their support for the National Park Services proposed funding of the Trail of Tears National Historic Trail. She worked closely with Oklahoma Senator David Boren on the issue of jurisdiction over the Arkansas River Bed, something the Cherokee Nation had been battling for several years prior to her coming into office. Mankiller thanked Boren for his work on behalf of the tribe, "Your continual support of our effort to equitably resolve this issue is important to the Cherokee Nation." Mankiller exchanged countless letters with Boren and others in both houses of Congress regarding the environment and other issues facing Native Americans.[17]

In addition to the relationships between Harris and Mankiller and policy makers on Capital Hill, each had considerable dealings with U.S. presidents. Harris has worked with both Democratic and

Republican presidents on issues facing Native Americans and has remarked that each time a new president gets elected the education process starts all over again. She has received letters thanking her for her service on behalf of Native Americans from a number of administrations, including Spiro Agnew, Gerald Ford, and Jimmy Carter. Harris also enlisted the help of former First Lady Rosalyn Carter in her quest to see passage of the Indian Child Welfare Bill, which sought to keep Indian children in Indian homes. In her interaction with such powerful people, Harris credits her experience as a congressional wife for helping her feel more at ease. According to one interviewer, "Being married to a United States Senator helped Harris see government as 'just another group of people trying to do a job.'" Although this holds true to a certain extent, her longtime friend and Democratic activist, Barbara Blum, credited Harris's "political sophistication" and her ability to forge personal relationships for allowing her to "more clearly see the issues than anyone else in the [Indian] movement."[18]

Mankiller interacted with top-level policy makers as well, and she too left her mark on the Washington political structure. Mankiller and Peterson Zah, who served as president of the Navajo Nation, were selected by other tribal leaders to co-chair meetings with tribal officials and members of government. In this capacity Mankiller eventually met with presidents Ronald Reagan, George H. W. Bush, and Bill Clinton. While she spoke with President Reagan to discuss his administration's approach to addressing problems facing Native Americans, she found little support from Reagan or the subsequent Bush administration. She described President Reagan as "not good on Indian issues," adding, "He did not have the tiniest interest" in them. When Bill Clinton ran for president in 1992, Mankiller actively supported him despite having once told former Oklahoma Governor David Walters, "It is my policy to not endorse any candidate for public office." She added, "We at the Cherokee Nation cannot become involved in partisan politics to that extent." Mankiller's support for the Clinton/Gore ticket earned her criticism from at least one of her constituents. In a letter to the editor of a local paper, George Wickliffe, a frequent critic of Mankiller, questioned her endorsement of Clinton in the

1992 presidential election and accused her of believing herself superior to other Cherokees and of telling them how to vote. Regardless
of Wickliffe's criticisms, Mankiller demonstrated strong show of support for Clinton and even participated in his 1992 economic conference in Little Rock. She offered her assistance to Clinton and expressed pleasure at hearing of his Cherokee ancestry. She wrote to
Clinton, "It makes me so proud that someone with Cherokee ancestry is now President of the United States." In response, Clinton
thanked her for the enthusiasm she had shown at his economic
conference and added a handwritten message to Mankiller, saying,
"You were great."[19]

Teaming Up

In light of the prominence of Harris and Mankiller and their Oklahoma connection, it is hardly a surprise that they have worked together from time to time on issues of mutual interest. They actually
met while Mankiller still lived in San Francisco, but their collaboration on behalf of Native Americans did not begin until Mankiller
became involved with the Cherokee Nation. They proved useful al-
lies in their joint support of issues affecting Native Americans, and
they also gave each other advice from time to time.[20]

In 1991 Harris wrote Mankiller to tell her about funding from
the W. K. Kellogg Foundation for programs dealing with community health and prevention. Harris described the initiative as "designed to promote partnerships between public health education
and practices." Another project that brought Harris and Mankiller
together came in 1994 when Harris asked the Cherokee Nation to
act as a consortium member in a proposal to the National Telecommunications and Information Administration. Mankiller agreed to
support the proposal, which would provide better internet access to
tribes. Harris also solicited Mankiller's support for an AIO repatria-
tion program that would "provide the opportunity for academics to
develop a large body of data of specific Native American groups"
and enable the information to be conveyed to the general public as
well as to the individual cultures. Mankiller responded that she believed this could be "a mutually beneficial collaboration between
Native Americans and the academic and museum communities."

Mankiller also became one of the early board members of the AIO Ambassador's Program, which Harris initiated in 1993 as a way to mentor young Native Americans in preparation to serve their communities. Harris and Mankiller endorsed Jerry F. Muskrat for nomination to the Tenth Circuit Court of Appeals in 1992. The prominence of both women emerges in the wording of the letter of support for Muskrat. Harris opened the letter of support stating that she wrote "on behalf of Wilma Mankiller, myself and others in the American Indian community." Indeed, both Harris and Mankiller had made national reputations for themselves and carried a lot of weight in political circles.[21]

Protecting the Environment

Aside from their other concerns, both Harris and Mankiller exerted considerable efforts on environmental issues. In the early 1980s, AIO began a two-year study entitled "To Assess Environmental Health Impacts of Development on Indian Communities and the Roles of Government Agencies Charged with the Responsibilities for Various Aspects of Environmental Protection and Individual Safety." Harris explained that AIO had found that "tribal governments are making daily decisions with far-reaching effects with very little information regarding the impacts of those decisions on the environment and health of the people." She said that AIO wanted to "increase the awareness of Indian decision makers of the environmental health impacts" related to development. To accomplish this, AIO, with funding from six federal agencies, sponsored a series of regional seminars to educate leaders on environmental problems and possible solutions. A seminar in San Diego had approximately forty-one tribes in attendance.[22]

AIO continued its work on environmental issues and responded to a request from the EPA to comment on a proposal regarding the administration of environmental programs on Indian lands. Harris did so by reminding William Ruckelshaus of the EPA that "Indian tribes are not subject to state jurisdiction unless *specifically* authorized by Congress." She admonished that "any attempt by the EPA to place Indian tribes under state jurisdiction would be strenuously opposed" and would detract from the larger goal of protecting the environment. Harris cautioned that the problem should "not try to be solved in haste with a 'broad brush stroke.'" A facilitator of education and environmental protection, AIO drew praise from many, including Wilma Mankiller. While still serving as deputy chief, Mankiller wrote to Harris to offer her advice on AIO's annual report. "I find your past work in tribal resources, environmental matters, and tribal governance both important and needed." She went on to say she thought AIO "can and should be the final word on Indian related economic development and information within its areas of expertise." Mankiller later encouraged AIO to become "even more involved in environmental actions."[23]

That AIO and Harris spent considerable effort to protect the environment is not surprising. Going back at least to the early 1970s, Harris had voiced strong concern over the future of the environment. Believing that Native Americans have something to teach other Americans when it comes to the environment, Harris explained that "American Indians' whole social and religious relationship to the earth and to the reproduction of the earth is totally ecology." Mankiller echoed a similar sentiment nearly twenty years later when she participated in the International People of Color Environmental Leadership Summit.[24]

At that conference Mankiller described the way in which whites and Native Americans have historically differed in their views of the environment. She explained, "To indigenous people, the environment and land are all connected," and they "understand clearly that everything in nature has its place and works to sustain" their lives. According to Mankiller, this put Native Americans into immediate conflict with European settlers. She concluded that the conflict continued between indigenous concepts of the interconnectedness of nature and humanity and the mainstream desire for progress. She said she could not understand why 80 percent of people said they believed something should be done about the environment yet politicians remained unwilling to support meaningful reform. Mankiller concluded her presentation by saying she no longer believed that people could wait for someone, a national leader or a prophet, to save the day. "There's only us," she admitted, and added that they must take charge to "preserve an environment that will be good for our children and our children's children." Shortly after attending the conference, Mankiller testified before Congress at a joint hearing of the Subcommittee on Health and the Environment and the Committee on Energy and Commerce. The following year Mankiller served on the Clinton/Gore National Environmental Committee. She urged other tribal leaders to support them in the 1992 presidential election and stated that the Clinton/Gore environmental policies reflected their "ancestor's teachings."[25]

Mankiller also devoted a good deal of attention to the Cherokee Nation policies regarding the environment. Along with the tribal council, she supported the efforts of Native Americans for a Clean Environment when they tried to stop a food irradiation facility from being built in Oklahoma. When the Cherokee Nation drew criticism for operating a "dump site," the executive director of tribal operations, Tommy Thompson, explained that the landfill, run by the tribe since Ross Swimmer established it in 1978, functioned as simply a "repository for domestic, household waste" and not toxic waste of any kind. He maintained that the Cherokee Nation had the "strongest environmental record of any tribe in the State of Oklahoma due to the leadership of the Council and the Chief." Mankiller did not hesitate to criticize environmental organizations, however, if she felt they were not doing enough. In 1993, when the tribal council passed a resolution for the Cherokee Nation to become a member of the National Tribal Environmental Council, Mankiller vetoed it. Citing internal problems within the organization as explanation for her decision, Chief Mankiller said that it had not yet become clear the extent to which the National Tribal Environmental Council would "prevent environmental destruction of Indian lands." Until the issues could be resolved, Mankiller made it clear she did not want to join.[26]

Health Care, Housing, and Discrimination

The concern of Harris and Mankiller over the environment paralleled their advocacy of Indian health issues. In a letter to Idaho Republican Senator James A. McClure, Harris blasted a proposed recommendation of the Appropriations Committee to reduce significantly the funding of urban Indian health care programs. Harris said, "Indian people do not stop being Indian simply because they live in the city." She implored McClure not to assume that those living in cities were "better off financially, educationally, or physically than their reservation counterparts," adding, "Nor is there less of a responsibility on the part of the government to assist them." Harris concluded her plea by describing the proposal to cut funding as "irresponsible" and said it would result in "even deeper human misery." Her concerns revealed the difficulties often faced by nonreservation Indians living in urban areas, an issue that Harris had fought to bring to the attention of policy makers since the 1960s. Part of Harris's frustration came from the fact that she had to repeat points to policy makers, often many times. Regardless of the verbal support given to improving conditions for Indian people, the actions of lawmakers often contradicted their rhetoric.

Mankiller had her own concerns about health care for Native Americans. As chief she opened new health-care clinics for the Cherokee and shared her experience with Indian health-care services with policy makers at the national level. Arizona Republican Senator John McCain requested that Mankiller testify before the Committee on Indian Affairs in an oversight hearing on Indian Health Service implementation of the self-governance demonstration project. Once again, Mankiller's experience with community development and health care as chief of the Cherokee Nation provided her expert credentials to testify before Congress.[27]

Senators McCain and Inouye asked Mankiller to serve as a member of the National Commission on American Indian, Alaska Native, and Native Hawaiian Housing. They praised her past work and commended Mankiller on the "intelligence and judgment" she brought to "every task" she undertook. McCain and Inouye expressed confidence that her contribution to the commission would ensure its success.[28]

Harris's and Mankiller's own experiences helped them empathize with others suffering discrimination. They strongly advocated on behalf of African Americans and all minorities who were subjected to prejudice. Harris, of course, had helped facilitate the integration of Lawton and has been a lifelong supporter of equal rights. One African American friend of Fred and LaDonna Harris from Lawton recalled staying with them in their home in Washington, D.C., on numerous occasions. John Henry Nelson, also a pioneering member of the Lawton integration effort, said that some of his other African American friends could not believe that Fred and LaDonna had invited him to stay with them in their home in the 1960s. From her desegregation work in Lawton to the nature of her individual friendships, Harris unequivocally condemned racial discrimination. She dismissed the melting pot theory as a myth because "if you are of a dark-skinned people, you do not melt into the society." Harris added that she believed American Indians "could help the blacks and Chicanos and others in understanding that being different is something beautiful." Because the civil rights movement created a climate conducive to Native American efforts to challenge their treatment by the federal government, it also led to the unfortunate tendency by some to see Native Americans as simply minorities. Harris pointed this out: "We are not just another minority. We are political governmental entities." She added that the Supreme Court "continues to uphold the fact that we are sovereign governments and that we have to be dealt with."[29]

In her support of civil rights, Harris not only recognized the commonalities among all groups who suffered discrimination; she also used the language of civil rights to point out the unique status of Native Americans. In effect, she connected the struggle of Native Americans for self-determination with the larger fight against all forms of oppression. In 1987 at the Constitutional, Roots, Rights, and Responsibilities International Smithsonian Symposium, Harris presented a paper entitled "Constitutional and Tribal Governance" in which she spoke of the need to preserve Native American heritage. She explained that her life's work had been "to work with Indian tribes in attaining their political, social, educational, and economic aspirations" and discussed the contributions of Native Americans to "United States and global society as a whole." Harris insisted that much of her work emerged from a "lifelong and deepening understanding of Native American traditions." She explained that all of what she did was a manifestation of her culture's ancient traditions, which taught her that "internationally as well as domestically, the voice of the smallest, weakest, and most vulnerable must be heard, that *all* people may live." Implicit in the concept of cultural restoration is the recognition of the importance of Native American heritage to an understanding of the present. By situating both her work and the contributions of Native American culture as a whole within a larger global framework, Harris articulated the significance of cultural preservation as a necessary component of civil rights. In short, cultural restoration offered a vital link to the future and offered Indians a way to participate in the mainstream while maintaining and celebrating their heritage.[30]

Indianness and Social Justice

Harris's ability to relate the suffering of others to her own experience with discrimination and intolerance is reflected in the varied causes both she and AIO have embraced. Whereas most of AIO's focus centered on Native Americans, the organization also reflects the wider concerns of its founder in that it has supported women's organizations, antiwar efforts, and the rights of indigenous people around the world. For example, in 1982 AIO passed a resolution condemning Israel's invasion of Lebanon. The resolution not only called on the United States to "provide the maximum in humanitarian assistance" to the victims in Lebanon, but also stated that "no justification exists for the bombing and shelling of areas in which civilians live" regardless of the presence of Palestinian guerrillas. AIO also joined Citizens Against Nuclear War (CAN). In a letter to the executive director of CAN, Harris commended the organization for its ability "to include the concerns of people of color and women's groups in the nuclear arms debate."[31]

Harris's personal concern over the issue of nuclear arms led to her involvement in other organizations, such as Global Tomorrow Coalition and Women for Meaningful Summits. She visited the Soviet Union as a part of her work toward a reduction of nuclear armaments and the creation of a better dialogue and understanding between the Soviet and American people. In a speech in which she recounted her trip, she opened by saying that, on embarking on her journey to the Soviet Union, she had taken with her "all of the knowledge and prejudice that a Comanche girl from Cotton County, Oklahoma would have." True to her style, Harris drew from her own experience to express commonality with the Soviet people. She made an insightful comparison between the bureaucracy that governed so many aspects of Soviet people's lives and the bureaucracy under which Native Americans live. She concluded by saying that her trip to the Soviet Union had humbled her. Her compassion for others and her ability to find some way to connect her experiences with theirs is what has made her such an effective humanitarian.[32]

Yet another indication of commitment by AIO and Harris to a broad range of humanitarian and civil rights concerns can be seen in a statement issued by AIO about the plight of indigenous people in Guatemala. It expressed concern over the involvement of the United States and asked that the United States government not resume military aid to the Guatemalan government. Citing both physical and cultural genocide against the Indian population in Guatemala, AIO condemned their treatment and pointed out that Guatemalan Indians, who accounted for 60 percent of the population, received no government representation. The position of AIO on the situation in Guatemala, as well as its stance on Israel's invasion of Lebanon, goes to the heart of Harris's political philosophy of helping all those who faced discrimination and were in need.[33]

Wilma Mankiller also has a strong record in her support of civil rights, which, in part, stemmed from her own negative experiences with racism. In fact, Mankiller recalled that the Black Panther Party was the first activist group she could really identify with because of their self-help approach and because they addressed problems that resonated with her own experiences. She said she had "never before seen any minority stand up to police, judges, and other white people." Mankiller's commitment to fighting against racism only deepened over time as her national stature afforded her greater opportunities for involvement. She served on the board of the South Africa Free Elections Fund, which provided financial support for voter education projects. According to one newspaper article, after her reelection in 1991, Mankiller "emerged as one of the most effective global leaders for human liberation and justice." Earlier that same year, Mankiller had also taken part in a civil rights march to celebrate Martin Luther King Jr.'s birthday. One woman wrote Mankiller a letter criticizing her for participating in the march with Patricia Ireland, Ted Kennedy, and Barney Frank: "Unfortunately, I'm afraid you have let all native Oklahomans down by walking hand in hand with this motley crew." Mankiller responded by telling the woman that "being liberal or conservative has nothing to do with being concerned about the growing racial intolerance in this country." She added that she indeed wanted "a world in which Dr. King's dream of equality for all people is finally realized."[34]

Mankiller received recognition for her civil rights efforts in 1992 when the Commission on Racial Justice presented her with an award. In response, Mankiller said she believed Native Americans and African Americans had a great deal in common because of the discrimination inflicted upon them. She pointed out that at different points in history each group had been "the subject of debates as to whether we were human or whether we had souls." Mankiller said, "We know about struggle and loss" but added, "We will continue on" until "racial hatred will no longer be tolerated anywhere in the world."[35] Mankiller's support for equality for all people brought her accolades from Indians and non-Indians alike and helps explain why she has been called a humanitarian leader rather than simply a Native American leader. Like Harris, Mankiller's work and her rhetoric reflected a broad commitment to social justice.

LaDonna Harris and Wilma Mankiller clearly brought different sensibilities to their work, but the way in which each harnessed her experiences into a larger advocacy for oppressed people engenders a striking commonality, one that is steeped in their conception of Indianness. The emphasis on the group, as opposed to the individual, and the belief in the interconnectedness of all things infused their perceptions of their work. Both women firmly situated their life experiences and work—including their efforts to improve federal Indian policy—within the context of their tribal heritage and traditions. They believed that their roles in national politics were rooted in tradition, which played a central role in defining the identity and image of each woman.

The Intersection of Feminism and Indianness

In September 1993 Cherokee Chief Wilma Mankiller cited "One Native prophecy," which foretold that "this is the 'time of the women,' a time when women's leadership skills are needed." Noting the differences in male and female approaches, she added, "Women, by and large, bring to leadership a greater sense of collaboration, an ability to view social, political and personal concerns in a uniquely interconnected, female way." Mankiller's statement reveals one component of the gendered imagery that came to so clearly define her public persona—just as it did that of LaDonna Harris.[1]

Though quite remarkable in their own right as Native American leaders, Harris and Mankiller operated within a particular political and social climate as women. The public persona of each was necessarily and inextricably tied to gendered imagery—Harris because she acted in an unofficial capacity as a congressional wife and as an extension of her husband's political persona and Mankiller because of the mystique surrounding her status as a female chief. In other words, Harris and Mankiller were not national leaders who happened to be women. They became national political sensations because of the way they negotiated contradictory gender constructs that defined women's roles in the U.S. political arena in the post–World War II era. Like white liberal feminists who at times emphasized their distinct power as "women" as a legitimizing force for their involvement in electoral politics, these "beloved women" challenged gender constructs in the name of Native American tradition. That understanding is paramount in situating them within the historical and political context to which they belong.

Use of Gender Imagery

Harris's entry into the political arena came through, and because of, her gender. As the wife of a politician, she played a particular type of role, one that she expanded and ultimately challenged through her own direct involvement in politics as an advocate for Native Americans. Still, her first involvement in politics hinged on her being a wife. She used a very traditional role to afford her own entry into the world of politics and activism; she would not have known and interacted with people such as Robert Kennedy, Hubert Humphrey, and Stewart Udall if she were not the wife of a U.S. senator. She drew on the private, social side of being a senator's wife to enter into political discourse with policy makers. It is important to note that Harris did not simply sit down one day and decide to play up a particular image to get what she wanted. The process came about in a far slower and less deliberate fashion. She realized in the early 1960s that she wanted to make people aware of the problems facing Native Americans. She also knew what people expected of her and which roles were available to her at that particular time. She and Fred made a striking political duo, and the manifestations of that public relationship afforded her a means by which her voice would be heard. That said, Harris possessed a remarkable sense of self-awareness in constructing an image to accomplish her goals. As she pointed out, she "knew that being a senator's wife had some power behind it" and used that power accordingly.[2]

Wilma Mankiller also employed gendered imagery in her political career with the Cherokee Nation. Pinpointing the exact nature of Mankiller's popularity and rise to national prominence poses certain difficulties, but she certainly made successful use of media interest in her as a female chief. A woman named Mankiller becoming chief of the second-largest and best-known tribe in the country during a period of renewed interest in Indian culture contained all the ingredients of a good human interest story. The real heart of her story, however, lies in how she used this interest to create a forum in which she could express her views on Native American rights, women's rights, and other issues. The use of gendered imagery by Mankiller is perhaps two-fold. First, she made her gender an issue by virtue of the sheer number of times she said "gender is not an issue" while simultaneously expressing surprise at gender-based opposition to her. Second, Mankiller used Cherokee history to legitimize her leadership within the tribe, when her election actually represented a departure from tradition.

Molding Tradition

In fact, the argument that Mankiller's election represented an extension of traditional roles of women in her tribe is really no different than the arguments made by nineteenth-century white female reformers to legitimize their involvement in the public realm. They, too, characterized their entrance into the public world of social reform as an extension of tradition. Advocating for temperance, regulation of child labor, and prostitution reform lent legitimacy to female activism. Indeed, they could and did justify their involvement in reform as a logical extension of the traditional role of women as moral guardians of the family. In the cases of both Mankiller and those nineteenth-century female reformers, traditional concepts of femininity were molded to legitimize a new behavior.[3]

Although considerable scholarship exists on female reform in the nineteenth century, only recently has scholarship on Native American gender roles begun to emerge. A major goal of this scholarship has been to debunk myths surrounding the role of

Native American women throughout history. The gist of this attempt to instill agency in Indian women and transcend the image of them as either "squaws" or "Indian princesses" has resulted in useful literature. One author has argued that, for the Cherokees to acculturate, "it was necessary to undermine the role of women in Cherokee society." She explained, "this bias against women was something the white man brought to Cherokee culture." Similarly, there have been a number of works that stress the power of women within their tribes and the significant role they played throughout history. It is interesting that many of these works argue that power should not necessarily be equated with participation in politics but rather should be evaluated as a part of the larger esteem a given society, or tribe, afforded women. According to this theory, issues such as marriage rights, religious influence, and community involvement should also be considered.[4]

It is striking that arguments emphasizing the agency of women and expressions of female power within traditional gender boundaries (whatever those may be) have long been made by women's historians and actually demonstrate more commonality than difference among Indian women and their European counterparts who settled in North America. In most cultures women have, in one way or another, found ways to express power in unofficial but legitimate terms. This should hardly serve to downplay the existence of sex-based oppression and discrimination. It should, however, be noted that more similarities exist, in this respect, between Native American women and their white counterparts in terms of private or familial-based expressions of power than is often recognized. For instance, Clara Sue Kidwell points out "the power of women in matrilineal societies included that of selecting men for positions of leadership." Although that is not true in the case of the European women who came to North America, it is the case that, just as white men dominated public life, Indian men "played the public roles in Native American societies."[5]

Mankiller stated on numerous occasions that no sexism existed among the Cherokee prior to contact. As a political move, she defended her own role in tribal government by explaining it as an extension of the powerful role women have historically played in the Cherokee tribe, and some scholars have lent their support to her contention. Susan Williams and Joy Harjo identify Mankiller's election as the first time a Cherokee woman had held such a position of power since the influence of Christianity and say that this was "due to the insecurity of men." They also characterized Mankiller as following "in the path of other Beloved Women" in the Cherokee tribe. Yet the very essence of the Cherokee having "Beloved Women" connotes that women achieving an equitable level of power and influence to that of men was exceptional in nature. The presence of Cherokee men in the public arena of politics and decision making was unremarkable in the very ordinariness of it. Mankiller's election as chief did pose a challenge to traditional Cherokee gender roles, regardless of the autonomy and even public power some Cherokee women exercised in the past. Absent from both Mankiller's portrayal of her role and that of Williams and Harjo is the recognition that Mankiller's accomplishment clearly exceeded traditional female representations of power within the Cherokee Nation. This is, in part, an indication of Mankiller's astute political maneuvering; by characterizing her leadership as a restoration of tradition instead of an aberration, she put her critics on the defensive and portrayed the Cherokee tribe as far more progressive on women's rights than mainstream white society.[6]

Nevertheless, the tendency to characterize Mankiller's tenure as chief as a return to tradition speaks to a larger problem in the area of Native American women's history, which is the fallacy promulgated by romanticized depictions of a distant past prior to the arrival of Europeans in North America in which all Indian women exercised a great deal of power. This is not to dismiss the fact that some groups of Native American women did exercise a greater degree of autonomy than white women, but rather to suggest there existed more similarities between the two groups in terms of the acceptable arena for expressions of power than has been indicated by many scholars. Certainly one could argue, for example, that Abigail Adams, the wife of President John Adams and mother of President John Quincy Adams, occupied something akin to "beloved woman" status. But just as it would be erroneous to take the status and respect afforded to Adams and apply that to an analysis of the roles of other women in the eighteenth century, so too is it inaccurate to take the experience of a small minority of beloved women and argue that all Cherokee women achieved a status of power equal to that of men. Scholarship that overemphasizes the power of Native American women prior to the influence of white culture ignores the diversity of tribal societies and the dynamic nature of human interaction. The larger point, however, is not to dwell on precontact manifestations of female power, but instead to explore how belief in that power shaped the image, as well as identity, of both Harris and Mankiller.

Female Leadership

Harris and Mankiller share two fundamental beliefs about female leadership that underpin their styles of interaction and participation in politics. First, both believe that Indian women have historically played a vital role within their tribes and that sexism came from white culture. For instance, Harris described Indian men and women as "equal until Euro-American society and religion came in." Likewise, Mankiller indicated that, "from the time of European contact, there has been a concerted attempt to diminish the role of indigenous women." On the basis of her discussions with other indigenous women, Mankiller said that they all believed "there was a point in time when there was greater equity between men and women." Second, each woman contends that women and men engage in leadership differently. In fact, Harris and Mankiller both argue that women are more collaborative and that they bring a different type of sensitivity to leadership. The significance of both beliefs is that at the heart of their activism and self-image is a gendered perception of politics. Being female and believing traditional Native American cultures esteem women lends a legitimacy and confidence not automatically found among many females in politics. In fact, most women in politics have had to overcome gender in order to succeed; Harris and Mankiller actually *used* their gender to succeed. Devon Mihesuah argues that "many modern Native women leaders point to their tribal religions and traditions as inspiration and justification for their position as leaders," which certainly holds true in the case of Harris and Mankiller.[7]

Mankiller has been instrumental in encouraging greater political participation among both Indian and non-Indian women. As she said in 1993, "Continued change will not occur without women leaders organizing, networking, debating, and singing our way into the next millennium, hand in hand with our young sisters." Describing Mankiller as a "role model for all Americans," New York Republican Congresswoman Susan Molinari invited her to speak at the "Women as Leaders" seminar in Washington, D.C. Representative Molinari expressed confidence that Mankiller's "inspirational words" would "impart wisdom and hope" to those participating in the seminar. Mankiller also demonstrated her support of women when she voiced objection to the confirmation of Clarence Thomas to the U.S. Supreme Court after University of Oklahoma law professor Anita Hill accused him of sexual harassment. She wrote to Senator David Boren and criticized the lack of female leadership in government. She questioned the ramifications of Thomas's confirmation, saying, "If a Yale educated law professor will not be believed when she complains about sexual harassment, what woman or girl can be encouraged to come forward with complaints about sexual harassment?" Adding that she felt strongly about the issue, she reiterated her concern that Thomas's confirmation would discourage females across the country from exposing sexual exploitation and harassment.[8]

Mankiller criticized not only the treatment of Anita Hill but also lamented the fact that more women did not get appointed as judges. She asked Boren to support Jane Wiseman for a federal judgeship in Tulsa, Oklahoma. The chief wrote, "I don't understand how we can continue to have gender inequity in judgeships when we have so may women qualified to serve in these positions." She added that she had been able to solve a similar problem in the Cherokee Nation "pretty quickly by appointing two women judges in the tribal courts." Boren responded that Wiseman would be among those he considered for the opening, and Wiseman also wrote to Mankiller thanking her for her help and advice.[9]

Harris also has actively supported women in politics throughout her career. She was, after all, one of the founding members of the Women's Political Caucus in 1971. Her lengthy stint as a political wife brought her into contact with numerous politically

active women. She easily befriended such women as Betty
Friedan, Gloria Steinem, and Barbara Blum. And ten years before
Mankiller became the first woman elected principal chief of the
Cherokee Nation, Harris wrote a letter of congratulations to another female leader of an Indian tribe. In a letter to Anne Sandoval, chairwoman of the Sycuan Band of Mission Indians, Harris wrote, "I'm glad to see a woman chairing an Indian tribe,"
adding, "It does my heart good." When Mankiller was elected
chief of the Cherokee Nation, Harris says she was pleased but not
surprised to see a woman chosen, given that a number of other
women had already served as leaders of their tribes. Harris's support
of women has continued for more than thirty years. Described by
one associate as a "Fearless Noble Comanche Maiden," Harris contributed significantly to the promotion of women's issues. She did
this both in her support of women and in her ability and willingness to expand assumptions about women in leadership positions.
Moreover, her work with the Women's Political Caucus, support of
the Equal Rights Amendment, and involvement with the feminist
movement further illustrates this commitment.[10]

Harris and Mankiller have received numerous accolades for their
work on behalf of women. Both were named women of the year by
different women's magazines, including *Ladies Home Journal* and
Ms. Magazine, and both have given numerous talks on the subject
of women's rights. Here again, they took the traditions from their
native cultures and applied them to their support for women's
rights. In fact, the intersection of Indianness and feminism is best
seen through an evaluation of how each woman has approached
the issue of feminism and women's rights.

Indigenous Support Network

That Harris and Mankiller developed a profound sense of themselves as Indian women and, at times, used it to band together is
clear in any examination of their interaction with each other and
with other Native American women. When Mankiller ran for chief
in 1987, for example, a prominent Native American activist, Ada
Deer, sent a letter to Harris and other members of the Women of
Indian Nations Political Action Committee (WINPAC) board

about the election. This organization encouraged the participation of Native Americans in all levels of politics but did not affiliate itself with any political entity or group. In regards to the pending election, Deer explained that Mankiller was "facing three male opponents" and urged the board members to make a personal donation to her campaign. When Mankiller won the election Harris sent her a congratulatory telegram. Harris and another friend, Ella Mae Horse, wrote, "Your sisters across the country are so extremely proud of you" and "Please know we are thinking of you and stand ready to help assure you a successful and productive term." The letter closed with an extension of their "most heartfelt congratulations" and "best wishes." As evidenced here, gender was a central component of the political identity and image of these women and also served as a basis for unity and mutual support. Such support proved a tremendous asset among the network of Native American women involved in politics.[11]

Deer is important for her accomplishments on behalf of Native Americans, but an examination of her work is particularly useful here in forging a better understanding of the network formed by contemporary Native American women in politics. Her relationship to both Harris and Mankiller provides insight into the centrality of the gender-based support network forged by these women. Like Harris and Mankiller, Deer urged women to play a larger role in politics, saying, "It is a man's world unless women vote." She encouraged women to support political candidates who "are striving to eliminate oppressions of all kinds."[12]

Harris has been a mentor to Deer throughout her career, and the two joked that every time Harris was named to one board or another, she would soon open the door for Deer to follow. In fact, both Fred and LaDonna Harris provided Deer with assistance. She stayed with them in their Washington home on a number of occasions, and they also aided her in her efforts to regain federally recognized status for her tribe, the Menominee, which had been terminated during the 1950s. Deer wrote a letter to LaDonna Harris, thanking her for all the help both she and Fred provided to the Menominee efforts at restoration. "Your encouragement, consultation, and advice really bolstered my work," she wrote. "I always marvel at your vision and foresight." Deer concluded the letter by calling Harris an inspiration for all Indian people: "You've won my perpetual Woman-Of-The-Year Award!"[13]

After securing restoration of reservation status for her tribe by the mid-1970s, Deer has since continued as a vital activist for the rights of Native Americans and later became the head of Native American Studies at the University of Wisconsin at Madison. She ran, but did not win, as the Democratic candidate for secretary of state of Wisconsin in 1978 and 1982. In 1993, she became the first female Native American assistant secretary of the interior for Indian affairs. When Deer ran for secretary of state of Wisconsin, the Harrises supported her. They wrote letters of support and engaged in fund-raising efforts on her behalf, writing, "We have known and admired her for many years" and "we respect her abilities as a leader." They described Deer as an American Indian woman who "has accomplished many firsts in her career." Quoted on the back of a pamphlet promoting her candidacy, a passage from *Ms. Magazine* described Deer as representing the "re-emergence of the Indian woman, who historically has filled positions of equal responsibility in a tribal society which operates on qualifications." To be sure, gendered language and assumptions about supposed traditional expressions of female power in native societies regularly informed positive depictions of Native American women in politics such as Deer and Mankiller.[14]

Deer met Mankiller in the early 1980s, and the two occasionally worked on projects of mutual interest and sought advice from one another. Mankiller testified in support of Deer's confirmation as the assistant secretary of the interior for Indian affairs in July 1993. She described Deer as a "courageous and tireless advocate of Native people" and as "always in tune to the needs of people." Mankiller said that, in her opinion, Deer's greatest contribution was the leadership she exhibited in the restoration efforts of her tribe and called Deer a "superior choice" for the position. After receiving confirmation for her new job, Deer continued to receive support from Mankiller.[15]

The following year Mankiller gave Deer advice on formulating priorities for 1994. After making some general observations and recommendations, Mankiller warned Deer of Oklahoma-based opposition to her because of her efforts the previous year to consolidate the Oklahoma Bureau of Indian Affairs (BIA) offices. Mankiller told her that Senator David Boren was "so angry he has threatened taking you personally to federal court" and added that the other United States senator from Oklahoma, Don Nickles, was "pretty pissed off" as well. Mankiller advised Deer to "always question the agenda and recommendations" of the BIA and to keep in mind that even as she "worked for the common good" as she always had, there were people who wanted to see Deer "fall and trip" to facilitate her removal from Indian Affairs. Deer clearly saw Mankiller as a sound advisor, as she expressed a few months later. Deer praised Wilma for her efforts at the 1994 White House Listening Conference in which numerous Indian leaders met with policy makers and members of the Clinton administration. Deer told Mankiller, "I trust your judgment and am in awe of your intelligence and common sense." She added, "You have already achieved so much in your life and I am counting on you to help me achieve our goals for Indian country."[16]

When Harris received the Lucy Covington Award for her lifetime contributions to bettering the condition of Native Americans, both Mankiller and Deer, along with feminist leader Gloria Steinem, participated in the awards ceremony honoring Harris. Here again, the significance of the support network emerges. These women identified heavily with their gender, and thus it represented a central bond that forged this support network. Harris thanked Mankiller for her presentation at the ceremony: "I know we will always be supportive of each other." Harris and Mankiller indeed have held each other in mutually high regard. In one article, Harris described Mankiller as someone other Indian leaders view "with great admiration, maybe sometimes with envy that she can do what she does," and Mankiller characterized Harris as a "remarkable stateswoman and national leader who has enriched the lives of thousands." She further described Harris as a "consistent and ardent advocate on behalf of indigenous people."[17]

The support network made up of women such as Harris, Mankiller, Deer, and others remains central to understanding the identity they brought to their leadership and the goals they accomplished. In 1993 Clara Nomee, madam chairman of the Crow Tribal Council, wrote to Mankiller concerning the role of Indian women leaders and their responsibilities to their respective tribal governments. She said that they "must stand and support each other in the area of tribal sovereignty." There were also numerous support organizations that emerged for Native American women. For instance, Women of All Red Nations (WARN) stresses the value of women within Indian tribal traditions. Winona LaDuke, one of the founders of WARN, described the organization as growing out of a recognition that more women needed to be involved in the American Indian movement. She added that WARN also sought to "bring back the traditional role of women in the Indian nations and in the leadership and guidance of [the American Indian movement]." This push toward reasserting "traditional roles" of Indian women mirrors the language employed by Harris and Mankiller and reflects the Indigenous feminist imperative behind the growing number of Native women elected to tribal offices in the late twentieth century.[18]

Second-Wave Feminism

To be sure, the lives of many Native American women differed markedly from those of white women, and, like other women of color and working-class white women, they could not separate their needs as women from broader social issues that oppressed the men in their communities as well—racism, sovereignty, and class. White middle- and upper-class college-educated women dominated the feminist movement and often defined "female issues" too narrowly to appeal to women of color and poor women, but the movement nevertheless had implications for women at large. It brought the issue of sex-based discrimination to national attention and fostered a dialogue that directly shaped perceptions of femininity and increased the options available to women. The feminist movement gave women like Harris and Mankiller a framework within which they could challenge assumptions about the appropriate place of women in society. In fact, the feminist movement created a host of new possibilities for women. By the mid-1990s, women still earned less money than men and remained underrepresented in every branch of the government. It is also true, however, that increasing numbers of women go to college, pursue advanced degrees, run companies, and do a number of other things that, prior to the feminist movement, were considered unusual.[19]

The friendship between Mankiller and Steinem, whose name is virtually synonymous with the feminist movement, illuminates an interesting connection between white and Native American feminists. The two developed a friendship after meeting through their work with the Ms. Foundation. Mankiller credited Steinem for encouraging her to write her autobiography. In her acknowledgments, Mankiller extended her "love and appreciation" to Steinem for her support. Her relationship to Steinem has brought even more publicity to Mankiller. What better irony than for feminists and critics alike to see Steinem, the best-known spokesperson of the movement, linked to a woman named Mankiller? The name brought substantial interest, and, in fact, even the *Wall Street Journal* quipped about her name. Saying that their favorite name on the list of those in attendance at Clinton's economic summit meeting was Chief Mankiller, they added their hope that she represented only the Cherokee Nation and not "a feminist economic priority." Mankiller also used humor about her name, often telling people that she had earned the appellation.[20]

Female Politicians, Female Issues

Although Harris represents a first in the expanding role of congressional wives and Mankiller became the first female chief of the Cherokee Nation, each functioned within a larger political climate they shared with a number of other contemporary women in politics. Two such women, Shirley Chisholm and Bella Abzug, provide useful comparisons to Harris and Mankiller because of the way in which each used her image as a feminist and a woman to take on "female issues."

Chisholm became the first African American woman elected to the U.S. House of Representatives in 1968. She also ran for president in 1972, the same year Fred Harris ran for the first time. Like Harris and Mankiller, Chisholm believed women brought special attributes to political leadership. In fact, she argued that women make better politicians because "they are not as likely as men to engage in deals, manipulations, and sharp tactics." For this very reason, she argued, more women should be in politics. Chisholm's language is reminiscent of nineteenth-century female reformers who also stressed the superior moral attributes of women. In each case, this subtle twist in sexist constructs was born of political expediency, because women have historically been forced to justify their presence in venues perceived to fall outside the scope of women's domain. An examination of Chisholm's rhetoric proves helpful primarily because of her use of feminism and gendered imagery during her career. She also drew a connection between racism and sexism, saying, "The cheerful old darky on the plantation and the happy little homemaker" constitute equally destructive stereotypes steeped in oppression. She urged women to see that involvement in the existing political struggle offered them the best way to instigate change and challenge oppression. Here is where her activism most resembled that of Harris and Mankiller. Chisholm also recognized the need to work within the system in an effort to change it.[21]

Another notable politician who challenged assumptions about female leadership was Bella Abzug, a Jewish congresswoman from New York who did not begin her political career until age fifty. Acknowledging that people described her as a "tough and noisy woman," a "prizefighter," and a "man-hater," Abzug consciously constructed an image that made her stand out and be heard. Abzug became notorious in Congress for her aggressive in-your-face style. She, too, lamented the need for more women to involve themselves in politics and, like many feminists in the early 1970s, believed that women had a number of concerns in common. Abzug dedicated the last few decades of her life to condemning war, fighting for the passage of the Equal Rights Amendment, and working for other "female" causes such as equal pay and adequate child care for working mothers. In addition to Abzug's outspoken personality, she also exhibited a loud persona in the manner in which she dressed. She wore colorful clothing and large hats that made her impossible to ignore. Physically, Abzug was not a woman most would describe as pretty, and this too provided a challenge to traditional assumptions and beliefs about women. Whereas scrutiny of unattractive male politicians seldom arises, the same does not hold true for women. Abzug challenged many very basic ideals of womanhood by being loud, aggressive, and unattractive.[22]

Roger Jourdain, the chairman of the Red Lake Band of Chippewa Indians, drew an interesting comparison between Harris and Abzug. After assuring Harris that there was no "physical comparison" between them, he said that "the same forceful manner in which you state 'our' case is quite like Bella's." Among her other numerous accomplishments, Abzug also introduced and helped pass House Resolution 9924, which created a National Women's Conference in 1976. Abzug described the conferences as the first "federally supported opportunity" for women "to assess their current status, identify the barriers that prevent women from participating fully and equally in all aspects of national life," and "develop recommendations for means whereby such impediments can be removed." That all women did not embrace such a conference is hardly surprising. Certainly this proved the case with one AIO female staff member who scratched a note to Harris at the bottom of Abzug's letter about the conference. She wrote: "This offends me someway. Maybe it is spending 5 [million] for what will probably be a mutual masturbation." As if anticipating Harris's reaction, she added, "I know, don't knock it."[23]

Legacy of Feminism

The letter from Abzug and the response of the AIO staffer demonstrate one of the clearest issues which emerged in the feminist movement: Women are by no means united in their perceptions of the problems that face them or the solutions to those problems. Still, it is because of the persistence of women like Shirley Chisholm, Bella Abzug, Gloria Steinem, Ada Deer, LaDonna Harris, and Wilma Mankiller that the role of women in politics has evolved so substantially, and the participation of women in mainstream politics continues to grow. The relationships that developed between these political women is also noteworthy because of the type of both public and private support they lent one another. Because of the pioneering roles of such women and their willingness to support one another, they have indeed contributed to the changing role of women in politics. Today, a congressional wife taking an activist role would hardly seem surprising, and although women have yet to achieve full equality, what seemed radical in the 1960s is today mainstream in terms of the opportunities available to women and new notions about appropriate gender roles. As opportunities for women continue to increase, stories about women in politics triumphing over sexism and accomplishing female firsts will become increasingly quaint, just as women in the military and in other venues previously dominated by men is increasingly unexceptional.[24]

Until that time, however, women such as Harris and Mankiller continue to serve as role models for others to follow. Mankiller, however, said she felt "uncomfortable with being cast as a role model" because people get upset if you fail to fulfill the image they have of you. "I can't do my work or live my life being conscious of the fact that some people view me as a role model," or "I would begin to suffer from paralysis." Despite her discomfort with being considered an exemplary person, Mankiller received numerous awards and other recognitions precisely for this reason. Similarly, Harris also deflected praise and said "any real Indian will say that an individual doesn't know the answers." Harris has, nevertheless, served as a role model for many women, including Deer. Kathryn Harris described her mother as a "great theoretical thinker" whose openness to "adventure and new experiences," as well as her "life-long curiosity and compassion," made her a tremendous role model for people from all sorts of backgrounds. For the wives of politicians, Harris set an example of informed activism and made it clear that wives had more to offer than folding bandages for the Red Cross or heading up social functions.[25]

The irony of Mankiller and Harris's prominence remains their successful manipulation of constructed notions of both gender and tradition. Mankiller's image, because of her name, her prominence, and her support for women's issues cannot be separated from her use of gender. Despite her claims that gender had nothing to do with leadership, it had everything to do with her national image as a leader. Similarly, gender opened the door for Harris's rise to national leadership. By the time that her organization, AIO, celebrated its twenty-fifth anniversary, Harris had been divorced for fifteen years and it had been even longer since she was a congressional wife. No doubt she projected a different image in 1995 than she did as the young wife of a rising politician. Yet it was, after all, her gendered image that first brought her national recognition. She continued to be one of the most respected advocates of Native American rights in the country and grew far less likely to have to cater to social expectations to get what she wanted. Indeed, gender role expectations, while still in existence at the end of the twentieth century, were far less rigid than they were in the late 1950s and early 1960s when Harris had her first taste of expectations for political wives.

The intersection of feminism and Indianness that shaped both the identity and image of LaDonna Harris and Wilma Mankiller made possible their respective challenges to accepted social and political norms by enabling them to view their activism as a traditional expression of women's tribal power, rather than as a challenge to traditionalism. Harris not only redefined the role of political wives but also helped erase stereotypes of both women and Native Americans. By characterizing her larger humanitarian efforts as an outgrowth of her tribal values, Harris helped make Native American beliefs and customs relevant to contemporary society. An AIO biographical description of Harris characterized her identity succinctly: she is one "who ultimately only seeks to be known as a Comanche woman." Mankiller drew on elements of feminist ideals and Cherokee tradition to create a new modern concept of the beloved woman who is politicized yet traditional. Taken together, Harris and Mankiller are the two most important Native American women in the second half of the twentieth century, both for their accomplishments and for their use of gendered imagery to justify and effect change.[26]

AUTHOR'S NOTE

When I began this work as a doctoral student at the University of Oklahoma, my goal was to better understand the importance of identity in the political lives of LaDonna Harris and Wilma Mankiller. Specifically, I wanted to explore how their sense of identity evolved over time, how that identity helped or hindered their careers as activists and politicians, and how their public images were shaped by the media and by changing conceptions of Native Americans in mainstream society. I found, as scholars always do, that the more questions I confronted the more I was able to raise, so by the end of my project it had become more complex, more frustrating, and more rewarding than I could have possibly predicted.

The complexities and frustrations stemmed in part from the difficulty of writing about living people and depending on their invaluable yet very fallible memories. Historians who write about persons long since passed away have an advantage in this regard, because the dead—at least those with no living relatives or friends to challenge an author's conclusions—are in no position to do so themselves. The living, on the other hand, have imperfect memories and sometimes have a vested interest in remembering events and/or their own importance in past events in a specific way. This is not to say that historians or authors have a monopoly on accuracy, of course. It is only to argue that the interplay between author and living subject is fraught with possibilities for friction and that it should come as no surprise that interpretive differences between the two can often become intense. Wilma Mankiller, for example, objected to some of the arguments in this book and decided against signing her interview consent forms. For this reason I was unable to use the interviews I conducted with her, her husband, and one of her brothers.

Other frustrations came from the field of Native American history itself, which has become intensely politicized and fragmented over the last decade. Some scholars believe that only Native Americans should write about Indians or that works adhering to the decolonization model should form the foundation of future scholarship about indigenous peoples. This is hardly the place to address these issues, except to note that they are passionately debated and have important implications for authors in the field. I was always taught, for example, that neither race, ethnicity, nor sex had anything to do with a scholar's conclusions, that evidence could be analyzed and interpreted by anyone, and that the more points of view presented within a given field of study the better. Being a woman who happens to write about women's history gives me no particular insight into the historical experience of being female. In fact, I owe much intellectual debt to the male historians of women who trained me.

Ultimately, my work offers one interpretation of the political lives of two influential Indian women. I tried to be respectful of their beliefs, and, in places where discrepancies exist between memories and documents, I have tried to give both views. This is especially difficult in examining issues surrounding ethnic identity formation in the early lives of these two women. My hope has been to avoid engaging in an argument of sorts with my research subjects over the point at which they experienced Indianness or the extent to which that identity emerged in childhood or grew more pronounced as a result of the particular historical circumstances each confronted. Harris and Mankiller are remarkable women who have effected great change, and this book has been an effort to help place them in the historical context to which they belong.

NOTES

Abbreviations

CACRSC	Carl Albert Congressional Research and Studies Center
CNA	Cherokee National Archives
CP	College Park, Maryland
FHC	Fred Harris Collection
LHC	LaDonna Harris Collection
MGP	Museum of the Great Plains
NAES college	Native American Educational Studies College
NARA	National Archives and Records Administration
NCIO Papers	National Council on Indian Opportunity Papers
OU	University of Oklahoma
Owens Collection	Sarah "Betty" Owens Collection
RG	Record Group
RSC	Ross Swimmer Collection
Swimmer private papers	Ross O. Swimmer private papers inherited from his secretary, Carol Allison
WHC	Western History Collection
WMC	Wilma Mankiller Collection

Introduction

1. Paula Gunn Allen, *The Sacred Hoop: Recovering the Feminine in American Indian Traditions* (Boston: Beacon Press, 1986), p. 43.

2. Wilma Mankiller and Michael Wallis, *Wilma Mankiller: A*

Chief and Her People (New York: St. Martin's Press, 1993), p. 14; LaDonna Harris, *LaDonna Harris: A Comanche Life,* ed. H. Henrietta Stockel (Lincoln: University of Nebraska Press, 2000), p. 11.

3. Susan M. Williams and Joy Harjo, "American Indian Feminism," in *The Reader's Companion to U.S. Women's History,* eds. Wilma Mankiller, Gwendolyn Mink, Marysa Navarro, Barbara Smith, and Gloria Steinem (Boston: Houghton Mifflin, 1998), pp. 198–99; Devon Abbot Mihesuah, *Indigenous American Women: Decolonization, Empowerment, Activism* (Lincoln: University of Nebraska Press, 2003), p. 143. See also Melanie McCoy, "Gender or Ethnicity: What Makes a Difference? A Study of Women Tribal Leaders," *Women and Politics* 12, no. 3 (1992): 57–68; Gary Anderson and Brad Agnew have written essays on Harris and Mankiller–respectively–which appear in *The New Warriors: Native American Leaders since 1900,* ed. R. David Edmunds (Lincoln: University of Nebraska Press, 2001). The essays highlight some of the accomplishments of these two women in the area of Indian advocacy.

1—"Freddie and the Indian"

1. "Freddie and the Indian" was a nickname given to Fred and LaDonna Harris by one of his colleagues in the Oklahoma legislature, which LaDonna viewed as a "form of acceptance." LaDonna Harris, *LaDonna Harris,* p. 54.

2. Malvina Stephenson, "LaDonna Harris May Be Answer to TV Myth," *Tulsa Daily World,* May 18, 1965, p. 10.

3. *LaDonna Harris,* p. 18; p. 2; The Dawes Severalty Act was an effort to end the collective ownership of land by Native Americans by essentially turning them into farmers and forcing them to assimilate into white society. As a result of this policy, American Indians lost more than 60 percent of their land between 1887 and 1934. See Frederick Hoxie, *A Final Promise: The Campaign to Assimilate the Indians, 1800–1920* (Lincoln: University of Nebraska Press, 1984); Janet A. McDonnell, *Dispossession of the American Indian, 1887–1934* (Bloomington: Indiana University Press, 1991); and Morris W. Foster, *Being Comanche: A Social History of an American Indian Community* (Tucson: University of Arizona Press, 1991), p. 103.

4. Foster, *Being Comanche,* p. 102.

5. Foster, *Being Comanche,* p. 20; *LaDonna Harris,* p. 3; Thomas W. Kavanagh, *Comanche Political History: An Ethnohistorical Perspective 1706–1875* (Lincoln: University of Nebraska Press, 1996) p. 41; LaDonna Harris, interview with the author, November 20, 2000, p. 6.

6. Foster, *Being Comanche,* p. 106; LaDonna Harris, interview with the author, November 20, 2000, p. 2; Terry Morris, "LaDonna Harris: A Woman Who Gives a Damn," *Redbook Magazine,* February 1970, p. 117.

7. *LaDonna Harris,* p. 21; LaDonna Harris, interview with the author, November 20, 2000, p. 3; p. 2; LaDonna Harris, draft of bio-

graphical profile, p. 2, series 1, box 4, LaDonna Harris Collection (hereafter LHC), Native American Educational Studies (NAES) College, Chicago.

8. Laura Harris, interview with the author, July 24, 2003; *LaDonna Harris*, pp. 21–22; *LaDonna Harris*.

9. Foster, *Being Comanche,* p. 130; LaDonna Harris, interview with the author, September 25, 2001; Joane Nagel, *American Indian Ethnic Renewal: Red Power and the Resurgence of Identity and Culture* (New York: Oxford University Press, 1996, 1997) p. 21; For a more general discussion of ethnic identity formation, see Fredrik Barth, ed., *Ethnic Groups and Boundaries: The Social Organization of Culture Difference*(Boston: Little, Brown, 1969).

10. LaDonna Harris, interview with the author, November 20, 2000, p. 1.

11. LaDonna Harris, interview with the author, September 25, 2001.

12. Laura Harris, interview with the author, July 24, 2003.

13. See Kevin Gaines, *Uplifting the Race: Black Leadership, Politics, and Culture in the Twentieth Century* (Chapel Hill: University of North Carolina Press, 1996); Neil Wynn, *The Afro-American and the Second World War* (New York: Holmes & Meier, 1976); August Meier and Elliott Rudwick, *CORE: A Study in Civil Rights, 1942–1968* (New York: Oxford University Press, 1973).

14. George Lynn Cross, *Blacks in White Colleges: Oklahoma's Landmark Cases* (Norman: University of Oklahoma Press, 1975), p. 29

15. Cross, *Blacks in White Colleges*; Ada Lois Sipuel Fisher and Danney Gobel, *A Matter of Black and White: The Autobiography of Ada Lois Sipuel Fisher* (Norman: University of Oklahoma Press, 1996); LaDonna Harris, interview with the author, March 11, 2002.

16. Cross, *Blacks in White Colleges,* p. 32; LaDonna Harris, draft of biographical profile, p. 1, series 1, box 4, LHC, NAES College.

17. For a discussion of the significance of Indianness in defining American culture (and the tendency of whites to mimic Indian rituals and culture), see Phillip J. Deloria, *Playing Indian* (New Haven, Conn.: Yale University Press, 1998): Fergus M. Bordewich, *Killing the White Man's Indian: Reinventing of Native Americans at the End of the Twentieth Century* (New York: Doubleday, 1996).

18. For a thorough biography of Fred Harris that charts the course of his political career, see Richard Lowitt, *Fred Harris: His Journey From Liberalism to Populism* (Lanham, Md.: Rowman & Littlefield, 2002); LaDonna Harris, interview with the author, November 20, 2000, p. 6; Fred Harris, interview with the author, October 2, 2001; Kathryn Harris Tijerina, interview with the author, July 28, 2003.

19. For a discussion of grassroots activism in the civil rights movement, see John Dittmer, *Local People: The Struggle for Civil Rights in Mississippi* (Urbana: University of Illinois Press, 1994).

20. A History of "The Group," June 7, 1965, p. 1, folder 1, Sarah "Betty" Owens Collection (hereafter Owens Collection), Museum of the Great Plains (hereafter MGP), Lawton, Oklahoma; p. 6; *LaDonna Harris*, p. 54; "The Group," p. 1, folder 1, Owens Collection, MGP; *LaDonna Harris*, p. 55.

21. "The Group," p. 1, folder 1, Owens Collection, MGP; p. 2.

22. "A Struggle for Equality—A Community View," booklet published by the Museum of the Great Plains to accompany an exhibit on the integration of Lawton, 2003, p. 21; "The Group," pp. 1–2, folder 1, Owens Collection, MGP; *LaDonna Harris*, p. 55.

23. "The Group," p. 2, folder 1, Owens Collection, MGP; "Minutes from the regular Wednesday night meeting of The Group," April 12, 1967, folder 2, Owens Collection, MGP; "A Struggle for Equality —A Community View," p. 21; Open letter from E. A. Owens, president of the Lawton chapter of the NAACP, July 6, 1966, p. 2, folder 1, Owens Collection, MGP.

24. Sarah "Betty" Owens, interview with the author, September 20, 2001; *LaDonna Harris*, p. 55; "A Struggle for Equality—A Community View," p. 21.

25. *LaDonna Harris*, p. 55; "A Struggle for Equality—A Community View," p. 22.

26. Kathryn Harris Tijerina, interview with the author, July 28, 2003.

27. John Henry Nelson, interview with the author, September 20, 2001.

28. "Charles Mangel, "The Remarkable Fred Harris," *Look Magazine*, March 18, 1969, p. 76; Maggie Gover, "We Called Ourselves THE GROUP: The Story of a Small GROUP of People Who Changed a City and Each Other," unpublished manuscript, p. 7.

29. *LaDonna Harris*, p. 54.

30. LaDonna Harris, interview with the author, November 20, 2000, p. 9; Fred Harris, interview with the author, October 2, 2001; LaDonna Harris, interview with the author, September 25, 2001.

31. "Onward!" Fred Harris, campaign literature, Oklahoma gubernatorial race, 1962, folder 5, box 50, Fred Harris Collection (hereafter FHC), MGP, Lawton, Oklahoma.

32. LaDonna Harris, interview with the author, September 25, 2001.

33. LaDonna Harris, interview with the author, November 20, 2000, p. 9; LaDonna Harris, interview with the author, September 25, 2001.

34. LaDonna Harris, interview with the author, November 20, 2000, p. 10; The teamwork of the Harrises brought them to the attention of journalist Myra MacPherson and inspired her to include them in her book on political couples. She notes the close relationship of

the Harrises as well as their political partnership. See Myra MacPher-
son, *The Power Lovers: An Intimate Look at Politics and Marriage* (New
York: G. P. Putnam's Sons, 1975), especially pp. 417–24; "Sooner Sen-
ator's Wife Wows Them," *Wichita Eagle,* March 20, 1965, p. 6B;
Wauhillau La Hay, "Wife Shares Political Triumph," *New York World
Telegram and Sun,* January 8, 1965.

35. LaDonna Harris, interview with the author, November 20,
2000, p. 10; Aulena Gibson, interview with the author, October 2,
2001; Laura Harris, interview with the author, July 24, 2003;
LaDonna Harris, interview with the author, September 25, 2001; Fred
Harris, interview with the author, October 2, 2001; Beverly Saffa Stapleton, interview with the author, September 23, 2001.

36. Fred R. Harris, *Potomac Fever* (New York: W. W. Norton,
1977), pp. 121–22; p. 104.

37. MacPherson, *Power Lovers,* p. 422; LaDonna Harris, interview with the author, September 25, 2001.

38. Ben H. Weaver to Fred Harris, April 1, 1963; Maynard I.
Ungerman to Fred Harris, April 4, 1963; Harvey P. Everest to Fred
Harris, April 22, 1963, folder 2, box 33, FHC, MGP; Harris, *Potomac
Fever,* p. 108.

39. Aulena Gibson, interview with the author, October 2, 2001;
LaDonna Harris, interview with the author, November 20, 2001, p.
24; Comanche Indian Tribe Resolution, July 2, 1955, folder 4, box 48,
FHC, MGP.

40. LaDonna Harris, interview with the author, June 24, 2003;
Foster, *Being Comanche,* pp. 136–37.

41. For a discussion of the effects of termination policy, see Alison Bernstein, *American Indians and World War II: Toward a New Era in
Indian Affairs* (Norman: University of Oklahoma Press, 1991); Donald
L. Fixico, *Termination and Relocation: Federal Indian Policy, 1945–1960*
(Albuquerque: University of New Mexico Press, 1986); Donald L. Parman, *Indians and the American West in the Twentieth Century* (Bloomington: Indiana University Press, 1994).

42. To U.S. Senator Mike Monroney from Fred Harris, March
11, 1957, p. 3, folder 3, box 47, FHC, MGP. A memo at the top of the
letter indicates that the same letter was also sent to Ed Edmondson,
Toby Morris, and Bob Kerr, pp. 2–3; LaDonna Harris, interview with
the author, June 24, 2003; Foster, *Being Comanche,* p. 137.

43. LaDonna Harris, interview with the author, October 15,
2003; Meryle Secrest, "No Vanishing Comanche," *Washington Post,*
December 15, 1964, p. B-1. When asked about this quotation, Harris
indicated that she has no recollection of saying that her culture had
been lost; Malvina Stephenson, "They Communicate in Comanche,"
Sunday Star, November 15, 1964; LaDonna Harris, interview with the
author, September 25, 2001.

44. LaDonna Harris, draft of biographical profile, p. 2, series 1, box 4, LHC, NAES College.

45. For an overview of the Great Society, see John A. Andrew III, *Lyndon Johnson and the Great Society* (Chicago: Ivan R. Dee, 1998); Irving Bernstein, *Guns or Butter: The Presidency of Lyndon Johnson* (New York: Oxford University Press, 1996); David Zarefsky, *President Johnson's War on Poverty: Rhetoric and History* (Tuskaloosa: University of Alabama Press, 1986); Lyndon B. Johnson, University of Michigan Commencement Address, May 22, 1964, *The Great Society: A Sourcebook of Speeches,* compiled by Glenn R. Capp (Belmont, Calif.: Dickenson Publishing, 1967), p. 18.

46. Minutes of the initial meeting of members of Oklahomans for Indian Opportunity, August 7, 1965, folder 33, box 282, Fred R. Harris Collection (hereafter FHC), Carl Albert Congressional Research and Studies Center (hereafter CACRSC), University of Oklahoma (hereafter OU).

47. John B. O'Hara to LaDonna Harris, September 16, 1965, folder 7, box 282, FHC, CACRSC, OU.

48. Daniel M. Cobb, "'US Indians Understand the Basics': Oklahoma Indians and the Politics of Community Action, 1964–1970," *Western Historical Quarterly* 33, no. 1 (2002): 46.

49. Constitution and by-laws of Oklahomans for Indian Opportunity, Inc., folder 5, box 282, FHC, CACRSC, OU.

50. Constitution and by-laws of Oklahomans for Indian Opportunity, Inc., folder 5, box 282, FHC, CACRSC, OU; D. L. Monchil to Fred Harris, October 5, 1965, folder 7, box 282, FHC, CACRSC, OU. LaDonna's effort to found an Indian college proved short-lived. The idea first occurred to her in the midst of an effort to get Oklahoma high schools to incorporate more literature on Native Americans into their curriculum. After a preliminary investigation into the possibility of establishing an Indian college, LaDonna concluded that the more pressing issue was the high rate of high school dropouts and the lack of Native Americans who received any college or university training at all. LaDonna Harris, interview with the author, June 24, 2003; Meeting of Oklahomans for Indian Opportunity, University of Oklahoma, June 14, 1965, folder 33, box 282, FHC, CACRSC, OU; Hal Gulliver, "LaDonna Harris," *Atlanta Constitution,* November 29, 1971, p. 4-A; LaDonna Harris, interview with the author, November 20, 2000, p. 16.

51. LaDonna Harris, interview with the author, November 20, 2000, pp. 13–14; Iola Hayden, interview with the author, March 27, 2001.

52. Meeting of Oklahomans for Indian Opportunity, University of Oklahoma, June 14, 1965, folder 33, box 282, FHC, CACRSC, OU.

53. Daniel M. Cobb, "The Last Indian War: Indian Community

Action in the Johnson Administration's War on Poverty, 1964–1969"
(Master's thesis, University of Wyoming, 1998), 117; Fred Harris,
"American Indians—New Destiny," 89th Cong., 1st sess., *Congressional Record—Senate* 112, pt. 7 (April 21, 1966): 8310.

54. Statement of Mrs. Fred R. Harris before the Education and
Labor Committee, 90th Cong., 1st sess., *Congressional Record—Senate*
113, pt. 14 (July 13, 1967): 9581; Virgil Harrington to Iola Taylor,
April 27, 1967, folder 3, box 283, FRC, CACRSC, OU. Iola Taylor later
changed her name to Iola Hayden.

55. LaDonna Harris, interview with the author, October 15,
2003; OIO Special Committee Meeting, July 25, 1967, OIO Corporation Book n. 1, Oklahomans for Indian Opportunity, Norman, Oklahoma. Harris recalled that the board's effort to remove Hayden from
her position was led by a tribal leader on OIO's board of directors who
was angry over the suggestion that tribes should elect their own leaders, ironically believing that this actually encroached on tribal authority. Significantly, Harris believed that the man went after Hayden because she—as the wife of Senator Fred Harris—was too difficult of a
target. LaDonna Harris, interview with the author, October 15, 2003.

56. Cobb, "The Last Indian War," p. 121.

57. "'Oklahomans for Indian Opportunity' and Economic Development: Feasibility Study Under OEO Contract N. B89-4285," October 18, 1967, Continental-Allied Co., Inc., courtesy of Iola Hayden
and Daniel M. Cobb, p. 18; p. 21; For a contemporary critique of the
War on Poverty, see Daniel P. Moynihan, *Maximum Feasible Misunderstanding: Community Action in the War on Poverty* (New York: Free
Press, 1969).

58. Harris indicated that, although she knew there was some
criticism of OIO, she was not fully aware of the extent of criticism
and jealousy at the time. LaDonna Harris, interview with the author,
October 15, 2003.

59. LaDonna Harris, interview with the author, September 25,
2001.

60. Fred Harris, "American Indians—New Destiny," p. 8311;
Fred Harris, interview with the author, October 2, 2001; LaDonna
Harris, interview with the author, October 15, 2003. Harris is quick to
point out that she and Fred were co-opting derogatory language as a
way to marginalize the racist overtones. This is quite similar to the
way in which Hispanic Americans reclaimed the word "Chicano" as
their own to erase the negative implications once carried in the usage
of the word.

61. Fred Harris, "American Indians—New Destiny," p. 8311;
Tom Malone, "Wife Helps Harris on the Warpath," unidentified
newspaper, folder 9, box 286, FHC, CACRSC, OU; "Sooner Senator's
Wife Wows Them," *Wichita Eagle,* March 20, 1965, p. 6B.

62. LaDonna Harris, interview with the author, September 25, 2001. It is important to note that Harris's own definition of "assimilation" means to no longer exist. For her, assimilation into mainstream society would be to give up her existence as a Comanche Indian. Although there are certainly other ways to define "assimilation", out of respect for Harris's beliefs and because the word "assimilation" is almost always used in a derogatory manner, the use of the word has been avoided where ever possible. Instead, "integration" has been used to describe attempts to help Native Americans participate in mainstream society. In places where "assimilation" is used by the author, it signifies only the participation in mainstream society and is not intended to imply wholesale loss or abandonment of culture.

63. Jean Simpson, "Sooner Senator's Comanche Spouse Captivates Capital Crowd," *Tulsa Tribune,* March 27, 1965, p. 2; "LaDonna Harris Loves Role of Key Aid to Senator," *Oklahoma Journal,* September 10, 1965, p. 5; Harris, "American Indians—New Destiny," p. 8313; Charles Mangel, "Warpaint for the Senator's Wife," *Look,* April 4, 1967, p. 24.

64. Mangel, "Warpaint for the Senator's Wife," p. 24.

65. Mary Ann Weston, *Native Americans in the News: Images of Indians in the Twentieth Century Press* (Westport, Conn.: Greenwood Press, 1996), p. 163.

66. Mangel, "Warpaint for the Senator's Wife," p. 24.

67. MacPherson, *Power Lovers,* p. 326; Ernest Woods to Fred Harris, May 1, 1967, emphasis original, folder 1, box 68, FHC, CACRSC, OU; statement of Robert Kennedy about the testimony of Harris on behalf of the American Indian, 90th Cong., 1st sess., *Congressional Record—Senate* 113, pt. 14 (July 13, 1967): 9581.

68. Statement of Mrs. Fred R. Harris before the Education and Labor Committee, *Congressional Record—Senate* 113, pt. 14 (July 13, 1967): 9581.

69. Fred Harris, interview with the author, October 2, 2001.

70. Dan Blackburn, "LaDonna Harris is a Senate Wife with More on Her Mind than Mid-Afternoon Teas," *Washington Post/Potomac,* May 24, 1970, p. 26.

2—An Activist in Her Own Right

1. Fred Harris, interview with the author, October 2, 2001.

2. Minutes from OIO meeting, January 20, 1968, OIO Corporation Book, n. 1, Oklahomans for Indian Opportunity, Norman, Oklahoma. Upon the resignation of Harris, the board of OIO voted to name her honorary president for life.

3. "Washington Event Involves Women in the War on Poverty," *Bridge* (magazine of the Unitarian Universalist Women's Federation),

September 1968, folder 22, box 285, FHC, CACRSC, OU; "What One Woman Can Do . . . About Poverty" (A few ideas collected at the May 15–17 War on Poverty meeting), *National Council of Women of the United States Bulletin,* June 1968, folder 22, box 285, FHC, CACRSC, OU.

4. "LaDonna Harris: Indian Powerhouse," *Playboy* 19, no. 2, February 2, 1972, p. 178.

5. There are two primary schools of thought regarding the best way to secure equal rights for women. One involves the pursuit of legal equality that would eradicate all legal distinctions between men and women—the Equal Rights Amendment is a good example. The other centers on a recognition of the differences that exist between women and men and therefore advocates equity over equality. Harris fit into both camps to a certain degree. She strongly supported the ERA and other efforts by women to achieve legal equality, but she also believed that women and men have different styles of leadership and confront other dissimilar life experiences that necessitate equitable—rather than equal—treatment; Sara M. Evans, *Personal Politics: The Roots of Women's Liberation in the Civil Rights Movement and the New Left* (New York: Alfred A. Knopf, 1979). Evans argued that the gendered division of labor relegated women to menial tasks and kept them out of the most prominent leadership roles and that the organizational skills women gained from their participation in the New Left and the civil rights movement provided them a framework from which to start their own movement; LaDonna Harris, interview with the author, September 25, 2001.

6. LaDonna Harris, interview with the author, June 24, 2003; Sara M. Evans, *Born for Liberty: A History of Women in America* (New York: Simon & Schuster, 1989), p. 291; LaDonna Harris, interview with the author, June 24, 2003.

7. Speech by LaDonna Harris, circa early 1970s, folder 24, box 305, FHC, CACRSC, OU, emphasis original.

8. LaDonna Harris, interview with the author, September 25, 2001.

9. Alice Echols, *Daring to Be Bad: Radical Feminism in America 1967–1975* (Minneapolis: University of Minnesota Press, 1989). Echols explores the plethora of differences that emerged among radical feminists and illustrates the failure of the movement to address these differences; Gloria I. Joseph and Jill Lewis, *Common Differences: Conflicts in Black and White Feminist Perspectives* (1981; Boston: South End Press, 1986). Their emphasis is on the divisiveness of race and class in the movement, concluding that women need to explore, accept, and learn from their difference; Christina Hoff Sommers, *Who Stole Feminism: How Women Have Betrayed Women* (New York: Simon and Schuster, 1994). Sommers argues that anyone who dared to criticize the movement found themselves dismissed as an enemy of feminism and equated with the conservative right.

10. Statement of LaDonna Harris, President of Americans for Indian Opportunity, to the United Steelworkers of America, Atlantic City, New Jersey, September 30, 1970, folder 8, box 286, FHC, CACRSC, OU.

11. R. C. Gordon-McCutchan, *The Taos Indians and the Battle for Blue Lake* (Santa Fe, N.M.: Red Crane Books, 1991), pp. 151–52; Alvin M. Josephy Jr., *Red Power: The American Indians' Fight for Freedom* (New York: American Heritage Press, 1971), p. 203. The other Indian members of NCIO included Raymond Nakai (chairman of the Navajo Tribal Council), Roger Jourdain (chairman of the Red Lake Chippewa Tribal Council), William Hensley (an Eskimo member of the Alaska State Legislature), Wendell Chino (chairman of the Mescalero Apache Tribal Council), and Cato Valandra (member of the Rosebud Sioux Tribe of South Dakota). Harris, *LaDonna Harris,* p. 81; LaDonna Harris Profile, box 23, Record Group (hereafter RG) 220, National Council on Indian Opportunity Papers (hereafter NCIO Papers), National Archives and Records Administration (hereafter NARA), College Park, Maryland (hereafter CP).

12. Statement of the Indian Members of the National Council on Indian Opportunity, January 26, 1970, in Josephy, *Red Power,* p. 206; statement of the Indian Members of the National Council on Indian Opportunity to the Chairman and Federal Members, January 26, 1970, pp. 1–2, box 23, RG 220, NCIO Papers, NARA, CP.

13. Gordon-McCutchan, *Taos Indians and the Battle for Blue Lake,* p. 151; Spiro T. Agnew to LaDonna Harris, January 29, 1969, box 1, RG 220, NCIO Papers, NARA, CP.

14. Wauhillau La Hay, "Agnew Better Watch Out for Those Comanches," *Washington Daily News,* August 4, 1969.

15. See Marcia Keegan, *The Taos Pueblo and Its Sacred Blue Lake* (Santa Fe, N.M.: Clear Light Publishers, 1991).

16. LaDonna Harris, interview with the author, March 11, 2002; Gordon-McCutchan, *Taos Indians and the Battle for Blue Lake,* p. 168; *LaDonna Harris,* pp. 88–89.

17. LaDonna Harris, interview with the author, March 11, 2002; Gordon-McCutchan, *Taos Indians and the Battle for Blue Lake,* p. 166; p. 168; Peter Iverson, *"We Are Still Here": American Indians in the Twentieth Century* (Wheeling, Ill.: Harlan Davidson, 1998), p. 140.

18. Gordon-McCutchan, *Taos Indians and the Battle for Blue Lake,* 169; Iverson, *"We Are Still Here,"* p. 140; Fred Harris, interview with the author, October 2, 2001; Laura Harris, interview with the author, July 24, 2003; LaDonna Harris, interview with the author, March 11, 2002.

19. Dan Blackburn, "LaDonna Harris is a Senate Wife With More on Her Mind Than Mid-Afternoon Teas," *Washington Post/Potomac,* May 24, 1970, p. 31; "LaDonna Eyes 'Red Power,'" March 26, 1970, *Times.*

20. Blackburn, "LaDonna Harris is a Senate Wife with More on Her Mind Than Mid-Afternoon Teas," p. 26; "Champion of the Indian —LaDonna Crawford Harris," *New York Times*, July 11, 1970, section L, p. 16.

21. "Reports of Committees at New Directions Conference," June 1972, series 1, box 3, LHC, NAES College.

22. Minutes from AIO meeting, January 16, 1971, OIO Corporation Book n. 2, Oklahomans for Indian Opportunity, Norman, Oklahoma; see George Castile, *To Show Heart: Native American Self-Determination and Federal Indian Policy, 1960–1975* (Tucson: University of Arizona Press, 1998).

23. President Richard Nixon's message to Congress on Indian affairs, July 8, 1970, in Josephy, *Red Power*, p. 225; pp. 228–29.

24. Terry Morris, "LaDonna Harris: A Woman Who Gives a Damn," *Redbook Magazine*, February 1970, p. 117.

25. LaDonna Harris, Testimony submitted to the Subcommittee on Indian Affairs, House of Representatives, April 11, 1973, pp. 3–4, series 1, box 32, LHC, NAES College.

26. LaDonna Harris, Testimony submitted to the Subcommittee on Indian Affairs, House of Representatives, April 11, 1973, pp. 3–4, series 1, box 32, LHC, NAES College.

27. Statement by LaDonna Harris on "Speaking Freely," March 28, 1971, series 2, box 35, LHC, NAES College.

28. Statement by LaDonna Harris on Contributions of Tribal People to the Contemporary World, date unknown, series 1, box 29, LHC, NAES College.

29. LaDonna Harris, interview with the author, September 25, 2001; Melvin Small, *The Presidency of Richard Nixon* (Lawrence: University Press of Kansas, 1990); LaDonna Harris, interview with the author, September 25, 2001.

30. LaDonna Harris to Albert M. Miller, June 2, 1978, series 1, box 8, LHC, NAES College, emphasis original.

31. Americans for Indian Opportunity, "Red Alert," 1976, series 1, box 9, LHC, NAES College; each of the issues mentioned were specific topics in AIO "Red Alert" papers, series 3, box 9-10, LHC, NAES College.

32. Rich Nafziger, "A Violation of Trust: Federal Management of Indian Forest Lands," Red Paper, Americans for Indian Opportunity, 1976, series 3, box 10, LHC, NAES College.

33. "Americans for Indian Opportunity," *Civil Rights Digest* (Spring 1971): 17.

34. LaDonna Harris to Benjamin S. Rosenthal and Paul Findley, August 30, 1976, series 1, box 32, LHC, NAES College; Manuel Lujan Jr. to LaDonna Harris, July 24, 1978, series 1, box 32, LHC, NAES College.

35. LaDonna Harris, interview with the author, November 20, 2000, p. 40.

36. LaDonna Harris, interview with the author, November 20, 2000, p. 39.

37. LaDonna Harris, interview with the author, November 20, 2000, pp. 17–18.

38. LaDonna Harris to Carl Albert, January 27, 1975, folder 16, box 215, CAC, CACRSC, OU.

39. Barbara Blum, interview with the author, September 12, 2003.

40. Beverly Saffa Stapleton, interview with the author, September 23, 2001.

41. Harris, *Potomac Fever,* p. x; *LaDonna Harris,* p. 111.

42. LaDonna Harris to Joe Sando, April 13, 1980, series 2, box 23, LHC, NAES College; *LaDonna Harris,* p. 112.

43. Iola Hayden, interview with the author, March 27, 2001; LaDonna Harris, interview with the author, September 25, 2001.

44. Rusty Brown, "How LaDonna Harris Faces a Turning Point in Life," *Albuquerque Tribune,* January 12, 1982, p. A-6; Kathy Newcombe, interview with the author, September 12, 2001; Aulena Gibson, interview with the author, October 2, 2001; Laura Harris, interview with the author, July 24, 2003.

3—Beloved Woman Politicized

1. Mankiller/Wallis interview, January 5, 1992, p. 3, folder 6, box 43, Wilma Mankiller Collection (hereafter WMC), Western History Collection (hereafter WHC), University of Oklahoma (hereafter OU).

2. Mankiller and Wallis, *Mankiller,* pp. 34–35.

3. Mankiller and Wallis, *Mankiller,* pp. 37–38, 44.

4. See Donald L. Fixico, *Termination and Relocation: Federal Indian Policy, 1945–1960* (Albuquerque: University of New Mexico Press, 1986); Susan Lobo, ed., *Urban Voices: The Bay Area American Indian Community* (Tucson: University of Arizona Press, 2002), p. 24.

5. Sam Howe Verhovek, "Mankiller's Life Chronicled in New Book: Chief of Cherokee Nation Went on Own Trail of Tears," *Journal Record,* November 5, 1993; Sam Howe Verhovek, "At Work with Chief Wilma Mankiller: the Name's the Most and Least of Her," *New York Times,* November 4, 1993, p. C1; Lobo, *Urban Voices,* pp. 19, 29.

6. "Chief of the Cherokee," p. 190, series 1, box 19, LHC, NAES College.

7. Mankiller and Wallis, *Mankiller,* p. 99; p. 103; Judith Anne Antell, "American Indian Women Activists" (Ph.D. diss., University of California, Berkeley, 1989), pp. 104–105.

8. Donald Fixico, *The Urban Indian Experience in America* (Albuquerque: University of New Mexico Press, 2000), p. 58; Susan Lobo, "Is Urban a Person or a Place: Characteristics of Urban Indian Country," in *American Indians and the Urban Experience,* ed. Susan Lobo and Kurt Peters (Walnut Creek, Calif.: AltaMira Press, 2001), p. 75.

9. Mankiller and Wallis, *Mankiller,* p. 115; Wilma Mankiller, foreword to *Urban Voices,* ed. Susan Lobo, p. xv; Fixico, *The Urban Indian Experience in America,* p. 24; David Farber, *The Age of Great Dreams: America in the 1960s* (New York: Hill and Wang, 1994); Edward P. Morgan, *The Sixties Experience: Hard Lessons about Modern America* (Philadelphia: Temple University Press, 1991).

10. Mankiller and Wallis, *Mankiller,* pp. 148-54; See Richard Griswold del Castillo and Richard A. Garcia, *Caesar Chavez: A Triumph of Spirit* (Norman: University of Oklahoma Press, 1995); Mankiller and Wallis, *Mankiller,* p. 154.

11. Mankiller and Wallis, *Mankiller,* p. 190; Paul Chaat Smith and Robert Allen Warrior, *Like a Hurricane: The Indian Movement from Alcatraz to Wounded Knee* (New York: New Press, 1996), pp. 12-13.

12. Smith and Warrior, *Like a Hurricane,* pp. 12-13; Iverson, *"We Are Still Here,"* pp. 149-51.

13. Fixico, *The Urban Indian Experience in America,* p. 180; Mankiller and Wallis, *Mankiller,* pp. 192-93; p. 157; Mankiller/Wallis interview for autobiography, November 5, 1991, p. 10, folder 5, box 43, WMC, WHC, OU; Troy Johnson, Joane Nagel, and Duane Champagne, eds., *American Indian Activism: Alcatraz to the Longest Walk* (Urbana: University of Illinois Press, 1997), pp. 30-31.

14. Mankiller and Wallis, *Mankiller,* pp. 203-4; Pit River Tribal Council to President Richard M. Nixon, August 30, 1970, box 71, RG 220, NCIO Papers, NARA, CP; Deputy Solicitor Raymond C. Coulter, Department of the Interior, to Raymond Lego, Pit River Tribal Council, November 18, 1970, box 71, RG 220, NCIO Papers, NARA, CP.

15. For a firsthand account of the events of October 27, 1970, see Daryl B. Wilson, "The Pit River Challenge," *Chronicles of American Indian Protest,* ed., Council on Interracial Books for Children (Greenwich, Conn: Fawcett, 1971), pp. 322-27; Mankiller and Wallis, *Mankiller,* p. 204; Johnson, Nagel, and Champagne, *American Indian Activism,* p. 30; Wilma Mankiller, *Every Day Is a Good Day: Reflections by Contemporary Indigenous Women* (Golden, Colo.: Fulcrum, 2004), p. 84.

16. Mankiller and Wallis, *Mankiller,* pp. 202-3.

17. Betty Friedan, *The Feminine Mystique* (New York: Dell, 1963). In this best-selling work, Friedan challenged the notion that women's greatest sense of fulfillment should come from being wives and

mothers and articulated the sense many women had that their lives were incomplete; Mankiller and Wallis, *Mankiller,* 157.

18. Mankiller and Wallis, *Mankiller,* p. 159; Mankiller/Wallis interview, November 5, 1991, pp. 14–15, folder 5, box 43, WMC, WHC OU; unidentified newspaper article, folder 1, box 5, WMC, WHC, OU; Mankiller and Wallis, *Mankiller,* p. 159.

19. Mankiller and Wallis, *Mankiller,* p. 159.

20. Mankiller and Wallis, *Mankiller,* p. 159; pp. 213–16; Gina Olaya, interview with the author, March 17, 2004.

21. Mankiller and Wallis, *Mankiller,* p. 219; Charlie Soap and Thomas Muskrat to Applicants, March 24, 1983, folder 3, box 37, WMC, WHC, OU; Wilma Mankiller to Housing Participants, October 6, 1983, folder 3, box 37, WMC, WHC, OU; Wilma Mankiller to Housing Participants, May 11, 1984, folder 3, box 37, WMC, WHC, OU.

22. Wilma Mankiller, sample chapter from "Coming Into Office," p. 4, folder 10, box 43, WMC, WHC, OU; Ross O. Swimmer, interview with the author, June 21, 2001.

23. Ross Swimmer, interview with the author, June 21, 2001.

24. Lynn Howard, interview with the author, October 17, 2001; Mankiller/Wallis Interview, January 5, 1992, p. 2, folder 6, box 43, WMC, WHC, OU; Ross Swimmer, interview with the author, June 21, 2001.

25. Mankiller/Wallis interview, January 5, 1992, p. 3, folder 6, box 43, WMC, WHC, OU; Gina Olaya, interview with the author, March 17, 2004.

26. Mankiller/Wallis interview, January 5, 1992, p. 3, folder 6, box 43, WMC, WHC, OU; p. 5; Mankiller, *Every Day Is a Good Day,* p. 150; p. 151; Mankiller/Wallis interview, January 5, 1992, p. 3, folder 6, box 43, WMC, WHC, OU, p. 6.

27. Mankiller/Wallis interview, January 5, 1992, p. 4, folder 6, box 43, WMC, WHC, OU; Wilma Mankiller, "Entering the Twenty-First Century—On Our Own Terms," in *A Voice of Our Own: Leading American Women Celebrate the Right to Vote,* ed. Nancy Neuman (San Francisco: Jossey-Bass, 1996), p. 213; Mankiller/Wallis interview, January 5, 1992, p. 9; "Cherokee Chief Fills Many Roles in Life," unidentified newspaper, circa 1992, folder 11, box 10 WMC, WHC, OU.

28. *Cherokee Advocate* 8, no. 3, election 83, p. 2; "Dreadfulwater Is Neutral in Runoff," 1983, unidentified newspaper clipping, Ross O. Swimmer private papers inherited from his secretary, Carol Allison (hereafter Swimmer private papers); for a discussion of Mankiller's political rhetoric, see Janis King, "Justificatory Rhetoric for a Female Political Candidate: A Case Study of Wilma Mankiller," *Women's Studies in Communication* 13 (Fall 1990): 21–38.

29. Mankiller/Wallis interview, January 5, 1992, p. 10, box 43, WMC, WHC, OU.

30. Mankiller/Wallis interview, January 5, 1992, p. 10, box 43, WMC, WHC, OU; Barbara Starr Scott and Wathene Young, political advertisement with quote from Rachael Lawrence, 1983 election, Swimmer private papers; "1983 Election," Ross Swimmer Collection (hereafter RSC), Cherokee National Archives (hereafter CNA), Tahlequah, Oklahoma.

31. Isabel Baker, interview with the author, July 14, 2001; Sandra Ketcher, interview with the author, June 12, 2001; Ross Swimmer, interview with the author, June 21, 2001; Sandra Ketcher, interview with the author, June 12, 2001.

32. Mankiller/Wallis Interview, November 14, 1991, p. 20 and p.11, folder 5, box 43, WMC, WHC, OU, p. 11.

33. Wilma Mankiller to Ross Swimmer, circa summer 1983, p. 2, Swimmer private papers; for a discussion of the scrutiny female politicians face including how they dress, see Cindy Simon Rosenthal, *When Women Lead: Integrative Leadership in State Legislatures* (New York: Oxford University Press, 1998).

34. Mankiller, *Every Day Is a Good Day,* p. 150.

35. Wilma Mankiller, "The Changing Role of American Indian Women Today," April 4, 1989, Honors Week keynote address, video recording, Northern Arizona University.

36. Mankiller and Wallis, *Mankiller,* p. 243. It should also be noted that despite numerous attempts, it was never possible to interview Barbara Starr Scott, Wathene Young, or Patsy Morton; Wilma Mankiller to Daniel Bomberry, August 12, 1983, folder 13, box 8, WMC, WHC, OU; whereas eastern Oklahoma is a conservative Republican stronghold, mainstream party politics does not appear to directly affect the selection of tribal officials. Candidates run on specific issues, and their affiliation with national political parties is typically of little consequence.

37. Mankiller and Wallis, *Mankiller,* pp. 236–38.

38. Ross Swimmer, interview with the author, June 21, 2001; Mankiller/Wallis Interview, January 5, 1992, p. 13, folder 6, box 43, WMC, WHC, OU.

39. Mankiller, *Every Day Is a Good Day,* p. 152.

40. Mankiller, *Every Day Is a Good Day,* p. 152; Mankiller/Wallis interview, January 5, 1992, p. 13, folder 6, box 43, WMC, WHC, OU; Cherokee Tribal Council meeting minutes, December 14, 1985, p. 8, folder 3, box 4, WMC, WHC, OU.

41. Cherokee Tribal Council meeting minutes, December 14, 1985, p. 14, folder 3, box 4, WMC, WHC, OU; Mankiller/Wallis interview, January 5, 1992, p. 15, folder 6, box 43, WMC, WHC, OU; Donna Hales, "First Woman Chief Begins Second Term," *Phoenix,* July 20, 1987.

42. Cherokee Tribal Election Committee meeting minutes, April 23, 1987, pp. 1–2, folder 2, box 18, WMC, WHC, OU.

43. Catherine C. Robbins, "Expanding Power for Indian Women," *New York Times*, May 26, 1987, p. C1; Jo Higginbotham, "Cherokee Autumn's Warrior," p. 12, April 11, 1994, folder 11, box 43, WMC, WHC, OU, emphasis original.

44. Mankiller/Wallis interview, January 5, 1992, p. 14, folder 6, box 43, WMC, WHC, OU.

45. Election Committee meeting minutes, July 21, 1987, p. 1, folder 2, box 17, WMC, WHC, OU; Mankiller and Wallis, *Mankiller*, pp. 249–50; p. xvii.

46. Mankiller and Wallis, *Mankiller*, p. 246; Gary Perceful, "Ms. Mankiller 'Thrilled' by Ms. Listing," *Tulsa World*, section A 19, December 17, 1987; Mankiller and Wallis, *Mankiller*, p. 20.

47. Wilma Mankiller to Carl Shaw, assistant to the assistant secretary, Indian Affairs, and director, Office of Public Affairs, December 28, 1993, folder 13, box 41, WMC, WHC, OU.

48. See Devon A. Mihesuah, *American Indians: Stereotypes and Realities* (Atlanta: Clarity Press, 1996), pp. 61–66; Laura F. Klein and Lillian A. Ackerman, *Women and Power in Native North America* (Norman: University of Oklahoma Press, 1995), pp. 222–29; Theda Perdue, *Cherokee Women: Gender and Cultural Change, 1700–1835* (Lincoln: University of Nebraska Press, 1998), pp. 38–39.

49. Perdue, *Cherokee Women*, p. 185; p. 3; p. 195.

50. For a critique of this tendency, see Cynthia Eller, *The Myth of Matriarchal Prehistory: Why an Invented Past Won't Give Women a Future* (Boston: Beacon Press, 2000); title and author unknown, p. 2, folder 25, box 45, WMC, WHC, OU. For a critique of this static view of gender relations among Indians, see Claudio Saunt, *A New Order of Things: Property, Power, and the Transformation of the Creek Indians, 1733–1816* (Cambridge: Cambridge University Press, 1999). Saunt argues that "balance, harmony, and tradition, so often used to describe Native American gender relations before the incursion of Western patriarchy, fail to describe the dynamic relationship between Creek men and women in the eighteenth century" (p. 140).

51. Mankiller, *Every Day Is a Good Day*, p. 102.

52. Lynn Howard, interview with the author, October 17, 2001; see, for instance, Connie Koenenn, "Heart of a Nation," *Los Angeles Times*, November 13, 1993, p. E1; Ross Swimmer, interview with the author, June 21, 2001. According to Swimmer, reporters wanted to refer to her as the first female chief of an Indian tribe but instead agreed to the wording "first female chief of a major Indian tribe" or "first female chief of the second largest Indian tribe," after learning that a number of other women served as chief or chairperson of their tribes; Lynn Howard, interview with the author, October 17, 2001.

53. "Chief of Tribe Eyes New Term" *Daily Oklahoman*, July 21, 1975, p. 16; "The Men Picked Her as Chief," unidentified newspaper,

February 13, 1976, series 1, box 5, LHC, NAES College; Jo Sandin, "Cherokee Chief Personifies New Face of Leadership," *Milwaukee Journal,* November 14, 1993. In this interview, as in many others, Mankiller jokingly insisted that she earned the name "Mankiller." She also related a story in which a young man, uncertain as to how to address her, suggested he call her "chiefette" because he believed "chief" was a masculine term. Instead, Mankiller suggested he address her as "Ms. Chief" or "mischief."

54. Linda Lowery, *Wilma Mankiller,* illustrations by Janice Lee Porter (Minneapolis: Carolrhoda Books, 1996), pp. 41–42.

55. Bruce Glassman, *Wilma Mankiller: Chief of the Cherokee Nation,* in *The Library of Famous Women* series (New York: Blackbirch Press, 1992), p. 39.

56. Susan Allison Gimmel, "Wilma Mankiller: A Chief and her People," *Oklahoma Woman,* November 1999, p. 4.

57. Mankiller/Wallis interview, January 5, 1992, p. 10, folder 6, box 43, WMC, WHC, OU; Mankiller and Wallis, *Mankiller,* p. 247.

58. The following works explore the divisions within the feminist movement: Echols, *Daring to be Bad*; Evans, *Personal Politics*; Joseph and Lewis, *Common Differences*; and Sommers, *Who Stole Feminism.*

59. John Ketcher, interview with the author, July 27, 2001; Lynn Howard, interview with the author, October 17, 2001; "Woman Chief Blazing an Indian Trail," *Mother Jones,* September 1986, p. 8; "Inaugural Address Charts Future Policy," *Cherokee Advocate* 10, no. 1 (January 1986): 11A.

60. Wilma Mankiller, "The Changing Role of American Indian Women Today."

4—Tribal Governance and Indian Identity

1. Mike Synar, Statement about Wilma Mankiller, RSC, CNA.

2. Mankiller and Wallis, *Mankiller,* p. xvii. For an overview of some of Mankiller's major accomplishments and challenges during her time in office, see Brad Agnew, "Wilma Mankiller," in *The New Warriors,* ed. Edmunds, pp. 220–27.

3. "Cherokee Nation Principal Chief Wilma P. Mankiller," Cherokee Nation Communications release, circa 1990–1991, folder 2, box 6, WMC, WHC, OU; Wilma Mankiller to Tom Bias, April 13, 1994, folder 11, box 1, WMC, WHC, OU.

4. United States Senator David Boren to Wilma Mankiller, October 6, 1986, folder 11, box 3, WMC, WHC, OU; Wilma Mankiller to Jim Joseph, executive director of Council on Foundations, January 28, 1985, folder 5, box 7, WMC, WHC, OU.

5. Mankiller and Wallis, *Mankiller,* pp. xxi–xxii; "Having a Good Mind: A Conversation with Wilma Mankiller," 1988, video recording.

6. Lynn Howard, interview with the author, October 17, 2001; Ellen Knickmeyer, "Wilma Mankiller: Cherokee Chief has Knack for Building Tribe's Success," *Daily Oklahoman,* December 28, 1987, p. 9.

7. To Wilma Mankiller, August 19, 1992, folder 1, box 8, WMC, WHC, OU. The names of individuals who wrote to Wilma Mankiller have been omitted to protect their privacy, unless they represented a particular group or organization or wrote to her in some other official capacity; to Wilma Mankiller, March 6, 1994, folder 15, box 2, WMC, WHC, OU.

8. Memo from Wilma Mankiller to Jerry Thompson, January 10, 1991, folder 10, box 17, WMC, WHC, OU.

9. Wilma Mankiller, testimony before the Subcommittee on Employment Opportunities, May 15, 1986, folder 18, box 34, WMC, WHC, OU; Roger D. Semerad, assistant secretary of labor, to Wilma Mankiller, June 27, 1986, folder 18, box 34, WMC, WHC, OU.

10. Mankiller/Wallis interview, January 27, 1992, p. 6, folder 7, box 43, WMC, WHC, OU; Mankiller/Wallis interview, January 27, 1992, p. 6, folder 7, box 43, WMC, WHC, OU; Lynn Howard, interview with the author, October 17, 2001.

11. Sandy Garret, Oklahoma state superintendent of public instruction, to Wilma Mankiller, February 3, 1992, folder 6, box 4, WMC, WHC, OU; Wilma Mankiller to Phyllis Wheeler, executive director of Tahlequah Project Inc., June 29, 1991, folder 2, box 4, WMC, WHC, OU.

12. Lynn Howard, interview with the author, October 17, 2001; Connie Koenenn, "Heart of a Nation," *Los Angeles Times,* pp. E1, E3.

13. "Self-Governance Compact between the Cherokee Nation and United States," July 2, 1990, signed by assistant secretary of the Interior, Eddie Brown and Principal Chief Wilma Mankiller, folder 16, box 18, WMC, WHC, OU; "The Tobacco Wars: Message from the Chief," *Cherokee Advocate* 16, nos. 7/8 (July/August 1992): 6.

14. Wilma Mankiller to Alan Parker, director of the National Indian Policy Center, February 20, 1991, folder 4, box 18, WMC, WHC, OU; Ross Swimmer to Wilma Mankiller, March 13, 1991, folder 1, box 26, WMC, WHC, OU.

15. Day Flower, educational director of the Pan American Indian Association to Wilma Mankiller, May 11, 1993, folder 9, box 16, WMC, WHC, OU; Chief Walking Bear of the Amonsoquath Tribe to Wilma Mankiller, October 20, 1993, folder 9, box 16, WMC, WHC, OU.

16. Luis Zapata to Wilma Mankiller, May 25, 1993, folder 9, box 16, WMC, WHC, OU, emphasis original.

17. Anthony Q. Vaughan, Mary Trail of Tears Long House, to Wilma Mankiller, April 23, 1993, folder 8, box 16, WMC, WHC, OU; to

Wilma Mankiller, March 9, 1993, folder 8, box 16, WMC, WHC, OU; to Wilma Mankiller, February 26, 1993, folder 8, box 16, WMC, WHC, OU.

18. Wilma Mankiller to Governor Zell Miller, May 4, 1993, folder 9, box 16, WMC, WHC, OU.

19. "Cherokee/Delaware Discussions and Chronology," prepared for meeting with Wilma Mankiller, March 30, 1994, folder 12, box 9, WMC, WHC, OU.

20. To Wilma Mankiller, May 22, 1994, folder 12, box 9, WMC, WHC, OU.

21. Tribal/State Tobacco Tax Compact between the Cherokee Nation and the State of Oklahoma, June 8, 1992, p. 2; Tribal/State Tobacco Tax Compact between the Cherokee Nation and the State of Oklahoma, June 8, 1992, p. 1.

22. Leaford Bearskin, chief of the Wyandotte Tribe to Wilma Mankiller, March 6, 1990, folder 18, box 17, WMC, WHC, OU; Leaford Bearskin to Wilma Mankiller, May 21, 1992, folder 16, box 17, WMC, WHC, OU; cartoon depicting Mankiller, folder 16, box 17, WMC, WHC, OU.

23. Wilma Mankiller to Leaford Bearskin, May 28, 1992, folder 16, box 17, WMC, WHC, OU.

24. Gary McAdams, president of the Wichita and Affiliated Tribes, to Wilma Mankiller, June 2, 1992, folder 16, box 17, WMC, WHC, OU; George Wickliffe, letter to the editor, circa spring 1993, unidentified newspaper, folder 2, box 5, WMC Collection, WHC, OU.

25. See Deloria, *Playing Indian*; see C. Matthew Snipp, *American Indians: First of this Land* (New York: Russell Sage Foundation, 1989); Nagel, *American Indian Ethnic Renewal,* p. 11; "Membership Soars during Last Four Years" *Cherokee Phoenix,* February 22, 1991, p. 1; to Wilma Mankiller, March 22, 1994, folder 11, box 1, WMC, WHC, OU; to Wilma Mankiller, November 29, 1993, folder 6, box 1, WMC, WHC, OU.

26. To Wilma Mankiller, January 6, 1991, folder 7, box 16, WMC, WHC, OU; to Wilma Mankiller, February 4, 1991, folder 7, box 16, WMC, WHC, OU; to Wilma Mankiller, December 30, 1993, folder 14, box 2, WMC, WHC, OU.

27. James A. Clifton, ed., *Being and Becoming Indian: Biographical Studies of North American Frontiers* (Chicago: Dorsey Press, 1989), p. 17; to Wilma Mankiller, February 20, 1991, folder 7, box 16, WMC, WHC, OU; to Wilma Mankiller, January 26, 1989, folder 6, box 16, WMC, WHC, OU.

28. The growing public fixation on Indianness is very much an outgrowth of modern noble savagery, which tends to romanticize Indians as being implicitly more environmentally conscientious, more spiritual, more pure, and historically more committed to gender equality than white Americans; unidentified letter to Wilma

Mankiller, folder 8, box 1, WMC, WHC, OU; Lynn Howard, former communications director for the Cherokee Nation, interview with the author, October 17, 2001.

29. To Wilma Mankiller, November 26, 1992, folder 1, box 8, WMC, WHC, OU; to Wilma Mankiller, September 14, 1991, folder 3, box 6, WMC, WHC, OU.

30. "Lawmakers Blasted by Cherokee Chief: Mankiller Cites Image Woes," *Daily Oklahoman*, February 23, 1992, p. 16; Wilma Mankiller to Michael Brown, president and CEO of Foxwoods Resort and Casino, January 9, 1996, folder 1, box 12, WMC, WHC, OU; "Woman Breaks Indian Stereotypes in Career," unidentified newspaper clipping, circa 1985, folder Mankiller, Wilma P., box 7, RSC, CNA; John Hughes, "Cherokee Nation Looks Up to Chief Mankiller," *Chicago Tribune*, May 14, 1986, p. 19.

31. To Wilma Mankiller, October 5, 1992, folder 5, box 6, WMC, OU; to Wilma Mankiller, February 22, 1993, folder 8, box 1, WMC, WHC, OU; from Wilma Mankiller, March 3, 1993, folder 8, box 1, WMC, WHC, OU.

32. Wilma Mankiller to W. T. Jeffers, World Changers, Inc., September 20, 1994, folder 17, box 2, WMC, WHC, OU.

33. To Wilma Mankiller, May 20, 1995, folder 4, box 3, WMC, WHC, OU; to Wilma Mankiller, August 18, 1991, emphasis original, folder 3, box 6, WMC, WHC, OU.

34. Lynn Howard, interview with the author, October 17, 2001.

35. To Wilma Mankiller, January 3, 1994, folder 13, box 41, WMC, WHC, OU; to Wilma Mankiller, May 12, 1995, folder 4, box 3, WMC, WHC, OU; to Wilma Mankiller, October 6, 1994, folder 1, box 3, WMC, WHC, OU; to Wilma Mankiller, March 29, 1994, folder 13, box 41, WMC, WHC, OU; to Wilma Mankiller, April 26, 1995, folder 13, box 41, WMC, WHC, OU.

36. To Wilma Mankiller, February 21, 1993, folder 8, box 1, WMC, WHC, OU; to Wilma Mankiller, July 13, 1995; to Wilma Mankiller, June 19, 1995, folder 5, box 3, WMC, WHC, OU; to Wilma Mankiller, March 13, 1993, folder 1 box 16, WMC, WHC, OU; to Wilma Mankiller, April 11, 1994, folder 11, box 1, WMC, WHC, OU.

37. "Mankiller Says She Won't Seek Third Term," *Cherokee Advocate* 18, no. 5 (May 1994): 1, 6.

38. Lynn Howard, interview with the author, October 17, 2001; Oklahoma Lieutenant Governor Jack Mildren to Wilma Mankiller, June 2, 1994, folder 11, box 1, WMC, WHC, OU.

5—Politics and Policy

1. LaDonna Harris, "Contributions of Tribal People To the Contemporary World," speech, date unknown, series 1, box 29, LHC,

NAES College; see Jere Bishop Franco, *Crossing the Pond: The Native American Effort in World War II* (Denton: University of North Texas Press, 1999); Bernstein, *American Indians and World War II*; Fixico, *Termination and Relocation*, p. 196.

2. For a discussion of Collier's Indian New Deal, see Kenneth R. Philp, *John Collier's Crusade for Indian Reform: 1920–1954* (Tucson: University of Arizona Press, 1977); LaDonna Harris, interview with the author, September 25, 2001; Harris, *LaDonna Harris*, p. 20.

3. LaDonna Harris to Ronald Van Dunk, Ramapuogh Mountain Indian Tribe, December 12, 1984, series 1, box 19, LHC, WHC, OU.

4. Mankiller and Wallis, *Mankiller*, p. 63.

5. See Castile, *To Show Heart.* He argues that Nixon essentially supported Indian self-determination as a public relations tool to boost his image among minority groups. Works that place greater emphasis on Native American activism in explaining the shift in policy to self-determination include Josephy, *Red Power;* Stephen Cornell, *Return of the Native: American Indian Political Resurgence* (New York: Oxford University Press, 1988); Smith and Warrior, *Like a Hurricane.* For an excellent overview of activism and self-determination, see Troy R. Johnson, "The Roots of Contemporary Native American Activism," *American Indian Culture and Research Journal* 20, no. 2, (1996): 127–54.

6. United States Senate Select Committee on Indian Affairs, "1953 Termination Resolution Finally Repealed," press release, April 21, 1988, series 1, box 22, LHC, NAES College; President Richard Nixon's message to Congress on Indian affairs, July 8, 1970, in Josephy, *Red Power,* p. 228.

7. LaDonna Harris to Congressman Peter deFrazio, March 30, 1988, series 1, box 23, LHC, NAES College; statement of Mrs. Fred R. Harris before the Education and Labor Committee, 90th Cong., 1st sess., *Congressional Record—Senate* 113, pt. 14 (July 13, 1967): 9581.

8. For a discussion of OIO community development efforts in the Cherokee Nation, see Cobb, "'US Indians Understand the Basics,'" 41–66; and "A War for Self-Determination: Culture, Poverty, and the Politics of Indian Community Action, 1960–1975" Ph.D. diss., University of Oklahoma, 2003); Ross Swimmer, interview with author, June 21, 2001.

9. Reuben A. Snake Jr., tribal chairman, Winnebago Tribe of Nebraska to LaDonna Harris, November 15, 1984, series 1, box 39, LHC, NAES College; Ernest House Sr., tribal chairman, Ute Mountain Tribal Council, to LaDonna Harris, October 6, 1987, series 1, box 22, LHC, NAES College.

10. LaDonna Harris to AIO mailing list, December 17, 1979, series 3, box 6, LHC, NAES College.

11. "New Federalism: The Role of the Indian Community," Red Paper, Americans for Indian Opportunity, 1981, series 3, box 11, LHC, NAES College.

12. "To Govern and to be Governed: American Indian Tribal Governments at the Crossroads," Americans for Indian Opportunity Publication, 1983, series 3, box 11, LHC, NAES College.

13. "Self Governance Compact between the Cherokee Nation and United States," October 1, 1990, folder 16, box 18, WMC, WHC, OU.

14. Wilma Mankiller, testimony before the House Interior Appropriations Subcommittee, March 27, 1995, folder 18, box 13, WMC, WHC, OU.

15. Laura Harris, interview with the author, July 24, 2003; Barbara Blum, interview with the author, September 12, 2003.

16. U.S. Senator Daniel K. Inouye, Senate Select Committee on Indian Affairs, to LaDonna Harris, March 26, 1987, series 1, box 37, LHC, NAES College; LaDonna Harris, interview with the author, March 11, 2002; U.S. Senator John D. Rockefeller IV to LaDonna Harris, October 31, 1986, series 1, box 37, LHC, NAES College; LaDonna Harris to U.S. Senator Jeff Bingaman, May 2, 1985, series 1, box 37, LHC, NAES College; Americans for Indian Opportunity Press Release, "Americans for Indian Opportunity Celebrates 30th Anniversary," 2000.

17. Wilma Mankiller to United States Senator Don Nickles, April 23, 1993, folder 6, box 3, WMC, WHC, OU; Wilma Mankiller to United States Senator David Boren, November 1, 1993, folder 2, box 2, WMC, WHC, OU.

18. LaDonna Harris, interview with the author, September 25, 2001; Spiro Agnew to LaDonna Harris, September 2, 1970, series 1, box 13 LHC, NAES College; Gerald R. Ford to LaDonna Harris, October 23, 1974, series 1, box 20, LHC, NAES College; Jimmy Carter to LaDonna Harris, February 21, 1978, series 1, box 20, LHC, NAES College; LaDonna Harris to Rosalyn Carter, November 9, 1978, series 1, box 20, LHC, NAES College; Jeanne Grimes, "Comanches Plan for a New Century," *Lawton Constitution,* January 16, 1999, p. 11; Barbara Blum, interview with the author, September 12, 2003.

19. Verhovek, "At Work with Chief Wilma Mankiller: The Name's the Most and Least of Her," p. C10; Wilma Mankiller to David L. Walters, September 3, 1986, folder 5, box 4, WMC, WHC, OU; George Wickliffe, letter to the editor, circa spring 1993, unidentified newspaper, folder 2, box 5, WMC, WHC, OU; Wilma Mankiller to President-Elect Bill Clinton, September 24, 1992, folder 14, box 10, WMC, WHC, OU; President-Elect Bill Clinton to Wilma Mankiller, December 17, 1992, folder 14, box 10, WMC, WHC, OU.

20. LaDonna Harris, interview with the author, September 25, 2001.

21. LaDonna Harris to Wilma Mankiller, January 27, 1991, folder 1, box 7, WMC, WHC, OU; LaDonna Harris to Wilma Mankiller, May 9, 1994, folder 11, box 1, WMC, WHC, OU; LaDonna Harris to Wilma Mankiller, June 2, 1992, folder 1, box 2, WMC,

WHC, OU; Wilma Mankiller to LaDonna Harris, June 5, 1992, folder 1, box 8, WMC, WHC, OU; LaDonna Harris to Jesse Jackson, president of the Rainbow Coalition, December 4, 1992, folder 1, box 2, WMC, WHC, OU.

22. LaDonna Harris to Perry Raglin, California Rural Indian Health Board, February 5, 1981, series 1, box 8, LHC, NAES College.

23. LaDonna Harris to William D. Ruckelshaus, administrator, Environmental Protection Agency, February 2, 1984, series 1, box 37, LHC, NAES College, emphasis original; Wilma Mankiller to LaDonna Harris, December 29, 1986, series 1, box 19, LHC, NAES College.

24. "Indian-ness: Beyond the Melting Pot," March 28, 1971, interview with LaDonna Harris by Edwin Newman, on WNBC-TV "Speaking Freely," series 2, box 35, LHC, NAES College.

25. Mankiller is not alone in her contention that Native Americans and whites have historically held conflicting perceptions of land and the environment. See Winona LaDuke, *All Our Relations: Native Struggles for Land and Life* (Cambridge, Mass.: South End Press, 1999); Donald L. Fixico, *The Invasion of Indian Country in the Twentieth Century: American Capitalism and Tribal Resources* (Niwot: University Press of Colorado, 1998); William Cronon, *Changes in the Land: Indians, Colonists, and the Ecology of New England* (New York: Hill & Wang, 1983). For an alternate view, see Shepard Krech, *The Ecological Indian: Myth and History* (New York: W. W. Norton, 1999); Wilma Mankiller, draft of presentation transcript, The First National People of Color Environmental Leadership Summit, October 24–27, 1991, p. 2, folder 9, box 2, WMC, WHC, OU; pp. 8–9; United States Representative George Miller to Wilma Mankiller, November 12, 1991, folder 12, box 6, WMC, WHC, OU; "Tribal Leaders Encourage Voter Participation, Endorse Clinton," *Cherokee Advocate* 16, no. 11 (November 1992): 8.

26. Wilma Mankiller to Whom It May Concern, May 10, 1989, folder 21, box 44, WMC, WHC, OU; Tommy Thompson, executive director of Tribal Operations for the Cherokee Nation, to Mike Haney, New Comer Band, Seminole Nation, October 1, 1991, folder 23, box 8, WMC, WHC, OU; Wilma Mankiller to John Ketcher and members of the tribal council, May 19, 1993, folder 2, box 45, WMC, WHC, OU.

27. LaDonna Harris to United States Senator James A. McClure, December 15, 1982, series 1, box 37, LHC, NAES College; United States Senators John McCain and Daniel Inouye to Wilma Mankiller, January 21, 1993, folder 6, box 3, WMC, WHC, OU.

28. United States Senators John McCain and Daniel Inouye to Wilma Mankiller, January 21, 1993, folder 6, box 3, WMC, WHC, OU.

29. John Henry Nelson, interview with the author, September 20, 2001; "Indian-ness: Beyond the Melting Pot," series 2, box 35, LHC, NAES College; Barbara Gamarekian, "A Long, Long Way From Oklahoma," *New York Times*, September 25, 1984, p. A22.

30. LaDonna Harris, "Constitutional and Tribal Governance," *The United States Constitution: Roots, Rights, and Responsibilities,* ed. A. E. Dick Howard (Washington: Smithsonian Institution Press, 1992), pp. 115–16; p. 126.

31. Americans for Indian Opportunity Resolution, 1982, series 1, box 25, LHC, NAES College; letter from LaDonna Harris to Karen Milhauser, February 8, 1987, series 1, box 27, LHC, NAES College.

32. LaDonna Harris, speech, circa mid-1980s, series 2, box 13, LHC, NAES College.

33. "Statement on Guatemala by Americans for Indian Opportunity," circa early 1980s, series 1, box 24, LHC, NAES College.

34. Mankiller and Wallis, *Mankiller,* p. 154; "Mankiller Presented Award for Efforts of Civil Rights," *Cherokee Advocate* 16, no. 11 (November 1992): 2; to Wilma Mankiller, January 1, 1992, folder 1, box 10, WMC, WHC, OU; from Wilma Mankiller, February 3, 1992, folder 1, box 10, WMC, WHC, OU.

35. Wilma Mankiller, written statement to Commission on Racial Justice in acceptance of an award, October 16, 1992, folder 10, box 2, WMC, WHC, OU.

6—The Intersection of Feminism and Indianness

1. Wilma Mankiller to "Dear Friends," September 1, 1993, folder 6, box 1, WMC, WHC, OU. Historically women in politics have been unable to avoid the issue of gender role expectations and stereotypes. See Jeane Kilpatrick, *Political Women* (New York: Basic Books, 1974); Chris Corrin, *Feminist Perspectives on Politics* (New York: Longman, 1999); and Sue Tolleson Rinehart, *Gender Consciousness and Politics* (New York: Routledge, 1992).

2. LaDonna Harris, interview with the author, November 20, 2000, p. 25.

3. See Nancy Burns et al., *The Private Roots of Public Action: Gender, Equality, and Political Participation* (Cambridge, Mass.: Harvard University Press, 2001); Lori Ginsberg, *Women and the Work of Benevolence: Morality, Politics, and Class in the Nineteenth-Century United States* (New Haven, Conn.: Yale University Press, 1990); and Ruth Bordin, *Woman and Temperance: The Quest for Power and Liberty 1873–1900* (Philadelphia: Temple University Press, 1981).

4. Maureen O'Dea Caragliano, "Beyond Princess and Squaw: Wilma Mankiller and the Cherokee Gynocentric System" (Master's thesis, San Jose State University, 1997), p. 76; see Gretchen M. Bataille and Kathleen Mullen Sands, *American Indian Women: Telling Their Lives* (Lincoln: University of Nebraska Press, 1984), p. 129; Glenda Riley, "The Historiography of American Indian and Other Western Women," in *Rethinking American Indian History,* ed. Donald

Fixico (Albuquerque, University of New Mexico Press, 1997); Perdue, "Writing the Ethnohistory of Native Women," in *Rethinking American Indian History;* Laura F. Klein and Lillian A. Ackerman, *Women and Power in Native North America* (Norman: University of Oklahoma Press, 1995); Rayna Green, *Women in American Indian Society* (New York: Chelsea House, 1992), Clara Sue Kidwell, "Native American Women," in *The Reader's Companion to U.S. Women's History,* eds. Mankiller et al., pp. 405–10. For a reevaluation of the biased sources on Indian women, see Patricia Albers and Beatrice Medicine, *The Hidden Half: Studies of Plains Indian Women* (Boston: University Press of America, 1983); Evans, *Born for Liberty,* pp. 298–99; Nancy Shoemaker, ed., *Negotiators of Change: Historical Perspectives on Native American Women* (New York: Routledge, 1995); Carolyn Niethammer, *Daughters of the Earth: The Lives and Legends of American Indian Women* (New York: Macmillian, 1977); Gretchen M. Bataille, ed., *Native American Women: A Biographical Dictionary* (New York: Garland Publishing, 1993); Marla Powers, *Oglala Women: Myth, Ritual, and Reality* (Chicago: University of Chicago Press, 1986); and Perdue, *Cherokee Women.*

5. Kidwell, "Native American Women," p. 407.

6. Williams and Harjo, "American Indian Feminism," p. 199.

7. LaDonna Harris, interview with the author, November 20, 2000, p. 42; Mankiller, *Every Day Is a Good Day,* p. 9; p. 8; see, for example, "LaDonna Harris: Indian Powerhouse," p. 178; Mihesuah, *Indigenous American Women,* p. 143; see also Virginia Sutter, "Today's Strength from Yesterday's Tradition—The Continuity of the American Indian Woman," *Frontiers* 6, no. 3 (Fall 1981): 53–57.

8. Wilma Mankiller to "Dear Friends," September 1, 1993, folder 6, box 1, WMC, WHC, OU; United States Representative Susan Molinari to Wilma Mankiller, March 5, 1993, folder 19, box 10, WMC, WHC, OU; Wilma Mankiller to United States Senator David Boren, October 15, 1991, folder 3, box 6, WMC, WHC, OU.

9. Wilma Mankiller to United States Senator David Boren, November 1, 1993, folder 2, box 2, WMC, WHC, OU; United States Senator David Boren to Wilma Mankiller, November 12, 1993; Jane P. Wiseman, district judge, to Wilma Mankiller, August 26, 1993, folder 2, box 2, WMC, WHC, OU.

10. LaDonna Harris to Anne Sandoval, chairwoman of the Sycuan Band of Mission Indians, January 28, 1977, series 1, box 20, LHC, NAES College; LaDonna Harris, interview with the author, September 25, 2001; Roger A. Jourdain, chairman of the Red Lake Band of Chippewa Indians, to LaDonna Harris, December 1, 1981, series 1, box 23, LHC, NAES College; LaDonna Harris, interview with the author, September 25, 2001.

11. Ada Deer to LaDonna Harris, May 22, 1987, series 1, box 19, LHC, NAES College; LaDonna Harris and Ella Mae Horse to Wilma Mankiller, August 13, 1987, folder 11, box 3, WMC, WHC, OU.

12. "Keynote Speaker Urges Political Involvement among Women," unidentified newspaper article, series 2, box 23, LHC, NAES College.

13. LaDonna Harris, interview with the author, September 25, 2001; Ada Deer, interview with the author, September 27, 2001. For a discussion of the Menominee tribe's effort to regain federal recognition, see Nicholas C. Peroff, *Menominee Drums: Tribal Termination and Restoration, 1954–1974* (Norman: University of Oklahoma Press, 1982); Ada Deer to LaDonna Harris, July 26, 1974, series 1, box 6, LHC, NAES College.

14. See Clara Sue Kidwell, "Ada Deer," in *The New Warriors,* ed. Edmunds, pp. 239–60; Campaign support letter from Fred Harris and LaDonna Harris, circa 1978, series 2, box 35, LHC, NAES College; "Ada E. Deer: Democrat for Secretary of State" election pamphlet, series 2, box 35, LHC, NAES College.

15. "Testimony of Principal Chief Wilma P. Mankiller, Cherokee Nation of Oklahoma, in support of Ada E. Deer for confirmation as assistant secretary of interior for Indian affairs, Senate Committee on Indian Affairs," July 15, 1993, p. 2, folder 13, box 19, WMC, WHC, OU, p. 3

16. Wilma Mankiller to Ada Deer, February 22, 1994, folder 15, box 13, WMC, WHC, OU; Ada Deer to Wilma Mankiller, June 27, 1994, folder 15, box 3, WMC, WHC, OU.

17. LaDonna Harris to Wilma Mankiller, October 10, 1994, folder 17, box 2, WMC, WHC, OU; Elizabeth Levitan Spaid, "Challenges of a Cherokee Chief: First Woman to Head Tribe Battles Poverty, Ill Health, and Lack of Jobs and Confidence," *Christian Science Monitor,* June 22, 1992, p. 14; Mankiller, *Every Day Is a Good Day,* p. 183.

18. Clara Nomee, madam chairman, Crow Tribal Council, to Wilma Mankiller, August 4, 1993, folder 1, box 10, WMC, WHC, OU; "Resources in Red Nations: A Conversation with Winona LaDuke, *RAIN* (February–March 1980): 6

19. See Evans, *Personal Politics;* Echols, *Daring to be Bad;* Joseph and Lewis, *Common Differences.* Biographies and autobiographies of Native American women provide some of the best insight into the disconnect between their lives and mainstream white feminism. See Johanna Brand, *The Life and Death of Anna Mae Aquash* (Toronto: James Lorimer & Co., 1978); Mary Crow Dog and Richard Erdoes, *Lakota Woman* (New York: Harper Collins, 1990).

20. Mankiller and Wallis, *Mankiller,* p. x; Connie Koenenn, "Heart of a Nation," *Los Angeles Times,* November 13, 1993, p. E3.

21. Shirley Chisholm, *Unbought and Unbossed* (Boston: Houghton Mifflin, 1970), p. 167; p. 163

22. Bella Abzug, *Bella! Ms. Abzug Goes to Washington,* ed. Mel Ziegler (New York: Saturday Review Press, 1972), p. 6. It is important

to note that the characterization of a strong and outspoken woman as unfeminine or manhating is one of the negative stereotypes political women have often been forced to confront.

23. Roger A. Jourdain, chairman of the Red Lake Band of Chippewa Indians, to LaDonna Harris, December 1, 1981, series 1, box 23, LHC, NAES College; United States Representative Bella Abzug to "Dear Friend," December 13, 1975, series 1, box 32, LHC, NAES College.

24. For a discussion of how the presence of women in even the most prestigious military academy in the United States is becoming less remarkable with each new class of cadets, see Lance Janda, *Stronger Than Custom: West Point and the Admission of Women* (Westport, Conn.: Praeger, 2002), pp. 198–200.

25. Mankiller/Wallis interview, January 27, 1992, p. 9, folder 7, box 43, WMC, WHC, OU; Harris, *LaDonna Harris,* p. 125; Kathryn Harris, interview with the author, July 28, 2003.

26. LaDonna Harris biographical profile, p. 1, folder 1, box 2, WMC, WHC, OU.

SELECTED BIBLIOGRAPHY

Archival Collections

Carl Albert Congressional Archives, University of Oklahoma, Norman, Oklahoma.
    Carl Albert Papers
    Fred R. Harris Collection and Papers (including papers of LaDonna Harris)

Cherokee National Archives, Tahlequah, Oklahoma.
    Cherokee Advocate
    Ross O. Swimmer Papers

Museum of the Great Plains, Lawton, Oklahoma.
    Fred R. Harris Papers
    Sarah "Betty" Owens Papers

National Archives and Records Administration, College Park, Maryland.
    National Council on Indian Opportunity Papers

Native American Educational Studies (NAES) College, Chicago, Illinois.
    LaDonna Harris Papers

Northeastern State University, Tahlequah, Oklahoma.
    Wilma P. Mankiller Newspaper Clippings

Oklahoma Historical Society, Oklahoma City, Oklahoma.
    Cherokee Advocate

Oklahomans for Indian Opportunity (OIO), Norman, Oklahoma.
    OIO Corporation Books, nos. 1 and 2

Western History Collection, University of Oklahoma, Norman, Oklahoma.
    Wilma P. Mankiller Papers

Interviews

(Note: All interviews were conducted by the author. Tape recordings and/or transcripts of each are in the author's possession).

Baker, Isabel. July 14, 2001. Tahlequah, Oklahoma.

Blum, Barbara. September 12, 2003. Telephone interview.

Deer, Ada. September 27, 2001. Telephone interview.

Gibson, Aulena. October 2, 2001. Lawton, Oklahoma.

Harris, Fred. October 2, 2001. Telephone interview.

Harris, LaDonna. November 20, 2000. Bernalilo, New Mexico; September 25, 2001. Telephone interview; June 24, 2003. Telephone interview; October 15, 2003. Telephone interview.

Harris, Laura. July 24, 2003. Telephone interview.

Hayden, Iola. March 27, 2001. Norman, Oklahoma.

Howard, Lynn. October 17, 2001. Telephone interview.

Ketcher, John. July 27, 2001. Tahlequah, Oklahoma.

Ketcher, Sandra. June 12, 2001. Tahlequah, Oklahoma.

Nelson, John Henry. September 20, 2001. Lawton, Oklahoma.

Newcombe, Kathy. September 12, 2001. Lawton, Oklahoma.

Olaya, Gina. March 17, 2004. Telephone Interview.

Owens, Sarah "Betty." September 20, 2001. Lawton, Oklahoma.

Stapleton, Beverly Saffa. September 23, 2001. Lawton, Oklahoma.

Swimmer, Ross O. June 21, 2001. Tulsa, Oklahoma.

Tijerina, Kathryn Harris. July 28, 2003. Telephone interview.

Books and Articles

Abzug, Bella S. *Bella! Ms. Abzug Goes to Washington.* Ed. Mel Ziegler. New York: Saturday Review Press, 1972.

Abzug, Bella S., and Mim Kelber. *Gender Gap: Bella Abzug's Guide to Political Power for American Women.* Boston: Houghton Mifflin, 1984.

Albers, Patricia, and Beatrice Medicine. *The Hidden Half: Studies of Plains Indian Women.* New York: University Press of America, 1983.

Allen, Paula Gunn. *The Sacred Hoop: Recovering the Feminine in American Indian Traditions.* Boston: Beacon Press, 1986.

———. "Sky Woman and Her Sisters." *Ms.,* September/October 1992: 22–26.

"Americans for Indian Opportunity." *Civil Rights Digest.* Spring 1971, p. 17.

Antell, Judith Anne. "Indian Women Activists." Ph.D. dissertation, University of California, Berkeley, 1989.

Andersen, Margaret L., and Patricia Hill Collins, eds. *Race, Class, and Gender: An Anthology.* Belmont, Calif.: Wadsworth, 1998.

Andersen, Terry. *The Movement and the Sixties: Protest in American from Greensboro to Wounded Knee.* New York: Oxford University Press, 1995.

Barth, Fredrik, ed. *Ethnic Groups and Boundaries: The Social Organization of Culture Difference.* Boston: Little, Brown, 1969.

Bataille, Gretchen M., ed. *Native American Women.* New York: Garland, 1993.

Bataille, Gretchen M., and Kathleen Mullen Sands. *American Indian Women: Telling Their Lives.* Lincoln: University of Nebraska Press, 1984.

Bernstein, Alison. *American Indians and World War II: Toward a New Era in Indian Affairs.* Norman: University of Oklahoma Press, 1991.

Blackburn, Dan. "LaDonna Harris Is a Senate Wife with More on Her Mind than Mid-Afternoon Teas." *Washington Post/Potomac,* May 24, 1970, p. 26.

Bordewich, Fergus M. *Killing the White Man's Indian: Reinventing of Native Americans at the End of the Twentieth Century.* New York: Doubleday, 1996.

Bordin, Ruth. *Woman and Temperance: The Quest for Power and Liberty 1873–1900.* Philadelphia: Temple University Press, 1981.

Braden, Maria. *Women Politicians and the Media.* Lexington: University Press of Kentucky, 1996.

Brand, Johanna. *The Life and Death of Anna Mae Aquash.* Toronto: James Lorimer & Co., 1978.

Brooks-Higgenbotham, Evelyn. "The Problem of Race in Women's History," in *Coming to Terms: Feminism, Theory, Politics,* ed. Elizabeth Weed. New York: Routledge, 1989, pp. 122–33.

Brown, Judith K. "Economic Organization and the Position of Women Among the Iroquois." *Ethnohistory* 17, nos. 3–4 (Summer/Fall 1970): 151–67.

———. "A Note on the Division of Labor by Sex." *American Anthropologist* 72, no. 5 (October 1970): 1073–78.

Brown, Rusty. "How LaDonna Harris Faces a Turning Point in Life." *Albuquerque Tribune.* January 12, 1982, p. A-6.

Burns, Nancy, Kay Lehman Schlozman, and Sidney Verba. *The Private Roots of Public Action: Gender, Equality and Political Participation.* Cambridge, Mass.: Harvard University Press, 2001.

Burrell, Barbara C. *A Woman's Place Is in the House: Campaigning for Congress in the Feminist Era.* Ann Arbor: University of Michigan Press, 1997.

Calhoun, Craig, ed. *Social Theory and the Politics of Identity.* Cambridge: Blackwell, 1994.

Cantor, Dorothy W., and Toni Bernay. *Women in Power.* Boston: Houghton Mifflin, 1992.

Carabillo, Toni, and Judith Meuli. *The Feminization of Power.* Arlington, Va.: Fund for the Feminist Majority, 1988.

Caragliano, Maureen O'Dea. "Beyond Princess and Squaw: Wilma Mankiller and the Cherokee Gynocentric System." Master's thesis, San Jose State University, 1997.

Caraway, Nancie. *Segregated Sisterhood: Racism and the Politics of American Feminism.* Knoxville: University of Tennessee Press, 1991.

Carroll, Susan J., ed. *The Impact of Women in Public Office.* Bloomington: Indiana University Press, 2001.

Castile, George Pierre. *To Show Heart: Native American Self-Determination and Federal Indian Policy, 1960–1975.* Tucson: University of Arizona Press, 1998.

"Challenges of a Cherokee Chief: First Woman to Head Tribe Battles Poverty, Ill Health, and Lack of Jobs and Confidence." *Christian Science Monitor,* June 22, 1992, p. 14.

"Champion of the Indian—LaDonna Crawford Harris." *New York Times,* July 11, 1979.

"Chief of Tribe Eyes New Term." *Daily Oklahoman,* July 21, 1975, 16.

Chisholm, Shirley. *The Good Fight.* New York: Harper & Row, 1973.

——. *Unbought and Unbossed.* Boston: Houghton Mifflin, 1970.

Churchill, Ward, and Jim Vander Wall. *Agents of Repression: The FBI's Secret War against the Black Panther Party and the American Indian Movement.* Boston: South End Press, 1988.

Clifton, James A., ed. *Being and Becoming Indian: Biographical Studies of North American Frontiers.* Chicago: Dorsey Press, 1989.

Cobb, Daniel M. "The Last Indian War: Indian Community Action in the Johnson Administration's War on Poverty, 1964–1969." Master's thesis, University of Wyoming, 1998.

——."'US Indians Understand the Basics': Oklahoma Indians and the Politics of Community Action, 1964–1970." *Western Historical Quarterly* 33, no. 1 (Spring 2002): 41–62.

——. "A War for Self-Determination: Culture, Poverty, and the Politics of Indian Community Action, 1960–1975." Ph.D. dissertation, University of Oklahoma, 2003.

Conway, M. Margaret, Gertrude A. Steuernagel, and David W. Ahern. *Women and Political Participation: Cultural Change in the Political Arena.* Washington, D.C.: CQ Press, 1997.

Cornell, Stephen. *The Return of the Native: American Indian Political Resurgence.* New York: Oxford University Press, 1988.

Corrin, Chris. *Feminist Perspectives on Politics.* New York: Longman, 1999.

Cott, Nancy F. *The Grounding of Modern Feminism.* New Haven, Conn.: Yale University Press, 1987.

Cronon, William. *Changes in the Land: Indians, Colonists, and the Ecology of New England.* New York: Hill & Wang, 1983.

Cross, George Lynn. *Blacks in White Colleges: Oklahoma's Landmark Cases.* Norman: University of Oklahoma Press, 1975.

Crow Dog, Mary and Richard Erdoes. *Lakota Woman.* New York: Harper Collins, 1990.

Deloria, Vine, Jr., and Clifford M. Lytle. *The Nations Within: The Past and Future of American Indian Sovereignty.* Austin: University of Texas Press, 1984; 1998.

Dittmer, John. *Local People: The Struggle for Civil Rights in Mississippi.* Urbana: University of Illinois Press, 1994.

Echols, Alice. *Daring to Be Bad: Radical Feminism in America 1967–1975.* Minneapolis: University of Minnesota Press, 1989.

Edmunds, R. David. *The New Warriors: Native American Leaders Since 1900.* Lincoln: University of Nebraska Press, 2001.

Eller, Cynthia. *The Myth of Matriarchal Prehistory: Why an Invented Past Won't Give Women a Future.* Boston: Beacon Press, 2000.

Evans, Sara M. *Born for Liberty: A History of Women in America.* New York: Simon & Schuster 1989, 1997.

———. *Personal Politics: The Roots of Women's Liberation in the Civil Rights Movement and the New Left.* New York: Alfred A. Knopf, 1979.

Farber, David. *The Age of Great Dreams: America in the 1960s.* New York: Hill and Wang, 1994.

Farber, David, ed. *The Sixties: From Memory to History.* Chapel Hill. University of North Carolina Press, 1994.

Fisher, Ada Lois Sipuel, and Danney Goble. *A Matter of Black and White: The Autobiography of Ada Lois Sipuel Fisher.* Norman: University of Oklahoma Press, 1996.

Fixico, Donald L. *The Invasion of Indian Country in the Twentieth Century: American Capitalism and Tribal Natural Resources.* Niwot: University Press of Colorado, 1998.

———. *Termination and Relocation: Federal Indian Policy, 1945–1960.* Albuquerque: University of New Mexico Press, 1986.

———. *The Urban Indian Experience in America.* Albuquerque: University of New Mexico Press, 2000.

Fixico, Donald L., ed. *Rethinking American Indian History.* Albuquerque:

University of New Mexico Press, 1997.

Ford, Ramona. "Native American Women: Changing Statuses, Changing Interpretations," in *Writing the Range: Race, Class, and Culture in the Women's West*, ed., Elizabeth Jameson and Susan Armitage. Norman: University of Oklahoma Press, 1997, pp. 42–68.

Foreman, Carolyn Thomas. *Indian Women Chiefs*. Muskogee, Okla.: Hoffman, 1966.

Foster, Morris W. *Being Comanche: A Social History of an American Indian Community*. Tucson: University of Arizona Press, 1991.

Franco, Jere Bishop. *Crossing the Pond: The Native American Effort in World War II*. Denton: University of North Texas Press, 1999.

Friedan, Betty. *The Feminine Mystique*. New York: Dell, 1963; 1983.

Gaines, Kevin. *Uplifting the Race: Black Leadership, Politics, and Culture in the Twentieth Century*. Chapel Hill: University of North Carolina Press, 1996.

Gamarekian, Barbara. "A Long, Long Way From Oklahoma." *New York Times,* September 25, 1984, p. A22.

Gimmel, Susan Allison. "Wilma Mankiller: A Chief and Her People." *Oklahoma Woman,* November 1999, p. 4.

Ginsberg, Lori. *Women and the Work of Benevolence: Morality, Politics, and Class in the Nineteenth-Century United States*. New Haven, Conn.: Yale University Pres, 1990.

Glassman, Bruce. *Wilma Mankiller: Chief of the Cherokee Nation*. Library of Famous Women series. New York: Blackbirch Press, 1992.

Gordon-McCutchan, R. C. *The Taos Indians and the Battle for Blue Lake*. Sante Fe, N.M.: Red Crane Books, 1991.

Green, Rayna. "American Indian Women." *Bridges of Power,* ed. Lisa Albrecht and Rose M. Brewer. Philadelphia: New Society Publishers, 1990, pp. 61–73.

———. "Native American Women." *Signs* 6, no. 2 (1980): 248–67.

———. "The Pocahontas Perplex: The Image of Indian Women in American Culture." *Massachusetts Review* 16 (Autumn 1975): 698–714.

———. *Women in American Indian Society*. Indians of North America series. General editor, Frank W. Porter III. New York: Chelsea House, 1992.

Gregory, M. K. "Wilma Mankiller: Harnessing Traditional Cherokee Wisdom." *Ms.,* August 1986, p. 32.

Gridley, Marion. *American Indian Women*. New York: Hawthorne Books, 1974.

Grimes, Jeanne. "Comanches Plan for a New Century." *Lawton Constitution,* January 16, 1999, p. 11.

Gulliver, Hal. "LaDonna Harris." *Atlanta Constitution,* November 29, 1971, p. 4-A.

Gutmann, Amy, ed. *Multiculturalism: Examining the Politics of Recognition.* Princeton, N.J.: Princeton University Press, 1994.

Hales, Donna. "First Woman Chief Begins Second Term." *Phoenix,* July 20, 1987.

Harmon, Alexandra. *Indians in the Making: Ethnic Relations and Indian Identities around Puget Sound.* Berkeley: University of California Press, 1998.

Harris, Fred. "American Indians—New Destiny." *Congressional Record—Senate.* April 21, 1966, p. 8311.

———. *Potomac Fever.* New York: W. W. Norton, 1977.

Harris, LaDonna. "Constitutional and Tribal Governance." *The United States Constitution: Roots, Rights and Responsibilities,* ed. A. E. Dick Howard. Washington: Smithsonian Institution Press, 1992, pp. 115–27.

———. *LaDonna Harris: A Comanche Life,* ed. Henrietta Stockel. Lincoln: University of Nebraska Press, 2000.

———. "Statement of Mrs. Fred R. Harris Before the Education and Labor Committee" *Congressional Record,* July 13, 1967, p. 9581.

Hewitt, Nancy. *Women's Activism and Social Change: Rochester, New York 1822–1872.* Ithaca, N.Y.: Cornell University Press, 1984.

Hoxie, Frederick E. *A Final Promise: The Campaign to Assimilate the Indians, 1880–1920.* Lincoln: University of Nebraska Press, 1984.

Hughes, John. "Cherokee Nation Looks Up to Chief Mankiller." *Chicago Tribune,* May 14, 1986, p. 19.

Isenberg, Nancy. *Sex and Citizenship in Antebellum America.* Chapel Hill: University of North Carolina Press, 1998.

Iverson, Peter. *"We Are Still Here:" American Indians in the Twentieth Century.* In *The American History* series. Wheeling, Ill.: Harlan Davidson, 1998.

Johnson, Troy R. "The Roots of Contemporary Native American Activism." *American Indian Culture and Research Journal* 20, no. 2 (1996): 127–54.

Johnson, Troy, Joane Nagel, and Duane Champagne, eds. *American Indian Activism: Alcatraz to the Longest Walk.* Urbana· University of Illinois Press, 1997.

Joseph, Gloria I., and Jill Lewis, *Common Differences: Conflicts in Black and White Feminist Perspectives.* Boston: South End Press, 1981; 1986.

Josephy, Alvin M., Jr. *Red Power: The American Indians' Fight for Freedom.* New York: American Heritage Press, 1970.

Kavanagh, Thomas W. *Comanche Political History: An Ethnohistorical Perspective 1706–1875.* Lincoln: University of Nebraska Press, 1996.

Keegan, Marcia. *The Taos Pueblo and Its Sacred Blue Lake.* Sante Fe, N.M.: Clear Light Publishers, 1991.

Kennedy, Robert. "Statement about the Testimony of Mrs. Harris on Behalf of the American Indian." *Congressional Record—Senate.* July 13, 1967, p. 9581.

King, Janis. "Justificatory Rhetoric for a Female Political Candidate: A Case Study of Wilma Mankiller." *Women's Studies in Communication* 13 (Fall 1990): 21–38.

Kilpatrick, Jeane. *Political Woman.* New York: Basic Books, 1974.

Klein, Laura F., and Lillian A. Ackerman, eds. *Women and Power in Native North America.* Norman: University of Oklahoma Press, 1995.

Knickmeyer, Ellen. "Wilma Mankiller: Cherokee Chief Has Knack for Building Tribe's Success." *Daily Oklahoman,* December 28, 1987, p. 9.

Koenenn, Connie. "Heart of a Nation." *Los Angeles Times,* November 13, 1993, p. E1.

Krech, Shepard. *The Ecological Indian: Myth and History.* New York: W. W. Norton, 1999.

"LaDonna Eyes 'Red Power.'" *Times,* March 26, 1970.

"LaDonna Harris Loves Role of Key Aid to Senator." *Oklahoma Journal,* September 10, 1965, p. 5.

"LaDonna Harris: Indian Powerhouse." *Playboy* 19, no. 2 (February 2, 1972): 178.

LaDuke, Winona. *All Our Relations: Native Struggles for Land and Life.* Cambridge, Mass.: South End Press, 1999.

La Hay, Wauhillau. "Agnew Better Watch Out for Those Comanches." *Washington Daily News,* August 4, 1969, p. 19.

———. "Wife Shares Political Triumph." *New York World Telegram and Sun,* January 8, 1965, p. 7.

"Lawmakers Blasted by Cherokee Chief: Mankiller Cites Image Woes." *Daily Oklahoman,* February 23, 1992, p. 16.

Lobo, Susan, ed. *Urban Voices: The Bay Area American Indian Community.* Tucson: University of Arizona Press, 2002.

Lobo, Susan, and Kurt Peters, eds. *American Indians and the Urban Experience.* Walnut Creek, Calif.: AltaMira Press, 2001.

Lobo, Susan, and Steve Talbot, eds. *Native American Voices: A Reader.* New York: Longman, 1998.

Lockwood, Frank L. "First Woman to Head a Major American Indian Tribe Speaks at Harvard." *Second Century,* April 1987, p. 4.

Lowery, Linda. *Wilma Mankiller.* Minneapolis: Carolrhoda Books, 1996.

Lowitt, Richard. *Fred Harris: His Journey from Liberalism to Populism.* New York: Rowman & Littlefield, 2002.

Mangel, Charles. "Warpaint for the Senator's Wife." *Look,* April 4, 1967, pp. 24–29.

Mankiller, Wilma. *Every Day Is a Good Day: Reflections by Contemporary Indigenous Women.* Golden, Colo.: Fulcrum, 2004.

Mankiller, Wilma, Gwendolyn Mink, Marysa Navarro, Barbara Smith, and Gloria Steinem, eds. *The Reader's Companion to U.S. Women's History.* Boston: Houghton Mifflin, 1998.

Mankiller, Wilma, and Michael Wallis. *Mankiller: A Chief and Her People*. New York: St. Martin's Press, 1993.

"Mankiller Presented Award for Efforts of Civil Rights." *Cherokee Advocate* 16, no. 11 (November 1992): 1.

"Mankiller Says She Won't Seek Third Term." *Cherokee Advocate* 18, no. 5, May 1994, p. 6.

Mansbridge, Jane. *Why We Lost the ERA*. Chicago: University of Chicago Press, 1986.

Margolies-Mezvinsky, Marjorie, and Barbara Feinman. *A Woman's Place: The Freshman Women Who Changed the Face of Congress*. New York: Crown, 1994.

Martin, Calvin. *The American Indian and the Problem of History*. New York: Oxford University Press, 1987.

Martin, Mart. *The Almanac of Women and Minorities in American Politics*. Boulder, Colo.: Westview Press, 2001.

McClary, Ben Harris. "Nancy Ward: The Last Beloved Woman of the Cherokees." *Tennessee Historical Quarterly* 2, no. 21 (1962): 352–64.

McDonnell, Janet A. *Dispossession of the American Indian, 1887–1934*. Bloomington: Indiana University Press, 1991.

Meier, August, and Elliott Rudwick, *CORE: A Study in the Civil Rights Movement, 1942–1968*. New York: Oxford University Press, 1973.

"Membership Soars during Last Four Years." *Cherokee Phoenix*, February 22, 1991, p. 1.

Mihesuah, Devon A. *American Indians: Stereotypes and Realities*. Atlanta: Clarity Press, 1996.

———. *Indigenous American Women: Decolonization, Empowerment, Activism*. Lincoln: University of Nebraska Press, 2003.

———, ed. *Natives and Academics: Researching and Writing about American Indians*. Lincoln: University of Nebraska Press, 1998.

Miller, Dorothy I. "Native American Women: Leadership Images." *Integrated Education* 15 (January/February 1978): 37–39.

Morgan, Edward P. *The Sixties Experience: Hard Lessons about Modern America*. Philadelphia: Temple University Press, 1991.

Morris, Terry. "LaDonna Harris: A Woman Who Gives a Damn." *Redbook*, February 1970, p. 117.

Nagel, Joane. *American Indian Ethnic Renewal: Red Power and the Resurgence of Identity and Culture*. New York: Oxford University Press, 1996; 1997.

Neuman, Nancy M., ed. *A Voice of Our Own: Leading American Women Celebrate the Right to Vote*. San Francisco: Jossey-Bass, 1996.

Niethammer, Carolyn. *Daughters of the Earth: The Lives and Legends of American Indian Women*. New York: Collier Macmillan, 1977.

Parman, Donald L. *Indians and the American West in the Twentieth Century*. Bloomington: Indiana University Press, 1994.

Perdue, Theda. *Cherokee Women: Gender and Cultural Change, 1700–1835*. Lincoln: University of Nebraska Press, 1998.

Peroff, Nicholas C. *Menominee Drums: Tribal Termination and Restoration, 1954–1974*. Norman: University of Oklahoma Press, 1982.

Philp, Kenneth R. *John Collier's Crusade for Indian Reform: 1920–1954*. Tucson: University of Arizona Press, 1977.

"Resources in Red Nations: A Conversation with Winona LaDuke." *RAIN*, February–March 1980, p. 6.

Rinehart, Sue Tolleson. *Gender Consciousness and Politics*. New York: Routledge, 1992.

Robbins, Catherine C. "Expanding Power for Indian Women." *New York Times*, May 26, 1987, p. C1.

Rosenthal, Cindy Simon. *When Women Lead: Integrative Leadership in State Legislatures*. New York: Oxford University Press, 1998.

Saunt, Claudio. *A New Order of Things: Property, Power, and the Transformation of the Creek Indians, 1733–1816*. Cambridge: Cambridge University Press, 1999.

Secrest, Meryle. "No Vanishing Comanche." *Washington Post*, December 15, 1964, p. B-1.

Shoemaker, Nancy, ed. *Negotiators of Change: Historical Perspectives on Native American Women*. New York: Routledge, 1995.

Simpson, Jean. "Sooner Senator's Comanche Spouse Captivates Capital Crowd." *Tulsa* [Oklahoma] *Tribune*, March 27, 1965, p. 2.

Simross, Lynn. "Hail to the Chief: The First Woman to Serve as Head of the Cherokee Nation." *Los Angeles Times*, September 18, 1986.

Smith, Paul Chat, and Robert Allen Warrior. *Like a Hurricane: The Indian Movement from Alcatraz to Wounded Knee*. New York: New Press, 1996.

Snipp, C. Matthew. *American Indians: First of this Land*. New York: Russell Sage Foundation, 1989.

Sommers, Christina Hoff. *Who Stole Feminism: How Women Have Betrayed Women*. New York: Simon & Schuster, 1994.

"Sooner Senator's Wife Wows Them." *Wichita Eagle*, March 20, 1965, p. 6B.

Stephenson, Malvina. "LaDonna Harris May Be Answer to TV Myth." *Tulsa* [Oklahoma] *Daily World*, May 18, 1965, p. 10.

———. "They Communicate in Comanche." *Sunday Star*, November 15, 1964.

Sutter, Virginia. "Today's Strength from Yesterday's Tradition—The Continuity of the American Indian Woman." *Frontiers* 6, no. 3 (Fall 1981): 53–57.

Thurman, Melvena, ed. *Women in Oklahoma: A Century of Change*. Oklahoma City: Oklahoma Historical Society, 1982.

"Tobacco Wars: Message from the Chief." *Cherokee Advocate* 16, nos. 7/8. (July/August 1992): 6.

Tsosie, Rebecca. "Changing Women: The Crosscurrents of American Indian Feminine Identity." *American Indian Culture and Research Journal* 12, no. 1 (1988): 1–37.

Van Biema, David. "Activist Wilma Mankiller Is Set to Become the First Female Chief of the Cherokee Nation." *To the Top*, 1985, p. 91.

Verhovek, Sam Howe. "At Work With Chief Wilma Mankiller: The Name's the Most and Least of Her." *New York Times,* November 4, 1993, p. C10.

———. "Mankiller's Life Chronicled in New Book: Chief of the Cherokee Nation Went on Own Trail of Tears." *Journal Record,* November 5, 1993.

Waldrop, Judith. "Mankiller's Challenge." *American Demographics,* June 1987, pp. 56, 58.

Wallis, Michael. "Wilma Mankiller." *Ms.,* January 1989, pp. 68–69.

Washburn, Wilcomb E. *Red Man's Land/White Man's Law: A Study of the Past and Present Status of the American Indian*. New York: Charles Scribner's Sons, 1971.

"Washington Event Involves Women in the War on Poverty." *Bridge,* September 1986.

Weisser, Susan Ostrov, and Jennifer Fleischner, eds. *Feminist Nightmares: Women at Odds: Feminism and the Problem of Sisterhood*. New York: New York University Press, 1994.

"What One Woman Can Do . . . about Poverty." *National Council of Women of the U.S. Bulletin,* June 1968.

Wilkins, David E. *American Indian Sovereignty and the U.S. Supreme Court: The Making of Justice*. Austin: University of Austin Press, 1997.

Wilkinson, Charles F. *American Indians, Time, and the Law: Native Societies in a Modern Constitutional Democracy.* New Haven, Conn.: Yale University Press, 1987.

Wilson, Daryl B. "The Pit River Challenge." *Chronicles of American Indian Protest,* ed. the Council on Interracial Books for Children. Greenwich, Conn.: Fawcett, 1971, pp. 322–27.

Woloch, Nancy. *Women and the American Experience*. 2nd ed. New York: McGraw Hill, 1994.

Wynn, Neil. *The Afro-American and the Second World War*. New York: Holmes and Meier, 1976.

Zankin, Susan. "Woman Chief Blazing an Indian Trail." *Mother Jones,* September 1986, p. 8.

INDEX

McGee, Bill, 98
McGovern, George, 62
McKay-Want, Rosalie, 82
Menominee, 148, 175
McLaurin, George W., 19
Mildren, Jack, 134
Miller, Zell, 122
Molinari, Susan, 173
Mondale, Joan, 31
Mondale, Walter, 31
Morton, Patsy, 96
Ms. Foundation, 179
Muskrat, Jerry, 159

National Association for the Advancement of Colored People (NAACP), 18–19, 23
National Council on Indian Opportunity (NCIO): creation of, 59–60; Harris's appointment to, 53; Harris's dissatisfaction with and New Directions Conference Committee Report, criticism of, 64–65, 72; inaction of, 63. *SEE ALSO* Taos Pueblo Indians, struggle to reclaim Blue Lake
National Commission on American Indian, Alaska Native, and Native Hawaiian Housing, 162
National Telecommunications and Information Administration, 158
National Tribal Environmental Council, 161
National Women's Advisory Council on the War on Poverty: Harris appointed chair of, 53
National Women's Conference, 181
National Women's Political Caucus (NCPW): formation of, 55
Native American Heritage: stories of and interest in, 19, 127–29

Native Americans: activism of, 83–86; discrimination against, 14–15, 19; Harris and stereotypes of, 44–49; Mankiller and stereotypes of, 113, 129–31; media depictions of, 35–36, 60–61; perceived as minorities, 43–44, 163; similarity of discrimination against African Americans and, 19–20, 82, 84; status of, 19–20; status of Oklahoma, 12, 41; stereotypes of, 11, 13. *SEE ALSO* federal Indian policy
Native American Women: identity of, 4; and sexism in tribal politics, 92–95, 99–101, 103–10; use of tradition for empowerment, 5, 7, 169–72
Native American Youth Center, Mankiller's work with, 87
Navajo Nation, 157
Nelson, John Henry, 163
Nickles, Don, 156, 177
Nixon, Richard M., 60–61, 63–66, 68, 85–86, 147, 149–50
Nomee, Clara, 177
Norman: effort to integrate, 19. *SEE ALSO* University of Oklahoma
Northeastern State University, 116–17

Oakes, Richard, 84–86
Occupation of Alcatraz, 85–86
Office of Economic Opportunity (OEO), 151; funding for OIO, 37; Harris's testimony in support of, 50
O'Hara, John, 38
Oklahomans for Indian Opportunity (OIO), 4, 53, 65, 67, 150; controversy surrounding, 42–43; founding of, 37; goals of and Harris as first president